Patrick Campbell

Travels in the interior inhabited parts of North America

in the years 1791 and 1792 in which is given an account of the manners and

customs of the Indians

Patrick Campbell

Travels in the interior inhabited parts of North America
in the years 1791 and 1792 in which is given an account of the manners and customs of the Indians

ISBN/EAN: 9783742845085

Manufactured in Europe, USA, Canada, Australia, Japa

Cover: Foto ©ninafisch / pixelio.de

Manufactured and distributed by brebook publishing software (www.brebook.com)

Patrick Campbell

Travels in the interior inhabited parts of North America

THE AUTHOR IN HIS TRAVELLING DRESS.

TRAVELS

IN THE INTERIOR INHABITED PARTS

OF

NORTH AMERICA.

IN THE YEARS 1791 *and* 1792.

In which is given an account of the manners and customs of the Indians, and the present war between them and the Fœderal States, the mode of life and system of farming among the new settlers of both Canadas, New York, New England, New Brunswick, and Nova Scotia; interspersed with anecdotes of people, observations on the soil, natural productions, and political situation of these countries.

ILLUSTRATED WITH COPPER-PLATES.

BY P. CAMPBELL.

EDINBURGH:
PRINTED FOR THE AUTHOR, AND SOLD BY JOHN GUTHRIE NO. 2. NICHOLSON STREET EDINBURGH.

MDCCXCIII.

PREFACE.

It may not here be improper to premise, that the following journal was not originally intended for the public eye, but merely for the author's own gratification and amusement; but on its being shown to several of his friends and acquaintance on his return home, they requested he should publish it, and thereby give to such of his countrymen as had any thoughts of emigrating to America, room to judge for themselves. If he has so far succeeded as to induce the wavering to continue at home, and direct those bent on leaving their country to the proper object, all his troubles and risks will be amply compensated, and his views in this expedition fully obtained.

The author set out from the Highlands of Scotland, with an intention to explore the interior inhabited parts of North America, attended with an old faithful servant, a Dog, and gun, only. As he travelled much in wildernesses, and in birch bark canoes, through lakes and rapid streams, where the mind could not at all times be inattentive to safety, and wrote in these canoes, and on the stumps of trees occasionally, as he went along, it is not to be supposed under these circumstances that arrangement of composition, the polish of language, and elegance of style could be much attended to; and as these were, was he more at leisure, beyond his reach, he made no attempt afterwards to attain them. He is therefore hopeful, that this fair and candid state of facts, will screen him from the attack of criticism; and that the public will make the proper allowances to a person situated as he was, not bred to literary pursuits, and engaged in one perpetual round of hurry, bustle, change of situation, and occasionally consequent confusion, and not expect from him that regular attention to method, just arrangement of argument, and that precision, nor in fine that correctnefs which are to be found in the works of learned and studious men, who have leisure and ability to revise, correct, and improve the rough manuscripts, before they send them to prefs.

But notwithstanding of these efforts of the author, with a view to serve his countrymen, he fears they must be all in vain, in that region which gave him birth, unless more effectual exertions shall be made, than is in the power of an individual, to save it from destruction; for although it be capable, with negative exertions only of the legislature, to be rendered a flourishing country, and of great service to the state, since every inhabitant has innumberable resourses of wealth furnished by nature at his door, were they permitted to make the proper use of them. But being deprived of that by the impolitic salt laws, and other oppressions, must drive them to despair, and ultimately tend to make them seek an asylum in the wilds of America. Even the humane law that is now passing in the House of Commons respecting the coal duty, unless care shall be taken to adapt it to the circumstances of those remote corners, by particular provisions suited to the nature of the case, will afford scarce any relief whatever, to the natives of the north west coast of Scotland; and in some cases, like the salt laws, which held out to view an appearance of indulgence and exemptions to them, operated in reality as the most effectual check to industry, that could be conceived, and as a snare for intrapping the people to their own undoing.

SHOULD the salt laws be repealed; or these, and the coal laws so modelled as to be applicable to the state of the country; and fhould the same thing happen with regard to the laws respecting corn, and wool, and a few other articles, which at present operate in the most cruel and impolitic manner upon the people, we might then see that part of the country, which at present exhibits only a melancholy scene of misery and distrefs, become the seat of industry, wealth, and happiness; unless, as he fears, the severity of landlords, may, in some instances counteract even the most beneficent intentions of the legislature. All ideas of emigration to other countries, will then, and not till then, intirely be abandoned. He leaves to any one not rotten or corrupted by minesterial influence, to judge whether attention to these domestic and salutary matters, or to wars and paying subsidies to foreign princes, would be most conducive to the happiness of the people, and prosperity of the British empire

CONTENTS.

	Page
From FORT WILLIAM in Scotland, to the city ST JOHN, New Brunswick.	1
ST JOHNS RIVER and TOWN, to FREDERICK TOWN,	19
From FREDERICK TOWN to the foot of the MERRIMASHEE RIVER and back again,	55
From FREDERICK TOWN to QUEBEC,	86
From QUEBEC to MONTREAL,	125
From MONTREAL to KINGSTON,	137
From KINGSTON to NIAGARA,	163
From NIAGARA to the GRAND RIVER and back again,	178
From NIAGARA to the GENESEE COUNTRY,	216
The story of DAVID RAMSAY,	226
From the GENESEE COUNTRY to NEW JOHNSTON on the MOHAWKE RIVER,	248
Method of finding out BEES in the woods,	258
From the MOHAWKE RIVER to NEW YORK,	282
From NEW YORK to the JERSIES and back again,	291
From NEW YORK to FREDERICK TOWN,	296
From FREDERICK TOWN to ST JOHN and the KENEBECASIUS,	310

From ST JOHN *to* ST ANDREWS. - - - - 348

From ST ANDREWS *to* GREENOCK *in* SCOT-
LAND, - - - - - - - - - - 368

Account of the ACTION *between the* STATES *of*
AMERICA *and the* CONFEDERATE INDIANS
on the 4*th November* 1791, - - - 377

REFLECTIONS *on the* BRITISH PROVINCES *in*
AMERICA, *with regard to their throwing
off their allegiance to the* MOTHER COUN-
TRY, *and their falling into the hands of
the* FOEDERAL STATES. - - - - - 385

TRAVELS
IN
NORTH AMERICA.

From FORT WILLIAM *in Scotland, to the city* ST JOHN'S, *New Brunswick.*

ON the 11th of June 1791, I set out from Fort William, and by easy stages arrived at Greenock on the 18th. Agreed with Mr James Hart, *junior*, owner of the brig Argyle, William Willie, master, for my passage to New Brunswick, in North America, at L. 18 for myself in the cabin, and L. 6 for my servant in the steerage; to be found in provisions and liquors. Here we were detained until the 2d of July, when we set sail, and found ourselves next Monday off the harbour of Lamlash in Arran. Passed by Ailsa, a high and stupendous piked rock in the sea, inhabited by Solan geese, and other sea fowl. Stretching along the North Channel, could see Ireland on the south, and the coast of Kintyre on the north; and by the time we entered the strait between the Mull of Kintyre, and the island of Rathring, the wind freshened straight a-head of us; and about night-fall began to blow very hard. We continued to beat about all night; the sea ran high, and the ship pitched so as to have overturned every thing in the cabin. Our young passengers, and my servant, became very sick; but I stood it out, which gave me good hopes of making out the voyage without being sea sick. The captain said he never saw a higher sea in that channel. The storm continued all the night, and next morning we fell back, and attempted to make the harbour of Campbelton, but could neither enter it nor any port in Ireland.

AFTER beating about the whole of that day, we returned and attempted to make the harbour of Lamlash; but with no better success. During the third night we were tossed backward and forward on a tempestuous sea, between the island of Arran and the coast of Galloway: and next morning, the wind being rather increased, we ran before it, under bare poles, and made for the Fairly roads, where we anchored about two o'clock, a. m.

Here we lay until the 8th, when at four o'clock, p. m. we weighed anchor, and stood for the South Channel; and stretching along the coast of Ireland, next morning we found ourselves off the harbour of Belfast. Continued our course along that coast; and leaving the Isle of Man on our left, had a fair view of the entrance to Newry, Dublin, and Waterford.

On the 12th we paſsed Cape Clear, the most southerly point of Ireland, entered the Atlantic Ocean, and bade adieu to all European prospects.

Off this Cape were to be seen a good many Solan geese, which were mostly of a grey, and but few of the common white colour.

After losing sight of land, the only birds we saw in the Atlantic, during our voyage, till we came to the coast, were those called by mariners *Sheer Water*, and *Mother carries Chickens*. The former very much resemble, and in my opinion are no other than a sort of sea gull, with a pretty long crooked bill; and the latter a marine swallow. But so numerous are these two kinds of birds in the Atlantic Ocean, that there is scarce a part of it where they are not to be met with.

It is somewhat singular that these birds ſhould be fond of grease, a food they cannot be accustomed to; yet when any of it is thrown overboard, which the sailors sometimes do to attract them, they come close to the ſhip to pick it up, and thereby become an easy prey to the sportsman.

AND as to the Buckers and Porpoises, large scools of them would come around, and play their gambols, very frequently within a few yards, and sometimes under the bow of our ſhip.

ON one of these occasions, the wind blowing very freſh, and the ſhip making great way, one of our men, who had been formerly on board a New England whaler, seeing a scool of them coming about the ſhip, seized a harpoon, ran up the bowsprit, and placing himself on the yard, struck one of them that paſsed below him. The Bucker gave but two or three plunges, when he got quit of the harpoon, bent as crooked as an S, and sprung away with redoubled fury.

WE could easily mark his course as he went along, by the blood streaming down his sides, and the rest of the Buckers in full chace of him. What came of him afterwards I know not; but the captain, and all the men on board, said, they would never give up the pursuit, until they would tear him in pieces. On my mentioning afterwards in company this circumstance, as very odd and singular, a gentleman then present corroborated what the seamen had affirmed, by telling me, that he himself had harpooned a Bucker, and before they could get tackle about, and hawl him up the ship's side, the one half of him was eaten by the rest.

Some days after this, these Buckers were gamboling around us in the same manner, and our harponeer, from his former seat, struck another of them with a force that drove the harpoon pretty deep into the body of the animal. It appeared to be very large, and of great strength; for with one spring he broke the harpoon, and made off, with the head fixed in his body, leaving us to regret the lofs of it; which we did very sincerely, as we had no other on board.

The principal amusement to be had in crofsing the Atlantic, is fhooting Sheer Water, and Mother carries Chickens, and fifhing the Buckers with harpoons, which come often in great fhoals about the fhip, and frequently continue for some time, seemingly in the most sportive mood, and playing their gambols round about the fhip, particularly if there be a smart breeze, and a moderate swell of the sea. Any person fond of such sport ought to provide himself well with harpoons, gigs, or grains, and he may depend upon having many opportunities of using them during the voyage. As to fifhing lines and hooks, most ships take care to be provided with them before they set out. I would also recommend shark hooks and chains, as these ravenous fishes are frequently to be met with; and when you enter the American coast, it is rare you can miss finding fish of different kinds.

NOTHING material happened till the 31st of July, when we came to the Azores, or Western Islands, subject to Portugal.

THESE islands, according to the information I had, produce wine grapes, lemons, and oranges, with various other kinds of fruits. The island of Corva, in latitude 40° and longitude 31°, west from Greenwich, appeared to be a high bold mountain in the middle of the sea, with steep precipices, and of difficult access. The island of Flora, somewhat larger, but more accessible, is distant from it about three or four leagues south east. Not far from the former we happened to be becalmed; and a little alarmed at finding ourselves drawn towards its bold rocky coast by the force of the current; but a gentle breeze springing up in the evening, we got clear of it and of our fears together.

AFTER we had left, and before we came to these islands, we saw various kinds of sea fishes besides the Buckers or Porpoises already mentioned; such as Sharks, Bonettas, Dolphins, Turtles, and Flying Fish. These last are a curious sort of small fish. They sometimes spring out of the water like a flock of birds; and if crofsing over a ſhip, they chance to strike against the sails or rigging, they inſtantly fall down on deck, give one ſhake, and then appear quite dead.

As to their size, they are no larger than a Herring; and the reason afsigned for their getting out of the water, and taking wing, is, that they may escape the Dolphin, who, (as an enemy,) pursues and devours them in great numbers, and being an eye witnefs to the following facts, I the more readily believe it.

A Dolphin that kept company with our ſhip for a considerable way, darted as quick as lightning through the water; and when my eye lost sight of him, I observed a Flying Fiſh spring up, to avoid, as I supposed, the Dolphin; who finding himself disappointed, immediately came back to his former station; along side of us.

At another time, being on deck, I saw a Dolphin spring nine or ten feet perpendicular above the the surface of the water, at one of these fiſhes pafsing by on wing; he struck him with his head, and threw him down, but did not catch him. Afterwards, I saw another of these fiſhes fly out of the side of a high sea in a straight line acrofs the trough, and into the opposite; but he was hardly out of sight when a Dolphin appeared in full chace of him, springing out of that spot from whence he had come, and into that into which he went. As we did not see him fly out again, we supposed he was taken.

The Dolphin is said not only to be the swiftest, but also the most beautiful of all fishes, so variegated, that whether in water, or out of it, he appears to the eye in a variety of of the most vivid and brilliant colours.

There is another fish in this ocean, which mariners call the *Balloch Fish*, who has a natural propensity, as they say, when he finds a man naked in the water, to seize his posteriors, and no other part; which is perhaps the reason for their giving him that name.

As we were coming towards the Banks of Newfoundland, we saw the phenomenon which mariners so much dread, a water spout, about a league distant from us.

The day being cloudy and dark, prevented my making any other remarks on it, than that it had all the appearance of a thick dark cloud, of a cylindrical form, whose lower end, as it entered into the sea, terminated in a small or sharp point, where it raised a huge spray, which the wind drove to within half a mile of the stern of our ship,

This phenomenon had scarcely disappeared, when a scene more rare, though more natural, was presented to our view. A sccol of Whales were observed a-head of us, and making straight towards us; immediately I loaded my gun with ball, and placed myself between one of the cat-heads and anchor, where I was so firmly seated as to be in no danger of being capsized. Two of them came so near the ſhip, that I had a distinct view of them under the water, and so close were they to one another, that they seemed to touch. They observed the ſhip, and paſsed her; but immediately got up in her wake, having their heads and bodies down in the water, and their tails above the surface, adjoining so closely, as if they were chained; so that they had every appearance of being then in the very act of copulation.

At the same time we had a view full as distinct of another pair, which came very near us. Though they were not in the same posture as the former, yet they were in so sportive and amorous a mood, as to be tumbling round and over each other; and however uncouth their careſses might be, no two lovers could seem more fond.

They copulate like land animals, and bring forth in nine months, sometimes two at a birth. Some of the mariners informed me, that they have at different times seen an old Whale and two young ones, swimming close by her side; whence they judged they were her own offspring.

We likewise saw a very large Turtle, apparently asleep on the surface of the water, where it lay motionlefs, and without any symptoms of life; but on our approaching, was awakened by the spray of the ſhip.

August 20. Being then in latitude 43° 23, longitude 59° 25, was the most boisterous day we had since we left the Fairly roads, and what at sea they call a hard gale, but on land a real storm.

I stayed on deck for a considerable time during the continuance of this storm, with a hold of the ſhrouds in each hand, admiring the great force and power the one element had over the other; tremendous billows succeeding and impelling each other, raised by the wind, and running, (according to the sea phrase) mountains high, with such awful rage and impetuosity, as can hardly be conceived by any but those only who are accustomed to the like sights.

The same day, and prior to making the above remark, as I was sitting alone in the cabin, casting up this day's reckoning, I heard an unusual noise on the quarter deck; and not knowing the cause or meaning of it, with some degree of emotion I looked up the companion door, which chanced to be open; and, in a moment, a high sea that rolled over the ſhip, came tumbling down the gangway into the cabin, and involved me in darkneſs. I immediately ran up upon deck, and found that the noiſe I had heard was occaſioned by the men running away from the sea, to preſerve themſelves from getting wet, and not from any dread of danger.

TOWARDS evening the storm abated, and continued to do so more and more during the night. The next day moderately calm, ſerene, and warm.

THE pleaſantneſs of the day induced the captain to order one of the crew to paye the ſhip's ſides; that is, giving it a new coat of tar with a bruſh. Whilſt employed in this buſineſs, he was ſuspended along the ſhip's ſide, down to the water edge, by a ſmall rope, fixed a-top to a tack's-pin on the rails; the other end ſet round his poſteriors so looſely, that a ſudden jerk of the ſhip, then under sail, might precipitate him in a moment into the regions below. Yet far from being the leaſt concerned or afraid, he ſeemed as if he had been ſitting at his greateſt eaſe.

I OBSERVED to him that I would not like to be in his situation. He damned his eyes if he had not rather be in that poſition, than on e'er a horſe or cart on the beſt road in Europe; that the ſharp back of the one, and heaving of the other, was extremely distressing; and if they came athwart a stone, and ne'er a rope at hand to lay hold of, he might be capsized and his brains knocked out. He sang and whistled alternately, and gave himself no sort of trouble about it.

WHEN he had finished the spot that he was working at, and wished to be removed to another, he called out, "Shift my sheets;" and as there happened to be none of the crew on deck at the time, but the man at the helm, he called out, " Hoa, there, Bill sings!" (which meant that Bill was calling.) This is owing to the peculiarity of their phrases; the words hallowing, or calling out, so common with landmen, are not known or used among them. For instance, if a man is sent to the topmast head to look out for land, vessels, or any thing they are in hopes of seeing at sea, he is desired to sing out when any such thing is in view. Accordingly, one of the crew came up, and shifted Bill's sheets, as he desired, but so loosely, that, had he not been his brother, I would have been apt to suppose that he was indifferent if Bill should fall into the sea: for which, I rated him, and secured it properly with my own hands.

AUGUST 22. Being in latitude 43° and longitude 64°, we sounded, and found bottom fifty-five fathoms. This day we lay to for some hours, during which we fiſhed and caught several Cod, some Tuſk and Halibut.

August 23. We made land, Cape Sable, the most southern point of Nova Scotia, bearing N. W. in latitude 43° 3, longitude, 64° 44.

Here we fell in with some American fiſhing schooners, whom we saw catching fiſh as fast as they could hawl them in. One of them hailed us, and aſked from whence? We answered from Glasgow. "Ay, ay," returned he, "that is from old Scotland; I have been there."

In the afternoon, as we were entering the mouth of the Bay of Fundi, we observed a large Shark, seemingly asleep, as he lay motionleſs on the surface. We made for him with guns, and just as we were on the point of firing, he got under water and made off. The captain and crew judged him to be about seventeen feet in length. Here we caught several of the sort of fiſhes called *Pollacks*. They are of the size of an ordinary Salmon, and are the same with those we in Scotland call *overgrown Seys*.

We had not proceeded far, when we met with and spoke a fine large top-sail schooner, going on an eastward course. The two masters addreſsed one another with speaking trumpets, by the word Hoa! Our friend aſked what that island was which he had paſsed?

The other answered, "It is one to the southward of Penobscot Bay, on the coast of New England. To this, with surprise, we replied, that we supposed it to be one of the Seal islands in the entrance of the Bay of Fundi. "Ye are wrong," (said he;) and without taking any further notice of us, scoured past us.

The weather being very hazy and cloudy, we could not see the island but at times, and even then but very indistinctly. As we supposed the captain of this schooner to be much better acquainted with the islands on these coasts than we, who were never there before, and wholly trusted to our charts, we concluded we had gone out of our course; which threw us into a state of doubt and uncertainty, whether we should proceed or go back. In this perplexity we remained for some minutes; but at last, after mature deliberation, we judged it would be our safest course to follow the schooner, in order to come to a farther explanation, which accordingly we did. The schooner, observing us bearing down on her with all the sail we could crowd, lay to till we came alongside of her. Then both the masters entered again upon the same subject; and after several questions and answers, *pro* and *con*, it came out in the end that they both were bound for the same port. Our captain told the other the information he got but a few hours before from the fishing schooner, at entering the mouth of the Bay, and urged it as an argument, to convince him of his mistake as to his reckoning. But the gentleman positively insisted, saying, "I am sure I am right, and you, notwithstanding your information, are wrong in your reckoning." Whereupon the latter, finding the former incapable of conviction, says to him in broad Scotch, " Well, well, gaung ye your gate, and I'se gaung mine." And having said this, immediately sang out, " Helm alee! fore fheet and top bowline, jib and stay sail fheets let go ;" wheeled about, and continued his former course, due north, for the Bay; which in the end proved we were right, and that at this time the master of the schooner had outrun his reckoning by two or three degrees; which was an unaccountable mistake, in a run of fourteen days, only from the West Indies.

Being becalmed and bewildered in fog the two following days, nothing material happened till the 26th, about noon. A fine clear day discovered to us that we had pafsed the island of Grandaman, and several lefser ones, in the dark.

This sound abounds with Whales. One of them got up in our wake, so close to our fhip, that all of us then standing on the quarter deck, were almost suffocated with the filthy rotten stench of his breath.

Solan Geese, of a larger size than those of Cape Clear, or the western coasts of Scotland, are very numerous here, and of different colours; some grey, and others white.

About four o'clock p. m. we had a very sudden and unexpected change, from very fair to very foul weather. As I was then sitting in the cabin, on hearing, all of a sudden, the loud call, of "All hands on deck," I was struck with no little surprise; and ran up to inquire into the cause of it; the mariners, pointing at a very dark lowering cloud, which appeared at some distance, said, it foreboded a storm, and would soon burst with violence; and then each falling to work in his proper department, with all the speed they could, handing the top gallant sails, and reefing the top sails, &c. they put the ship in such trim as they thought necessary for preparing her to ride out the storm they dreaded.

The men, after trimming their sails, were hardly come down on deck, when the heavens darkened so much, that day seemed almost as dark as night; and instantly the lightning began to flash, the thunder to roar awfully, and the rain to pour like a torrent; but happily for us the wind was moderate.

August 27. About ten o'clock p. m. I happened to be on the quarter deck, and beheld the most beautiful scenery that can be conceived, appearing in the west; flashes of lightning, so frequent as two or three in a minute, not accompanied with thunder or storm; and at so great a distance as not to be dreaded; so that one could contemplate the scene without emotion.

THE firmament, illuminated by the frequent flashes, appeared in all the variety and brilliancy of colour imaginable. It was the grandest scene I ever beheld, and such as may be more easily conceived than described; but it was of no long duration; for a thick fog coming on, veiled it from our sight.

MUCH pleased with the singular grandeur of this phenomenon, we retired to rest, in full hope that the approaching morning sun would enable us to know where we were. But about three in the morning the scene changed; we were suddenly awakened by the voice of the mate, whose watch it was, singing out as loud as he could, " All hands on deck." We sprang out of bed, and were hardly on foot when we found the ship strike. She struck again. All ran up to the deck except the captain and I, who waited to put on our clothes. It occurred to me that I heard of people suffering much by being naked on a similar occasion; I therefore resolved, whether we went to the bottom, or were cast on a rock or a desert

C

island, my clothes ſhould go along with me; so I waited to put them on.

When we got upon deck, the fog was so close and thick, that we could not see the ſhip's length from us. Her head had got on one of the rocks surrounding us, yet bore but lightly on it; and all the rest of her was a-float. All hands set to work; the sails handed; the poles and oars on board instantly laid hold of. We puſhed so hard against the rock, that by the help of these, we kept her from striking with any force; and our efforts were so far succeſsful as to ſhove her head off from the rock; but her stern then was in danger of coming on another.

We ſhifted immediately to it, and by similar efforts preserved it also.

When we got clear of this bold rock, we sounded, and found fifteen fathoms water. We suffered no material damage, as the bow of the ſhip was the only part that struck.

It happened to be low water at the time, and fortunately for us, a perfect calm; and the force of the tide, which drew us on the rock, was greatly abated; yet not so much but there was still a current, which was preſsing her on. But by the favour of a gentle breeze springing up a-head, we got clear, though not of all danger; for the darkneſs of midnight, and continued fog, kept us still under the dread of falling foul of another rock.

We continued in this dismal situation till morning began to dawn, and the rising sun dispersed the fog.

The breeze continuing in our favour, we soon made out Partridge island; a small clump, of about 100 yards over, lying in the offing of the harbour of St John's; on which there is an elegant light-house, which shows afar off, and directs mariners with safety into that port.

Here a pilot came on board and took charge of our ship.

Betwixt the island and shore there is a bar, over which no vessel can pass but when it is high water; and as it was low water then, we kept beating about till the tide made, in the dusk of the evening, when we had depth enough of water to carry us over this bar; and after a fine passage, of fifty-six days from Greenock, but fifty only from the Fairly roads, entered the harbour with great safety.

St John's River and Town.

When you enter the Bay of Fundy, and as you proceed in it, your view on all sides is bounded by the horizon. Underneath an endless space of forest, of miserable spruce, seemingly fit to be inhabited only by wild beasts; the soil so thin and poor as not to produce any t ing else; the coast rocky, and in appearance dangerous to a stranger; but such as are acquainted, can be at no lofs for a secure harbour, with which the Bay abounds on all sides, until you come to the famous harbour of St. John's, about 150 miles from the entrance of the Bay. This barrennefs of coast, I am informed, is not peculiar to this province alone, but prevails from the foot of the Mifsifsippi, over all the coast of America, to the gut of Canso on the east end of Nova Scotia. The industry, and the art of man, have given it a different appearance in the cultivated parts, which in former times, when in the rude state of nature, and without an inhabitant, were as barren as those we are describing; and there is no doubt, but in procefs of time, the same attention and cultivation, will render it equally pleasing to the sight, and profitable to its inhabitants.

The city of St John's lies on the east side of the grand river of that name, where it enters the Bay of Fundy, situated on a broad point, more than half surrounded by a Bay on the eastward. The town is well planned; the streets cut at right angles; but from the unevennefs and ruggednefs of the sloping ground on which it is built, does not appear regular to the eye. It consists of about five hundred houses, all of timber, well painted. They have a neat appearance, and some of them even elegant; generally consisting of two stories high. The shops, store, and wharfs, numerous and commodious. They have two churches, also of wood; the largest not yet finished; but when it is, may contain a numerous congregation; and so well painted on the outside is this church, that, without a strict examination, any spectator would conclude it to be built of stone and lime.

OPPOSITE to St John's lies the village of Carleton, on the west side of the river, on the borders of a beautiful bay, that ebbs dry at low water; in which is built a timber weir, or what in Scotland is called *a yerr;* wherein a great deal of Herring, Gasparoes, Bass, and Shed, are caught, sometimes two or three hundred barrels at a time. All the property of the inhabitants, conform to the number of souls in a family, share and share alike. And on the other, or St John's side, there is another large weir, intersected with lesser ones within, of which every inhabitant who takes the trouble of repairing and upholding it, has right to a share. And there are sometimes caught in this weir, more than the whole town will consume, and find casks and salt to cure.

ABOUT a mile above the town, is a narrow strait of only sixty yards over, which hems this great body of water in between two high rocks, and occasions a fall of eight feet at low water; but when the tide is in, it rises here to thirty-two feet, and admits vessels almost of any burden to pass and repass.

At the foot of this fall, amazing quantities of Herrings or Gasparoes, are caught, with what they call scoop nets; which are nothing but a sort of bag-net, tied to a hoop of the same circumference with that used by farmers fans in this country, for winnowing their corn, affixed to a long pole, which they dip in the water, and scoop up full of fish, throw them a-shore, and then fall to it again; and so go on in this way, till either they tire of the work, or have the quantity they wish. And at times are so successful, that a man often catches twenty barrels in a day.

As this fishing is free to every body, many idle people flock to it from a distance to make profit; and even farmers to supply their own families. They have casks and salt ready on shore, wherein they pack and cure the fish as they hawl them in.

The Salmon fishery at the town is no less extensive, and carried on with small nets twenty or thirty fathoms long, and thirty or forty mashes deep. This fishery, which is solely the property of the town, is yearly let in lots; and freeholders only have a right to draw for one.

These lots cost but two shillings each, payable to the clerk for his trouble; and if one happens to draw a good lot, he may either fiſh it himself, or let it to another. One lot, called *The Devil's Hole*, has been let this year at 450 Salmon; and I have heard several gentlemen say, that they have known a net hold a **hundred** Salmon of a day.

The fiſh here are not scringed nor dragged for, as in other places. The nets are set at low water on the ſhore; both ends fixed; that without to a heavy stone or anchor, and the end within, a-ſhore, chiefly in the eddies, in the same way that small trammels are put on the sea ſhores in Scotland for catching trout. When the tide makes, and these nets become a-float, the scools of fiſh that puſh up the river, strike with such amazing force, and in such numbers, as to raise a considerable part of it out of the water. So numerous are Salmon here, that three thousand, I have been told, were caught in a day in this way; and that the best fiſh, unleſs of an extraordinary size, will fetch in the market but a ſhilling;— the general run is but from ten to fifteen pounds weight, though there are some of between twenty and thirty.

Besides these I have mentioned, there are two other sorts of fiſh, called *Shed* and *Baſs*, caught here in vast numbers, generally weighing from three to five pounds.

On the banks of the bay, are found abundance of Cod and Ground Fiſh. The Salmon and Herring, though of a smaller size, are said to be as fat as those of Europe. The Gasparoes are a species of Herring, which puſh up the rivers in May, and spawn in freſh water; are much larger, but of poorer quality.

On the whole, there can be little doubt, that in course of time these fiſheries will be great articles of commercial intercourse, as they are already of considerable magnitude.

From this port they annually export between two and three thousand barrels of Salmon, and as many Herring or Gasparoes. Furs, to the value of L. 4000, of which six thousand Moose Deer ſkins make a part. Some of these animals are said to be fourteen or fifteen hands high. Masts and spars for the Britiſh royal navy in the following proportions; one inch thick in every three feet in length in masts; one inch to every four feet in spars or yards; and one inch to two feet in bowsprits. Last summer one spar was ſhipped on board the Lord Mansfield of Greenock, of thirty-two inches square, and 128 feet long. On hearing of this extraordinary stick, my curiosity prompted me to go to the mast yard to look at it; but it was put on board some days before; so that I was sorry at being deprived of the pleasure I expected from the sight of such an uncommon stick. However, I saw several which were ninety feet long, and thick in proportion. In short, there is no place upon the continent that abounds more with these articles, so necesary for our navy, nor where they are to be had better in quality, or easier for transportation, than at St John's. Lumber of various kinds is to be got here.

SHIPS are built not only in this, but also in different bays and creeks up the river, which are of two, three, or four hundred tons burden, carpenter's measurement, all of black birch.

I HAVE been on board a ship, then on the stocks, of three hundred tons, that had not a stick of any other wood in her whole hulk; and another brig of two hundred tons, just then launched, whose cabin and state rooms were finished in the neatest manner I have seen, all of black birch, equal in beauty to mahogany.

THESE vessels, when fitted for sea, are loaded with lumber, and dispatched either to Britain or the British West Indies. If to the former, often both ship and cargo are sold; but if to the latter, the cargo only. They take freight from thence for Britain, whence, if the ship is not sold there, she returns to her own port again, laden with the various commodities of that country.

It is the most fortunate thing in the world for these new colonies, that the old ones shook off their allegiance to the mother country, as they have a free trade with the British West Indies, and supply them with lumber, which the others, in consequence of their independency, are debarred from.

September 1. Leaving St John's, I came to the Indian house a little above the falls, where I went on board a small schooner, bound to Frederick town, which lies about ninety miles up the river.

About a mile above this Indian house, the river is much narrower. A ridge of high and steep rocks of lime stone, on each side, confine the waters; though not so much but that vessels may pass and repass with great safety either at high or low water.

Observing a little hut in the face of the rock, I went a-shore and took some refreshment. I had a short conversation with the landlord, whose name is Lorine, a mason by trade, and originally from Dumfries in Scotland. Adjoining to his house, (or rather cave,) in this romantic situation, he built a lime kiln and store house; and having abundance of lime stone, from the surrounding rocks, and large junts of wood, carried down the river to him at a small expence, he went on in burning lime, by which, I was informed, he not only made a good living, but also realized what might be deemed for him a considerable fortune.

A LITTLE above this place the river widens gradually, till it becomes equally broad with many arms of the sea, or salt water lochs on the west coast of Scotland. We proceeded up the river this day but twelve miles, when the wind died away into a perfect calm.

SEPTEMBER 2. After we had pafsed major Coffy's beautiful seat, pleasantly situated on a point, on the west side of the river, we landed on a point of low land, where one man, and three boys from eight to twelve years of age, were employed in mowing the rankest and strongest natural grafs I ever saw.

HERE I was informed, that two men coming down the river, attacked an old Bear and two young ones swimming acrofs the river, which they killed.

ANOTHER man, in his boat alone, met a Bear swimming acrofs, struck him with his axe, and wounded him; but by the force of the stroke the axe fell overboard. The wound exasperated the Bear to such a degree, that it was with the utmost difficulty the man could keep him from boarding him, and in the struggle bit one of his fingers; but at last, he shoved off his boat and got quit of him.

This day we landed and dined at an inn kept by one Roger, a Bostonian, who rents the place from a settler, at L. 27, 10s. currency. He raises a great deal of hay on this lot, which besides produces all sorts of grain.

Mr Roger told me, that rather than throw away his dung, he meant to lay it out on his meadow ground; though it yielded him already two tons *per* acre. He hoped by this improvement to make it return two and one half tons at a cutting. And when I recommended to him to lay his dung on his corn, rather than his grafs land, his answer was, that it was rich enough already, and that dung would spoil it.

Every mile we advanced up the river, on this day's journey, the prospect was more extended. The lands appeared better and closer inhabited; the islands and flats on each yielding the most luxuriant and greatest quantities of natural grafs I ever saw; and the foggage, for the most part, rich clover.

While dinner was getting ready, I took a stroll along with the landlord to two neighbouring farms, situated on a brae above the flats. One of these settlers told me, that he had but one Cow when he came there, about six years ago, but that now he has twenty head of black cattle, besides horses, poultry, and hogs.

The returns in their new cleared land, he said were not considerable, owing to weeds, which the soil throws up when unshaded by woods, and exposed to the influence of the sun and air. They are much pestered with Squirrels, of which they have several kinds, and very destructive to grain. Here I first saw the flying Squirrel, which is a curious animal, whose wings pretty much resemble those of a Bat, and are smoother than any velvet.

Having viewed every thing that was to be seen around this place, we returned to the inn, and after dinner went on board the vessel, where I slept that night.

Next day we sailed up the river several miles, but the wind slackening, we came ashore. From thence I travelled by land, which I preferred to going by water, as it gave me an opportunity of seeing and knowing more of the country.

This morning, in a field of Indian corn, I shot a bird, whose colour, shape, bill, head, and eyes, convinced me that he was as perfect a Woodcock as was ever seen in Europe, though somewhat smaller; owing, as I supposed, to his not being full grown. I showed him to several gentlemen, and inquired if they knew what sort of bird it was; but none could tell me, or acknowledge that they had ever seen any of the kind; but colonel Ting, a good looking, jolly, hoary headed gentleman, who said it was a Woodcock; that he had never seen any before in this country, though he often had in the province of New York; and that he believed they were to be seen there in all seasons of the year. Also ſhot two other beautiful birds, called *Hei-ho*, whose plumage is beautifully variegated. They are about twice the size of a Thruſh, and much of that ſhape.

AFTER leaving colonel Ting's place, I came to one Squire Peter's, who has an extensive plantation on the same side of the river. I aſked several questions of this gentleman about farming, which he answered in a very satisfactory manner; among the rest, that they might cut two crops of hay in a season on the same spot; but as one cutting afforded them plenty for their own use, it was not worth any man's while to be at the trouble or expence of making hay for sale, as it would only fetch five dollars a-ton, making in sterling, about twenty-one ſhillings; for a-ton of hay is 128 stone, of sixteen pounds, Dutch weight, each. At this rate, he would, after all his labour and expence, hardly get twopence *per* stone. A ton feeds a Cow for the season.

In this climate they have no more rain than is absolutely necefsary. A tradesman of Frederick Town told me, that he had wrought there thirty-four days last summer, and that of these he was only stopped from his work one day by rain.

The islands and flats, which are numerous and extensive, on each side of the river, yield great crops of grain and roots of various kinds; and an astonifhing quantity of grafs without any sort of manure. Some of the old settlements in Maugerville have been cropt annually for fifty years back, without so much as one handful of dung to help the vegetation; and are at this day, and will probably be to the end of time, as good as ever.

This, no doubt, is principally owing to the river overflowing and flooding the land, and enriching it in the spring; but the upper-lands on heights, such as are dry and un-flooded by any water, will, in course of long cultivation, require manure to make them produce rich and plentiful crops.

The schooner in which I first embarked, bound to Frederick Town, being detained for want of winds, and likely to make a tedious voyage of it, I fhifted from her on board the post-boat, along with the other pafsengers. We were all very social and happy. They mostly continued on board; but I walked a great part of the way, and when a-head of them, made excursions into the different plantations in the neighbourhood; and, when tired, returned to the boat.

In one of these excursions, many stories were told me of the bears in this country; one of which, as being somewhat curious, I shall relate.

On an island, called *Spoon island*, which I had pafsed a day or two before, there were seven bears killed in one day. A gentleman and his son, near a house in which I then lodged, had been out working at hay, having pitch forks and rakes; and seeing a monstrous bear, quite close to the river, they prefsed so hard upon him as to drive him into the water. They then thought they had him secure, as there was a boat near them, to which they immediately ran; and having pursued and come up with him, they struck and pelted him with the pitch forks and fhafts till they broke them to pieces. The exasperated monster now, as they had no weapon to annoy him, turned the chace on his adversaries; and fixing his fore paws upon the gunnel of the boat, attempted to get in. They did all they could to keep him out, but their efforts were in vain;—he got in. So that at last they had nothing else for it, but either to jump out into the water, or stay in the boat and be torn to pieces. They chose the former, and swam a-fhore. The Bear, now master of the boat, whence the enemy had battered him, was so severely galled with the strokes and wounds he had received, that he made no attempt to follow, but continued in the boat; otherwise he might have soon overtaken them, and have had ample revenge, as he could swim three times faster than they.

They immediately ran to the house for guns, and when they came back, saw him sitting in the boat, and dipping one of his paws now and then in the water, and wafhing his wounds; on which, levelling their pieces, they fhot him dead.

The landlord of the house I put up at, when this story was told, fhowed me one of the paws of this Bear, which, on account of its great size, he kept as a fhow; and added, that he was as big as an yearling calf. So that one may easily conceive the havock and destruction committed in a country so much infested with such monstrous and ravenous animals, especially on Sheep, the simplest and silliest of all creatures, which fall an easy prey to beasts of far lefs strength and size. Many of these harmlefs, yet useful animals, were destroyed by Bears in this very neighbourhood, where one man sustain-

E

ed the lofs of thirty of his Sheep within a fhort space; and even young cattle often were devoured, and carried off by them: yet they prefer Swine, when they can get them, to any other meat.

Going along with my landlord to view his farm, and entering the fkirts of the wood, he hollowed out pretty loudly, "Canaan! Canaan!" and presently a parcel of Sheep came fkipping out from a remote corner, and surrounding him, fawned upon him. He put his hand in his pocket to see if he had any salt to give them, but had none.

As I imagined it was queen Anne he called, I looked very attentively among the flock to see if I could discern the one he honoured with the royal title; and when I could not see any one seemingly superior to the rest, I afked him which of them he called queen Anne. At which he laughed immoderately, and told me, that I was led into the mistake by his manner of pronouncing the word Canaan; which is universally used in this country when they call in their Sheep.

This man had but few milk Cows, only six in number; but of an exceeding good kind. I pointed out the one I thought best of them, and afked him what he valued her at. He said ten pounds; but was sure he would not get near that money for her.

She would surely fetch it in any part of the world I have been in; and might be deemed a good Cow in any part of England I have seen.

This gave me an idea of the cattle of this country; but I saw none that would equal them during my stay in it.

After satisfying myself with every thing necefsary to be seen in this part of the river St John, I left my coat in the boat, it being as warm and sultry as with us in Scotland, in the heat of summer, and proceeded in my waistcoat and trowsers twelve miles on foot. It being Sunday, I met a great many genteel well drefsed ladies and gentlemen going to church; some on horseback, and some, family-way, in carreols; and all on the canter, scampering away as if posting.

I proceeded on the road, which had hitherto continued on the river side, but now struck off from it, and led into a thick wood; on the edge of which there was a house, and a girl standing on the road side by it. I afked her if this was the road to Frederick Town, and what distance it was from hence? She answered in German, that fhe could not speak Englifh. I then addrefsed her in that language, but could not make myself understood. Whether it was owing to the broken way in which I exprefsed myself, or that it was a very different dialect of that tongue she was bred to, I know not; but so it was, that after making several efforts on both sides, she went off, seemingly in confusion at not understanding me, and left me to pursue my journey; but no sooner had I entered this dreary wilderneſs, than the many stories I had heard of the Bears recurred to my mind, which made me so apprehensive as to be at a stand whether to return back or push forward. I chose the latter. My dog, who was along with me, and to whom I trusted much, in case of being attacked, kept ranging about for game, and but rarely in my sight; so that I had constantly to call on him to keep him in, lest a Bear should spring out of the wood on me in his absence; for (it being Sunday as before said,) I left my gun along with my servant in the boat, and began to cut a stout stick with my pocket knife; while bent down at this work, such was my apprehension, that I kept constantly looking around me, lest a Bear should seize me by the posteriors.

AFTER being fortified with this stick, I proceeded on without any farther concern. Had I been so well informed as I afterwards was, I would have been under no such apprehension; as it is very rare that a Bear, no way molested by man, will attack him, unlefs fhe happens to have young cubs; in that case, it is dangerous to go near her den. But no fhe Bear would keep her young so near a place so much frequented by her mortal enemies, the human species, as that road was.

This road did not lead above two miles, when it came down again to the river side at the Ferry, when I entered on board a large scow to crofs to Frederick Town.

The first person I met with there was the Ferryman, an Italian, which gave me a strange idea of the medley the inhabitants of this part of the country are made up of; but he spoke pretty good Englifh, having been here for several years, and pofsibly no other man of his nation except himself; nor have I seen any Germans who understood not Englifh, except the girl I lately mentioned.

I crossed the river in the scow, and arrived in Frederick Town three hours before the post-boat, wherein I left my clothes; paraded backwards and forwards looking for its arrival. The people seeing me half naked, stared at me, and put many questions, which I answered perversely, until the cold of the evening after sunset made me borrow a great coat from a Mr M'Leod, landlord of the house I put up at.

SEPTEMBER 4. Upon enquiry I was informed that my relation lieutenant Dugald Campbell, afsistant engineer, who resided within five miles of Frederick Town, had pafsed through it two days ago to visit his farm on the Nafhwack river, about eighteen miles from hence; and was expected to return that day by the same route. I waited his return, and took several 'strolls through that town and neighbourhood, and viewed the governor's inclosures and potatoe fields.

THE soil is poor, and has been long cultivated by French and Indians. It appears to be nothing else than banks of sand thrown out by the river. But I am informed the back fields, more distant from the water, which I had not time to view, are of good quality.

THE governor's house is situated about half a mile from the center of the town, up the river, and near the middle of his farm. The town itself is stretched on a flat and sandy foundation along the river's side, on a point forming an obtuse angle. Many of the houses have a noble appearance; but are scattered and detached from each other.

THE barracks are surrounded with a piquet, about fourteen feet high, put endways in the ground, so strait and close that a cat cannot get through; and so firmly as to secure every thing within, like a rampart.

The river is broad and shallow at this town, and the boats poled at crossing. Here I saw several Indians with their wives and children, selling small baskets and birch bark canoes. One of the women appeared to be a white one.

September 5. Being informed, that my relation Dugald was to be in town this day, to settle some workmen's accounts, I crossed the river in order to meet him, before he could be informed of my arrival in this country.

I was ferried in a small boat, by a man who called himself a Scotch Irishman, the greatest rap I as yet had met with. He said he would ferry me on account of my being an old countryman. Having promised him a sixpence, at landing I gave him a quarter dollar to change, which he pretended to search for through different houses, and coming back without it, he said he would return me the balance when I came back at night. He used all the art and chicane in his power to retain the money; on which we were like to come to blows. But when all shifts failed him, he put his hand in his pocket, and brought out the change, and begged I would employ him in re-ferrying me when I should return. I told him that I would rather give a shilling to another than one copper to such a rascal as he was. After parting with this consummate knave, I fell in with a captain Agnew, son to the doctor of that name, who overheard the dispute with the Scotch Irishman, and told me he knew him to be a great rascal.

This gentleman and his father bought several large properties in this country; and though he had been over the different provinces of North America, and had seen many parts of Europe, was bred in the south of Scotland, and mostly resided in England, yet he preferred this place to any he had ever been in. He gave a high account of the climate and soil, and said the winter months, to him, were the most pleasant of the whole year; particularly February and March. The serenity and clearness of the sky and air, and warmth of the sun, without a single cloud to obscure it, were really delightful. Indeed I have had the same account from almost every body; but they all agree, that while the north west winds continue, the cold is extremely keen and penetrating; and if a person be not aware of it, he may get frost bitten. But when the wind shifts to any other point of the compass, they may work or walk out as lightly clad as we in Scotland do in the summer months. More agreeable weather I never saw, nor felt such warmth as I have done since I came to this place.

This gentleman shewed me a dwelling house he is just now building, directly opposite to Frederick Town, most pleasantly situated at the foot of the river where it enters into the river Nashwack. The former is a pretty large river, navigable by canoes; and has many pleasant settlements on both sides of it for forty miles up.

After viewing this gentleman's rising mansion house, which has every appearance of being a very handsome one, with underground cellars of stone, and the rest of wood, I went over his inclosures, and the low grounds of his farm, and saw the manner in which he carried on his improvements.

Among other particulars, he told me that this country was very famous for Sheep. As they were a beneficial stock, he meant to have a pretty large flock, at least three score; and as the Ewes in this province are so prolific, when well kept, as to bring forth two Lambs at a time, his stock would soon increase.

His property, which is very extensive, is pleasantly situated, and at the same time very advantageously for disposing of all its produce. The wood he cuts down to clear his lands is purchased by the garrison for firing, whereby he has a double advantage; and all the hay he can make, which in a little time will amount to several hundred tons, will be

F

bought up by the town and garrison, where he also will find a ready market for many other articles his farm or estate may yield.

AFTER gratifying my curiosity, and viewing every thing that was to be seen in this place, the gentleman very politely afked me to dine with him; which, for want of time, I declined; and having thanked him for his civility and politenefs, I parted with him, and walked up a new road through a wildernefs of eleven miles extent, to see the Highland settlements on the river Nafhwack, and came to the house of a captain Shaw, a native of old Scotland, and county of Invernefs, where I slept that night.

SEPTEMBER 6. Captain Shaw, at whose house I was entertained very hospitably, is married to a Yanky young lady, by whom he has four boys and two girls. The mother is bare headed, and so blooming and well looking, that I supposed her to be a maiden, until I heard the children call her Mama. I fell into the like mistake often; as all the married women here go bare headed, except when drefsed.

THE captain, who is an intelligent gentleman, being the preceding day employed with his men, clearing and burning wood off his lands, came home in the evening as black as a collier. This, I find, is the general practice and employment of all the industrious gentlemen farmers in this part of the country; and indeed the state of their lands, and the produce thereof fully evince their laudable attention.

AFTER breakfast, and captain Shaw's fhowing me how he carried on his improvements, I was conducted by him to another gentleman's house, two miles from thence up the river, a captain Symon's, where we were told several gentlemen were to dine that day, and among the rest, my relation Dugald Campbell. As we were going along, we fhot a couple of Pheasants, beautiful birds, larger than a Moorfowl, and nearly about the size of a Heath Hen.

WHEN we arrived at captain Symon's, a New England loyalist, we found my relation there, who recollected me at first sight.

BEING very desirous to see his farm, which was but five miles farther up the river, with every other settlement I could on the Nafhwack, captain Symon said, he would give me a horse on condition of coming back by four o'clock to dine at his house; to which we agreed. Accordingly we set out, and on our way, called at a captain Archibald M'Lean's, originally from Mull, a captain French's, to whose daughter Mr M'Lean was married, and a Dr Drummond's, brother-in-law to the engineer my relation.

Here I met a lieutenant Dugald Campbell of the king's American Rangers, with several other gentlemen, settlers in this place. On our return, we found the above gentlemen, and three or four more at captain Symon's; dined, played cards, supped, and smoaked tobacco. We had a very plentiful and genteel dinner, but neither wine nor punch, as the produce of these new settlements cannot as yet afford this luxury.

Our drink was grog, and rasp rum, served up in wine decanters, and drank out of glafs tumblers. I was afked several times if I chose to have sugar, which I declined, as every other person present did; the rasps gave the rum such an agreeable relifh, as to make it unnecefsary.

We pafsed the evening very agreeably; three of the gentlemen and I slept here that night; the rest went to their own houses.

Here I was told that the Highlanders settled up this river, were in many respects not a whit better than the real Indians; that they would set out in the dead of winter, with their guns and dogs; travel into the deep recefses of distant forests; continue there two or three weeks at a time, sleeping at night in the snow, and in the open air; and return with sleas loaded with venison; yet withal, were acknowledged to be the most prudent and industrious farmers in all this province of New Brunswick, and lived most easy and independent.

The Salmon fishing on the river is very useful; and angling, and Trout fishing is not only serviceable, but delightful and amusing. Captain Symon told me, that he knew two Frenchmen, in one canoe, in the month of July, to spear in one night ninety-six Salmon, with torch light. And one of these men told him this was nothing to what he had seen, *viz.* that three canoes, in one of which he himself was, had speared at the same season of the year, seven hundred Salmon in one night. So that it was an easy matter for the first settlers here to catch, in the season, as many Salmon as would serve their families, which every farmer here has hitherto done; but since the country is settled, the Salmon fishing on this river is much upon the decline.

The engineer to whom I told the Frenchman's story, hardly thought it credible that such a thing could happen on this river; but had not the least doubt that it might on the Merrimashee, which probably was the one he meant.

The lands on many parts of this river, or, as they are called here, creeks, are rich and fertile; the flats extensive and easily improved; but they were pestered with a small black fly, which they call the Hefsian fly, that totally destroyed their wheat, and hurt some other grain for two or three years back; but this year they seem to think they are falling off, and will soon be quit of them. This destructive insect has, by degrees, over-run all America, and but rarely continues above three years in one place.

A MAN fifhing in a canoe, is reckoned a wretched fifherman, if, when he spears a Salmon, he wets himself, and goes afhore with the fifh. An expert hand pulls them into his canoe until it be brim full, and then paddles afhore to unload. When this is done, he falls to work again, and continues till daylight, attended with fuccefs.

NEITHER Wolves nor Bears are numerous in this part of the country, and the Moose Deer are banifhed to some distance; but those fine birds which they very improperly call Partridges, being much more like Pheasants, or Heath Fowl, or rather a species between the two, are numerous here.

OF Pigeons, in the season, may be seen from any eminence ten thousand flocks, or as far as the sight can reach. They are smaller than with us, and in some places caught with nets, in the same manner I have seen the Germans catch Fieldfairs, who probably introduced that custom into this country.

The warmth of the sun, the serenity and mildness of the weather continue, and astonish me, as I have never seen the like in any country I ever was in. It infeebles and enervates me much, and evinces that I am not fit for enduring a warmer climate; yet the inhabitants by no means complain, and tell me they have often seen such weather for six weeks without intermission. But in such fine weather as this, a frost often sets in at night that often spoils their potatoe crops; I mean so as to stop its growth, and hurt buck wheat and other grain.

SEPTEMBER 7. Captain Symon conducted me the length of captain Shaw's, where I parted with him and lieutenant Dugald Campbell, one of the gentlemen who were with us last night.

WE proceeded to the Ferry, where I again met with captain Agnew and a Hessian officer, who, I was told, was married to his sister. The captain again asked Dugald and me to dine with him, before I should leave the country.

HAVING crossed the Ferry and dined at McLeod's, we proceeded up the river five miles to Dugald's house, and on our way thither I waited on general Carleton the governor.

As I had conceived a very good opinion of this province from the specimen I had seen of it, and that I knew a great many people from the corner of Scotland I had come from, were in use for some years past of emigrating to the American states; that many more were preparing to do the same; that a Mr Simon Frazer, a young gentleman from Poictu, in Nova Scotia, told me at Fort William, a few days before I set out from that place, on his way to Greenock, that he was employed to engage vefsels for sixteen hundred he had on his list, ready to embark for America; and that eight hundred more were preparing to follow the next year, which I knew was not owing to wantonnefs or desire of change of situation on their part, but principally to the inhumanity and opprefsion of their landlords, who either distrefsed them, or screwed up the rents to a pitch they could not pofsibly pay. Of this I could not be mistaken, as I knew many of the people in this predicament, and some of them I had seen wringing their hands, crying most bitterly, deploring their miserable families, and the state they were reduced to.

HUMANITY fhudders and fhrinks with horror at the recital of their sufferings; and as I judged they would be as well here as in any part of the States, I resolved to wait on his excellency, general Carleton, the governor, and know from him what encouragement these people might look for, did they come to this province, and prefer being under the British government, and king's dominions, to those of the United States; and when I waited on him, and put that question, his answer was, " That they fhould have every thing dependent on him, such as lands, gratis, in any one spot they would pitch upon, not occupied already, in quantities proportioned to their stock."

HE spoke of 500 acres to some, lefs or more, conform to their capital and rank; that however desirous he would be of such a thing, he would not keep it for them, but give it to the first settlers that offered. I told him that I by no means desired he fhould, as I could not say whether they would accept of it or not; that all I could do was to acquaint such of them of it as intended to emigrate, on my return to Scotland, and let them judge for themselves; that as I liked the country, and was partial to the British government, I much wifhed that they would accept of his Excellency's proposal, rather than go to the States, as already said; made my bows, and came away for the engineer's house, where I remained some days, and visited several families in the neighbourhood; captain Lee, an Englifhman, Mr Gardener and Mr M'Gibbon, Scotchmen; to all whom I was much obliged for their politenefs and attention; and preparing for my journey, to the foot of the Merimafhee river, of which I had heard so much, that, though distant 150 miles, I determined to see it, and therefore engaged John and George M'Gregors, two smart young men, born in the forty-second regiment, whose father had been a serjeant in that corps, and killed last war, they being well acquainted with that river, and the course I was to take.

SQUIRE LYMON, of whose politeneſs and attention to me I cannot say enough, came here to wait on me, and he and the engineer were kind enough to agree to go along with me to see the settlements on the said river.

WE therefore set out, croſsed at Frederick Town, and proceeded up the river Nafhwack, to Squire Lymon's house, where we staid that night.

THIS gentleman is of such rank, and so highly respected in these parts, that he is delegated a member to the Provincial Aſsembly, and has the charge of carrying on the public roads on this river, and opening a communication between it and the Merimafhee. From captain Lymon's we again visited captains French and M'Lean, and lodged at Dr Drummond's. Here we staid some days; during which we dined in these families. Went over the Doctor's and engineer's farms, which are separated only by the small river Tay. They have a deal of interval; deep, rich land, that never got, and I suppose never will require manure. I was astonifhed at the loftinefs of the timber growing thereon; and I am convinced many of the large pine trees would measure from three to four feet diameter, of which they rarely make any other use than log canoes. On these intervals sometimes two crops of hay are cut in a season.

Here I saw a Beaver dam; and as my Dog made a great deal of work about it, we judged some of the family had been at home, but kept under large logs of trees that happened to be there; so that we did not see them.

In the pool, below these logs, were a good many fine large Trout, swimming about at their ease, and seemingly undisturbed, as if no creature molested them, which gave us reason to suppose, what has been often affirmed by many, that the Beaver does not eat fifh, but wholly subsists on the bark of trees. Were it otherwise, the fifh would not live in the same pool with them.

This is the only running stream of any magnitude I ever saw them settled in. Their general method, (which I have seen in several places down this creek,) is to dam up any low spot, through which a small brook of water glides; by which a pool, or small sheet of water may be formed. From this pool they make canals in different directions, by which they can lead considerable logs of trees to form their dam. The earth they take out of these they use as mortar to fill the crevices betwixt the logs, and stop the water. Their broad flat tail they use as a trowel to batter it up, as well as to form their habitations.

The natural sagacity of this creature is so well known, and so fully described by other travellers, that it is unnecesfary to enlarge on it here. It is, however, worth remarking, that when a hunter falls in with any of those dams, and wifhes to know if any Beavers live in them, he cuts down a small slap in the dike, and comes in a day or two to the same place; if they are there, he will find the slap made up.

An Indian who goes to look after Beavers, ties up his Dogs, and will not allow any of them to follow him, which if he did, and the Beaver got hold of any one of them, he would cut clear out whatever piece he got hold of, and so disable the Dog, and perhaps render him uselefs ever after.

A Beaver's tail, which is about four or five inches broad, and between one and two thick, is reckoned by many a delicious morsel, and sells high to white people; but, to me, it was too lucious, and appeared more of a gristly nature than real fat.

It is said, that if one of them be caught in a steel trap by one of the feet, he will cut that off which is held, and thus get away. As the trap only spoils the animal, and is of no advantage to him that lays it, I find that this method of catching them is discontinued.

I have seen a tree cut by a Beaver, and was much surprised at the size of some of the chips about it, some of which I took up, and found them to be about half an inch broad, and two lines thick; and, by way of curiosity, fhowed them to several persons in that country, who said they had often seen many such before.

They have four large broad fore teeth, two above and two below. The Hares in our country have teeth somewhat resembling them.

In all parts of this creek are Pheasants and Hares innumerable. Wherever I went I fell in with them, and fhot some.

In autumn they can kill as many as they please of the former. In this place where I am now writing, Dr Drummond tells me, five or six broods of them were hatched last summer, quite close to his house, and came mornings and evenings to feed through his fields and potatoe ground, of which he shot from day to day what served his family

A Gentleman in this neighbourhood also told me, that the preceding year, two gentlemen, from the river St John's, had been upon a visit to his family; that next day being Sunday, and consequently an idle day, he and they, to amuse themselves, went out with their guns, took different routs, and strove who should kill most Pheasants; that when they returned in the evening, and counted their game, they had above forty of these fine birds.

It is a practice, not uncommon in this country, to catch Hares by the following contrivance. In winter, when all kind of herbage is buried under the snow, a tree is cut down, which, in the course of their perpetual ranging about all night for food, they find out, and feed upon the buds and small branches of it. When the sportsman finds this, he places a number of gins around the tree, on these branches; by which it is no uncommon thing to find eight or ten of them caught against next morning. They are not so large as those of Britain, nor so small as Rabbits, but seem to be a species between the two, and are milk white in winter, but of a deep brown in summer.

From FREDERICK TOWN *to the Foot of the* MERIMA-SHEE RIVER *and back again.*

HAVING now got every thing ready for our journey to the Merimashee, we proceeded up the river Nashwack, through the settlements of the forty-second regiment, which is closely inhabited on beautiful spacious flats on each side of the river.

I FOUND them happily situated, each on his own property, and glad to see one come so lately from their native country. Their greatest want, and what they complained most of, was women for their young men; they begged of me to recommend some hundreds of them to come, and that they would engage that they should all get husband, or masters, before they should be three weeks in the country, proportional to their rank and age.

I MENTIONED to one that I was told every winter they would set out to the distant forests, and continue there for two or three weeks, and sleep on the snow in the same way the Indians do. He said it was very true, and that ne'er a winter since he settled on that river, but he had a thousand weight of Moose meat in his house, and that in general they all were so; that a good Moose would weigh eight hundred weight, and a Kerraboo about four hundred.

I now found the information I had formerly got of them to be well founded, as I could see they had abundance of stock and crop to supply their wants. Their habitations and inclosures neat, comfortable, and commodious. One of them told me, that one of his fields produced thirty bushels of bear for every one sown, but that he had given it a little manure, as the soil is somewhat thin and sandy. I have seen other fields of oats, which, they affirmed, would return twenty-fold, which I find to be the average increase on this, and St John's river, in wheat, oats, and bear, when no manure is given.

We called at several places as we went along, and dined at Mr Angus Mackintosh's, the highest settler on this river. He is a very decent man, originally from the county of Invernefs, and was a serjeant in the seventy-first regiment. His wife told me, they had every necefsary of life in abundance on their own property, but there was one thing which she wished much to have; that was heather. And as she had heard there was an island in the gulf of St Laurence, opposite to the mouth of the Merimafhee river, where it grew, and as fhe understood I was going that way, fhe earnestly entreated I would bring her two or three stalks, or cows, as fhe called it, which fhe would plant on a barren brae behind her house, where fhe supposed it would grow; that fhe made the same request to severals going that way, but had not got any of it; which fhe knew would greatly beautify the place; for, said fhe, " This is an ugly country that has no heather; I never yet saw any good or pleasant place without it."

She was so decent a woman, and so earnest in this matter, that I would go many miles out of my way to procure it for her; but as the island fhe mentioned, which produced it, was several scores of miles from fhore, I had no chance of seeing it.

After dinner, our hospitable landlady having furnifhed us with a parcel of fine frefh eggs for our journey, we set out, and encamped at night about the middle of the portage. The men set to work, and in an instant hewed down wood, and set up a fire; cut the crops of a species of ever green wood, which they call *varr*, of a most agreeable and aromatic odour, of which our beds were made, and covered with our Bear fkins. On this we slept. We ranged upon the one side, with our soles to a fire, kept up all night, and the men in the same situation on the other. Got up very early next morning, and proceeded through a large tract of hard woodland of good quality, and easily cleared.

DESCENDING on the opposite side we entered a valley, the immense pine trees of which were the loftiest I had ever seen, and so numerous, that I supposed the whole British navy might be supplied with masts and spars from it. Many of the trees we supposed to be from seventy to eighty feet high to the first branches, and three feet diameter. One tree in particular, the engineer supposed to be four feet through. Crossed two small rivers, the Nagudagun and Waametick, or Tax's river, which last takes its name from an Indian chief of the Meekmack nation, called Pier Tax, who sometimes had resided on it, and falls into the Merimashee below the eastern portage.

BETWEEN nine and ten o'clock a. m. we arrived on the banks of the Merimashee, put up a fire and breakfasted. Coming through the wood this morning I shot a fine large Polecat, or Martin, and a half dozen of Pheasants. While we were at breakfast, we saw many Salmon and Trouts jumping in the pool by us, and a flock of large grey Ducks, resembling those called in Scotland Sheldrakes.

AFTER breakfast we returned our horses, and embarked on board two canoes made of birch bark, which is very common in this country, and proceeded down the river on our voyage. The river as we went along is broad, fhoal, and of a clear gravelly bottom, and rare to find a pool deep enough to come over a man's head of six feet high; so that we made very little use of our paddles, but poled as we went along. Pafsed many fine islands and large links of deep, rich, interval land. We made a considerable way this day and encamped at night on an island. Slept soundly at the root of a large tree till about one o'clock in the morning. A heavy fhower then fell and obliged us to put our Bear fkin over us to secure us from it. We continued our nap till an hour or two thereafter, when I, happening to be awake, heard some strange animal call two' or three times pretty close to us, and seemed coming towards us. I gently put at the engineer, awakened him, and afked him what creature it was. He, without giving an answer, instantly sprang up, seized upon his gun, awakened the men, and watched its coming; but the night being very dark, could not see him pafsing by, calling now and then as he went along. They said, the call was that of a Moose Deɛ and resembled more the call of a young than an old one.

From this place we set out very early next morning, and paſsing a small island, we heard a loud plunge in the water, which drew our attention to that place, and found it was occasioned by a Cow Moose, and Calf, croſsing from thence to the main land, with such expedition that I had not time to turn about in the canoe to fire at her before ſhe got into the wood. I proposed to get aſhore and follow her; but they said it was in vain; because being once started, ſhe would go a great way before ſhe would stop.

We landed upon a point to take breakfast. Whilst the kettle was a-boiling, Captain Lymon having hooks and lines in his pocket, lopped a branch off a tree, with which he fiſhed, and caught more fine Trouts than we could use. While he was at this work, I took a stroll into the wood, to see the soil and nature of it. And wherever the wood was any thing open, the graſs and weeds were breast high, and obstructed my paſsing through it; which made me return to our encampment sooner than I otherwiſe would have done.

In these excursions I rarely ventured without my double barelled gun loaded, so as to be prepared for any wild animal I might chance to fall in with.

ALL along the banks of this river, are seen great quantities of hops growing spontaneously, and as luxuriant as those cultivated in the most fertile part of England, and small onions, with which we used to season our fish. In the evening we arrived at a house built by a set of wood cutters, employed by a Mr Fraser, merchant on this river, where the small river Kain falls into the Merimashee.

THE two brothers, John and George M'Gregors, whom I employed to accompany me in this expedition, were well acquainted with the navigation and fisheries on this river. The former was one of five fishermen, who, with the afsistance of a few Indians, caught seventy tierce of Salmon in the space of ten or twelve days; they would have continued the fishing longer, but rain came on and swelled the rivers, which induced them to give it up for that season.

ON the river Kain, the Salmon are so plenty that many may be caught in a few hours; for the same young man afsured me, that he has known 300 taken thereon with a net in one day, by placing the net at the foot of a pool, and beating the fish down the river into it.

WHILST our things were a-carrying to this hut, where we encamped, I went a-fishing, and was so succefsful as to catch many more fine large Trouts than we had occasion for; therefore left some on the shore, and threw several into the water again.

I OBSERVED, that there is a great deal of interval and good lands on both sides of the river as we came along. Having here a deal floor to lie on, we went to bed, and slept soundly and comfortably till morning. Then setting out pretty early, we set up sails in both canoes, and alternately sailed, poled, and paddled, till we came to a place some miles below, where there were several vessels, hogsheads, tubs, &c. for curing Salmon, still uncarried away; here we stopt, boiled our kettles, and breakfasted. Thereafter proceeded on our voyage down the river, whose banks on each side are covered with woods, mostly evergreens, and some hard wood intermixed. Many parts are high, and in other places low, with some well lying interval; particularly the parts called the Sugaries, from a deal of sugar being made on them. Many more streams falling into this river below the Kain than above, heightened the prospect all along, till we arrived at the point where the river Renow falls into the Merimashee on the north side. Here we saw an Indian and his Squa making some small, but very neat baskets of Porcupine quills of various colours. Their method of dying the quills is as follows: They pick up small pieces of cloth of every colour they can find. These they scrape down as small as they can, and boil separately in kettles, till the dye is extracted from the wool; then put in the quills in them. This dyes them, and gives them as fine colours as can be wifhed;—indeed I never saw any more brilliant.

The river Renow is broad, but fhoal at the foot, and seems to be a very beautiful little one, where a neat and beneficial settlement for a fifhery might be made. Here we put up sails, and joined both canoes together for our greater security, and that there might be no danger of oversetting.

From this place down to the island of Barnaby, several miles below, the river is navigable for small craft; and from thence to its entrance into the gulph of St Laurence, for thirty miles, for fhips of any burden.

The late Mr Davidson, al.a. John Goodsman, having obtained large grants of lands here, built a dwelling house, some offices, and a store house. The soil is rather thin and poor, as is common in this country on the coast; and the place seems more eligible for carrying on the fifheries, than for cultivation; for which purpose he placed crofs nets on stakes fixed in the channel of the river, to prevent the Salmon from going up; which occasioned many disputes and quarrels betwixt him and the Indians. He also erected saw mills on the north east branch of the river, for manufacturing the woods; and from thence exported large quantities of fine planks, masts, spars, &c. Besides the considerable trade he carried on in different articles of timber, he annually exported, caught on this branch of the river, from twelve to fifteen hundred tierce of Salmon. He was the first settler in this place, and to him it was owing, that many settlements there afterwards took place. He was a man of genius and great abilities; and though his views, as a schemer, were said to be too extensive, yet he was in such high esteem, and so well beloved, that he was made a member of the House of Assembly, and deemed one of the ablest and cleverest men in it. The surveyor of the customs told me, that in this river were shipped in one year 3800 tierce of Salmon.

In the evening we arrived at the house of Mefsrs James Fraser, and John Tom, merchants on the island of Barnaby, where they kept stores and different kinds of merchandise proper for the country; ship masts and spars for government; deals and all other kind of wood for foreign market. The ship Cochran, from Greenock, Robert Burn master, and a brig from Shelburn, were just then taking in their lading.

Mr Fraser is judge of the inferior court of common pleas; and this being a court day, several of the neighbouring gentlemen were assembled, and after the court business was over, dined at his house. Though dinner was over with them before we arrived, yet as they had not broke up, we had the good fortune of falling into their company, and conversing with them on the state of this part of the province, respecting improvements in agriculture, fisheries, game, &c. &c.

Besides Mr Fraser, and his partner Mr Tom, there were present on this occasion, Mr Nicolson an Irishman, collector and deputy surveyor; Mr Reid a Scotchman; Mr Robeshot a Frenchman; squire Taylor, squire Wilson, Americans; Mr Laurence, Mr Andrew, an Englishman, a liner of masts and timber, for which he has L. 200 a-year from this company, besides bed and board; captain Collick, a hearty jolly fat Pensylvanian; and Mr le Dernier, the sheriff, a Swifs; a smart, lively, sensible little man, once superintendant of Indian affairs, who, having lived for seven years among the Indians, acquired their language, and spoke it with ease and fluency; a great sportsman, and perfectly expert in their manner of fishing, hunting, and calling in the game.

We staid here all night, and next day took a view of the company's mast yard, stores, and every thing to be seen about this place. Judge Lymon, after satisfying his curiosity, went to visit Mrs Davidson, and see the saw mills.

The extent of this island is only 150 acres; very flat, all sandy, having little of any other soil, and covered with young birch wood and pines. When the French posseſsed this country, it seemed to have been cleared land; but being uninhabited, it ſhot out in wood. It lies at the fork of the two branches of the Merimaſhee, about thirty miles from where it enters into the gulph. The tide, which rises here about six feet, flows up to Renow river, fourteen or fifteen miles above it. The land on each side is level, or has a gradual and easy ascent; the wood mostly pine and birch; though there are some spots of large and hard wood. The river here is about a quarter of a mile broad, of a muddy and sandy bottom; and having neither stones nor rocks, seems to be as safe a navigation as is in the world.

The settlements thereon are but few, and none as yet above twelve miles from the forks. Every one has a right to fiſh on his own property to a certain extent of nets; and few or none exercise this right without vast advantage and profit.

Mr le Dernier told me he had seventy tierces of Salmon caught on his lot, with only one set net of about thirty fathoms to the back; and many others were nearly in that proportion; but that his was among the best stations on the river.

Sweep nets have been tried, but did not (as they say,) repay them for the expence and trouble; so they gave them up, and continued that kind of nets which gave no other trouble than setting them at night, and taking the fish out of them in the morning. These are set on poles, which are fixed in the bottom, and standing upright. And I am informed, that from this river 3000 tierces of Salmon, caught in this way, had been shipped two years ago; but that last year and this have not answered so well; and that on the Restigush river, which falls into the bay of Chaleur, forty miles to the northward of this, they catch a great many more, and these of a larger size; for it takes only from twenty to twenty-five Salmon of the latter river to make a tierce; whereas from thirty-six to forty of those of the former are required to make one.

There are a great many streams of lesser note in this part of the province, where a deal of Salmon are caught. The mouths of the rivers and all along the coast, abound with almost all the varieties of fish in the sea; and as for Lobsters and Oysters, they are so numerous, as to become a nuisance, destructive to the nets and the fish therein. Wild Geese, Brants, Ducks, and all the variety of water fowl, are in such numbers, that a good sportsman in a few hours may load a canoe with them.

Mr le Dernier the sheriff, who is as indefatigable and expert a sportsman as can be met with in any country, told me, that he himself annually lays up for winter store, two tierces of Brant and Wild Geese, as many of Salmon, and as many of Herring, besides other fish, Moose, Keraboo, and other venison. The latter need not be salted, as they are killed in winter, and the frost preserves them; but the Brant, which is like a lump of butter for fat, and the Geese, are shot in September and October, and therefore require to be pickled to preserve them. When plucked they are split on the back, and barrelled up, and when they have occasion to use them, they are steeped in water for a night or two, to thaw and carry off the salt, when they become fresh, sweet, and as fit to be roasted or stewed as the day they were caught.

As the method of shooting the Wild Geese, Brants, and other sea fowl in this place, is somewhat curious and uncommon, it will not perhaps be amiſs to give some account of it, which is as follows:

On any point of land between two creeks, bays, or (which is best,) between two rivers, the sportsman slips off a tree, a twig, or small branch, the small end of which he fixes in the sand, quite close to the water edge, to the height of the bird he means to represent; near to it he fixes two or three other sticks to the height of the body; round these sticks he wraps some sea weed, so as to resemble as much as poſsible the wings and tail of the bird; and the upper end of the stick, the neck and head, I mean that which formerly adhered to the tree; so that to view it at a distance it will very much resemble a bird. He sometimes makes two or three of these decoys close to each other, which being seen by the birds at a distance, as they fly along, entice them to come on, and take a sweep around, supposing them to be some of their fellows. At a proper distance he makes a pit in the sand, and around it places some ſhrubbery or small bunches of the crops of trees, to cover himself when he sits, that he may not be seen by them. This is always done on the windward side of the point, which, for the most part, sea fowls are fondest of frequenting. A flock of them in paſsing by, suppose these objects to be real birds, and come close up to them; on which the sportsman fires, and if he happens to kill one or two, he places them in the water, with a sharp pointed stick, one end of which is fixed in the sand, the other under the chops of the bird, which holds up his head as if alive, and the motion of the surge keeps him heaving up and down, and from side to side; so that now it is next to impossible to discover the deception.

The next flight that comes, alight close by this one, on which he readily fires sitting; and every one he kills, he places close by the other, in the same manner with the first. This he continues to do, till in a few hours he may have the full loading of his canoe, or as many as he chooses to carry home. The birds are so numerous in these bays, and flocks of them so frequently passing from one point to another, that scarcely would there be an end to this diversion, at which, indeed, the Indians are most expert.

The manner of hunting the Moose Deer in the rutting season, is as follows: The Moose at night is fond of feeding on a sort of grass that grows at the bottom or sides of ponds of lakes.

The sportsman ranges from pond to pond, and lake to lake, until he find by their track that which the Moose frequents; he then places himself in a proper situation on the side of that pond or lake. He is provided with a slip of birch bark, about a span broad, which he rolls up in the form of a funnel; and when the proper time of night comes, putting the small end of it to his mouth, he blows through it, and gives the call peculiar to this animal; if the Moose is within hearing, he answers the call, and comes ruſhing through the wood with such rapidity and noise, that he is heard at a considerable distance; all the young sapplings, branches, or buſhes giving way to his great strength in his career. If he is any way doubtful, he stops and listens; the sportsman then calls and calls again, through his birch funnel; and if the Moose Bull does not know the sound, though within gun ſhot, he comes no farther. The huntsman finding this, has recourse to another deception with the same instrument. He blows in the water, and makes it bubble up; so as to resemble the water bubbling by the breath of an animal feeding in it; then putting his finger in the small end of the funnel, he dips it into the water and raises the full of it; then removing his finger, he pours it back again in a small stream; thus making a noise as if a Cow Moose was piſsing. When the Bull hears this, he runs with such fury and force, that the sportsman, for fear of being trodden down, is often obliged to step to a side, till he dafh into the water, where he becomes more visible by its reflection, and having now full sight and time to take his aim, he fires and kills him on the spot.

In winter they hunt them with dogs, when the crust of the snow is so hard as to hold up the dogs, while the weight of the Moose sinks him to the bottom. When closely pursued, and no pofsibility of escaping, he runs about in a circle until he beat down the snow and make a path, within which he keeps to beat off the dogs, and often kills some of those that happen to come within this circle and his reach. His horns are of an enormous length and thicknefs at the root. I have seen one horn of a Moose Deer, which I am convinced would weigh from sixteen to twenty pounds.

The Keraboo is another kind of Deer, much of the same colour with that of the Moose, but not near the size. I have seen many of their fkins, which are of a very dark gray; but none of them alive. Their antlers or horns are somewhat similar to those of the red Deer. They inhabit the coldest countries; are numerous in Newfoundland, the extensive country of Labrador, lower parts of Canada, Nova Scotia, and New Brunswick, but never farther south. They eat no grafs, but live on the poorest and most barren mofses. So that, by every information I have had, I consider them to be the Rein Deer of this country, but not domesticated as those of Lapland and Rufsia are.

They have a particular way of walking on the snow, by which they sink no deeper than stout Dogs, owing, as I have been told, to the form of their hoofs, and to their manner of placing them when they run or walk in deep snow. I have seen their tracks, which are as large as a Bull's.

The huntsmen therefore stalk them, much in the same way as they do Red Deer in Scotland; with this difference only, that the Keraboo are fond of extensive plains clear of wood, and herd together in droves. When the sportsman finds them in a plain of this kind, he cuts a bunch of branches of young trees, which he carries before him to hide him from their sight, and goes on so slowly that his motion is not perceived by them; and when he comes within fhot he fixes it in the ground, and lays himself flat behind it; from this place he fires, and as he is covered by the bufh, they do not see what occasions the report. If he either mifses or kills dead, they are not disturbed. He may therefore charge and fire again, while he continues to kill or miſs, as already said; so that it is not unfrequent to fire half a dozen of ſhots in this way. But if he only wounds, and one of them whistles, which is the sign of alarm, they set off in a gang; and ten to one if he sees them more that day.

The Luservi and Carcaseu are of the Cat kind, and much the size of a Lamb six months old. The Lucervi is of a light grey colour, and in figure a perfect Cat, with strong broad paws, and very long ſharp claws. They have no tail, but a small stump of the size and length of one's little finger. They are very numerous here, as I have seen a great many of their ſkins with merchants wherever I went. They are not mischievous but when attacked, and seldom attack Sheep, though full master of their strength. The real Wild Cat is also here; but not near in such numbers as the former.

The Carcaseu, as I am told by some people, is still a larger animal; his hue is jet black, very hairy, ſharp ears, with a rough, buſhy tail, somewhat resembling that of a Fox, but not quite so long, with ſharp claws like those of a Cat.

This animal has something of the Monkey in him, and plays many of his tricks. The following stories of his pranks are only a few of many which are related of him.

A MAN who had been alone in the woods, had occasion to go a start away from the place at which he had encamped at night, and thinking it troublesome to carry his blanket and tomahawk along with him, left them there until he fhould return. The Carcaseu had come in his absence and carried away both blanket and tomahawk; when the man returned, he mifsed them, and finding no track about the place but that of the Carcaseu, he followed it, and at a considerable distance found the snow had been stirred and heaped up; he had the curiosity to examine it, and there found his own blanket; but the tomahawk he never got.

ANOTHER man, on the like occasion, being in a similar situation, had left his blanket, tomahawk and powder horn. When he came back, he found his blanket had been burnt to afhes in the fire he had left, and his powder horn and hatchet a-mifsing. On looking around him, he saw a Carcaseu in the next tree, which he fired at and fhot dead. On examining it, he found his head singed, and both his eyes burnt stone blind, which was owing to his putting the powder horn in the fire, to see if it would burn, and staying too near it till it blew up about his face; and when frantic with the pain and blindnefs, he ran up the first tree he met, and dared not come down in case worse fhould befal him. And hence it is that sportsmen in this country are so very careful of leaving nothing of value near a fire in the woods, lest this tricky animal find it out and burn it.

A Mr Higginbottom, who had been a long time an Indian trader in the Magdalen mountain, which bounds lower Canada and this province, told me he had once left a pack of fkins in a forsaken solitary hut, which the Carcaseu found out, untied the packages, and carried off every one of them.

That, to mislead and deceive the owner, he raised the snow in heaps, he supposes in a thousand parts about the place. That he, Mr Higginbottom, ripped up a great many of these in hopes of finding some of the fkins concealed under them, but never yet found so much as one of them.

This strange mischievous creature is a great pest to the Indians, who are expert enough in making traps of various constructions, sufficient to hold all sorts of wild animals that frequent the corner they happen to be in; yet fhould they make a chain of traps ten miles long, and that the Carcaseu fell in with any one of them, he will range about until he demolifhes one and all of them, and seems uneasy while one is remaining. He hides the sticks of which they are composed, in such a manner that it is the next thing to a miracle to find out any one of them; and how he can remove logs of a considerable weight, is no lefs surprising.

The Indians in New Brunswick and Lower Canada call him the *Black Devil*; and as an instance of their knowledge of his bad tricks, when a merchant cheats or circumvents them in a bargain, they call him a Carcaseu.

I do not suppose they are numerous, as I have not seen above half a dozen of their fkins; and as I have not heard of their being in the south, I judge them to be inhabitants of a cold country only.

Having set out on our way home from Mr Frazer's, who furnifhed us very hospitably with some provisions and necefsaries, we arrived in the evening at a deserted house at the foot of the river Renow, where it empties itself into the Merimafhee. We put up there that night, and as it rained a great deal, we deemed ourselves lucky to be under a dry roof.

We proceeded up the river, and saw three Moose Deer crofsing it; a Cow and young, and a Bull Moose; and though the water where they crofsed had been between three and four feet deep, they treaded through with as much ease as if it had been but as many inches; and as they had gone in some sort of haste into the wood, it was thought needless to follow them.

On this day's course I observed a great many places where fishing cruives or chests could be built with very little trouble or expence, and with a certainty of success. The water spreads so wide as to be on many fords not above four inches in the deepest part; we could not get the canoe up without touching and dragging her along the bottom. If it should so happen, as no doubt it will, when settlements take place in the country above, that cruiving the river will be opposed; yet if one man had a property of one of the long islands on this river, and the land on the opposite shore, it is to be supposed he might cruive betwixt it and the shore, while the channel on the other side of the island were left open, and permit the fish to proceed up the stream. Many of these islands are so long, that if a chest were placed at the head, such fish as chanced to come up that channel would be apt to push forward at any hazard, rather than return and attempt another course. The channel is smooth, and the gravel and beach so small, that pickets, or stakes of wood, might be driven endwise into the bottom, and so close, that the fish could not pafs. Many of the pickets, if not the whole, would readily stand from year to year. There is little danger of their being carried away by speats during the fishing season; as generally the rains falling then seldom or never swell the river to such a height as would endanger them; or supposing any breaches were then made they could be soon repaired. And in the event the whole of these pickets should be driven away by the ice and trees floating down the river, in time of the freshes, the trouble and expence of replacing them would be but small; as two men having wood at hand could make up the whole in a few days.

Coming up this grand and beautiful river, I observed several fine islands that escaped my notice going down, where cruives might be made in the water in this way. Also large intervals; and a vast extent of rich lands, admitting of easy improvement, where many hundreds, and even thousands of families might find comfortable settlements; so that, upon the whole, I think it as eligible a place for a settlement as any I have as yet seen in America.

The great risque would be, and which has already hurt the lower settlements on this river, that the vast abundance of fish might induce the settlers to apply more to the fishing than to the cultivation of their lands.

On the small rivers Kain and Renow, they fish in the following manner: At the foot of a certain pool they place a net acrofs; beat down the fish for a number of miles from above, and then sweep the pool. And changing in this manner from one pool to another, they hardly leave a fish in these small rivers, till the next speat bring up what will supply their place.

The Rustiguich, which is a large stream, falling into the bay of Chaleur, as already observed, is fished in a way that is a little more curious. As the Indians have no large nets of their own, and claim an exclusive right to the fifhing, they apply for the loan of one to some white man who has one, and for which he is to get a proportional fhare of the fifh. When a proper net is obtained, they place it acrofs a certain large pool, near the foot of the river. Having done this, they go with a number of canoes up the river, sometimes eight or ten miles, each being provided with a boiled Salmon in it; and when they get up as far as they intend, they range their canoes in proper order from side to side of the river, and crumble out the boiled Salmon as fast as they are able, till the water appears white and muddy by it. They then fall to work, and beat down the fish with their poles and spear shafts, keeping pace with the crumbled fish as they go along, until they come to the large pool, at the foot of which the net is set, and then they scringe the pool.

GEORGE M'GREGOR, on whose veracity I could depend, told me, that he himself had seen 900 Salmon taken out of that pool at one time in this manner, and that he got thirty or forty of them from the Indians for mending a few holes in the net. And his account is corroborated by another man, who told me, that upon another occasion, he had seen 1100 taken out of the same place in the like manner. Having encamped and slept all night on the banks of the river, we set out pretty early next morning, and as we were going up, we made the same observations as the day before, in regard to the soil and fishing. As I was travelling on the banks of the river, I observed two Wigwams; I went in to see them, and found both of them without an inhabitant. The families had been then either fishing or hunting. The furniture of these temporary habitations consisted of several dishes made of birch bark, finely ornamented, and boxes of Porcupine quills, as I supposed for sale. Besides these, I saw a root drying, which the Indians use as a cure for many complaints, and took a piece of it along with me. The name they give it, I think, is Calomet*. It has a strong spicy taste, an aromatic scent, and heats the stomach almost as much as a dram. It is either the root of the sedge, or something very like it.

We arrived at the Portage and dined. Left the canoes there, and proceeded on foot to the Nashwack river. Shot three or four pheasants; and found a large Moose Deer's horn, lately dropped off, by the side of the path, which, I suppose, would weigh above a stone weight. Having met our horses about midway, we mounted and arrived an hour or two after night fall at the house of our former landlord, Angus M'Intosh, with whom we staid that night.

Next morning, beginning to breakfast, I was surprised to see him bring in a large kebuck, as I supposed of cheese, of about twenty pounds weight. I asked him, when did he make that cheese? he answered, in spring last. I observed to him that I had seen many a farmer in my country who had threescore of milk Cows, but never knew them to make a cheese of that size at that season of the year. He said it took more than that number of his Cows;—that he milked above an hundred to make that cheese. This I could

* *Calamus aromaticus*, I suppose.

not divine, as I knew he had only four milk Cows, which I saw that morning, until he began to slice it down, when, to my great surprise, I found it to be a loaf of maple sugar, made in the form, and of the colour of a cheese; which proved what he had said to be true, as he had pierced that number of trees to make it.

Here I saw the finest melaſses I ever tasted, extracted from the same tree, far superior to that made of the sugar cane, and nighest to honey in taste of any thing I know.

Continued our journey. Called on Dr Drummond, captain M'Lean, and captain French. The latter told me, that some years he caught ten barrels of Salmon on a pool in the river before his house, besides what served his family, in one season; but that yearly they are turning fewer, as the settlements increase; and that the people destroy most of them in the spawning time, as there is no attention paid to prevent it in this province.

The gentlemen in this settlement have very fine spacious farms, which in a few years must turn out to a very great account.

Captain French, who holds one of these, rarely keeps a servant. He himself and son, who is also a half pay officer, manage and carry on the work without, while his wife and daughters do the dairy, and that within. By laudable attention and industry, he lives in affluence, and independent of the trouble and expence of servants, while many of his brother officers who trust to them, get in debt, become poor, and the next thing to bankruptcy.

In the neighbourhood of my good friend Captain M'Lean, was a farm to be disposed of, which, from the low price afked for it, the quality of its soil, and its pleasant situation, I was very near induced to purchase. It belonged then to a half pay officer, whose father died in the Vermount State, and left him a good pofsefsion, which he was obliged to occupy or lose. His farm here consisted of 550 acres, twenty-five of which were clear, which could not be done but at a considerable expence, though lefs to him than to others, as he wrought the greatest part of it with his own hands. There was an island in it on which he could annually cut twelve tons of hay. More of the island could be cleared at a small expence; so that triple the quantity could be made on it. Besides this there was a pool in the river on which he usually caught a barrel of Salmon more than served his family. All this I could have had, and was offered to me for fifty pounds, Halifax currency; which is five pounds lefs than Sterling. But as I was determined to engage in nothing of the kind till I ſhould return home, I declined it. The owner, whom I fell in with next year, told me he sold it for that money. I proceeded down the river, called on Captain Shaw, lieutenant Dugald Campbell, and in the evening arrived at Frederick Town; and next day waited again on the governor, who confirmed what he had formerly said in regard to lands, with the addition, that to some he would give even a thousand acres, if their stock was proportional to it. He said, he did not doubt but I would see finer lands on the lakes and southern parts of Canada, but it was much more out of the world than any part of this province, from whence every inhabitant had acceſs of seeing or hearing from the mother country almost every day.

From the governor's I went to the engineer's house, where I staid for some days, preparing for my journey through the wilderneſs and mountains to Lower Canada.

From FREDERICK TOWN *to* QUEBEC.

I was now to encounter a journey, the dangers and difficulties of which would stagger many, more accustomed than I was to travelling in this country, and inured to the ways necessary, through impenetrable forests, a savage wilderness, and mountains covered with snow; and what I deemed little better was, that I had to go from 270 to 300 miles, by water, through broad and rapid streams, broken with stones and rocks, which made it both unsafe and intricate to get up against them in a small birch canoe, that could hardly carry my Dog besides the poleman, or navigator, and myself. Of all this I was informed by others, as well as by my nephew, the engineer, who pressed me much to wait until next May, when I might, without any danger of being overtaken by snow in the mountains, get through with more safety; and mentioned that lord Fitzgerald, who had undertaken such a journey a year or two ago, from Frederick Town to Quebec, in the dead of winter, was well provided with a small party, snow shoes, and every thing necessary for

well ~~provided with~~ a small par-
oes, and every thing necefsary for

such an undertaking; that he had large Dogs to carry their provisions on tobagans on the snow; and that before he crossed the mountains, which there rise one above another, for more than an hundred miles, he himself, and two or three more who pushed on, thought it advisable to send back the rest; that by the time they descended into Canada, their provisions were so far exhausted, and their clothes so torn to rags by the bushes, and no game falling in their way, that they began to despond, and at length lost all hopes of ever seeing a human creature again; with these gloomy thoughts, they continued for eight or ten days, still pushing on, and directed by their pocket compasses, until providentially they fell in with the snow shoe track of an Indian, who had been hunting very deep in the woods, which they followed, and it led them to his Wigwam, and after they refreshed themselves there, that the Indian conducted them to Quebec. His lordship was about a month on this journey, though he was in hopes, when he left Frederick Town, of making it out in half the time.

It is much easier travelling in winter in the woods of this country than in summer; as the snow covers the ground hemlock, and most of the under brush, swamps, creeks, lakes, fallen trees, logs, &c. which otherwise would obstruct the passenger, and retard his progress more than any one who has not seen it can conceive; and though I had entertained some thoughts of making a straight course, as lord Fitzgerald had done, which I afterwards understood no one had ever accomplished but himself, yet on hearing of his disasters, I changed my purpose, and resolved to follow the course of the water, however dangerous the rapid currents in many places might be, as far as it would lead, and shorten my passage by land through the mountains and deserts to Canada, by the short way that lord Fitzgerald took, or at least meant to take. I do not suppose the distance between Frederick Town and Quebec to exceed much 200 miles; but that which I was now to take is above 400. I therefore got provisions and every other necessary ready, and engaged my old conductor, George M'Gregor, who is one of the best canoe men in the province, and was acquainted with a part of the way, to go along with me. At the same time the engineer, having occasion to visit the barracks on Preskeel, and at the Grand Falls, took the opportunity of conducting me that length, which is reckoned to be 180 miles of the way. We accordingly set out on the 7th of October, he in his own canoe, poled by his servant, and I in another, conducted by

George. My servant was obliged to travel as far as he could by land. And when we were under the necefsity of crofsing from the one side of the river to the other, on account of the badnefs of the channel, or rapidity of the stream, it was requisite to land me while the canoe was sent for him, as it could not carry us both at a time.

In this way we kept on our course, and on the first day pafsed many spacious fertile islands, averaged at about 100 acres extent each, flat as a bowling green, mostly covered with the loftiest hard timber imaginable, delightfully situated, the soil deep and of the richest quality, the country closely inhabited; and when night came on we encamped in the woods, in preference to going to any of the neighbouring houses. The scent of our provisions brought, as we supposed, some wild animals about us; but my faithful Dog kept watch all night; and he once barked so close, that he seemed to have some large animal at bay, which he durst not attack, probably a Bear. Next morning we were told that one had been lately seen about that place. Dogs are very useful upon such occasions, and few people here go any distance into the woods without one.

October 8. On our way this day, both sides of the river continued closely inhabited;

the face of the country descended with an easy slope, like that we had paſsed yesterday, but the islands smaller and fewer in number. We saw several flocks of large black Ducks with red bills, but they were so ſhy as not to allow us to come within ſhot. Towards evening the land became more precipitate, and the mountains descended to the water's edge. We put up at a place called Paey York, in which a Major Murray had once resided. He had built a dwelling house, barn, and a large grist and saw mill, and made several other improvements; but as the land was so poor as to yield no crop worth while without manure, he left it, and had let his mills at L. 50 *per annum*; but they unfortunately took fire last summer, and were reduced to aſhes; so that if he himself, or some other adventurer, does not rebuild them, it is said he will not get a sixpence for his property, notwithstanding the considerable expence he has been at.

OCTOBER 9. The river, for a considerable part of our way this morning, was entirely confined with mountains, and there were no settlements; but further on it opened again, and the country was inhabited. Towards noon we fell in with a large party of Indians, who were encamped on the banks of the river, making canoes, and preparing for going down the river with their wives and families. Many of the daughters were handsome buxom wenches, with lively expreſsive features, all with their hair tied, and better dreſsed in their faſhion than any I had yet seen. The engineer's canoe being a little leaky, we stopped here and got it repaired. Many of the Indians spoke French, but scarcely a word of Engliſh; the engineer conversed with them in the former language, as did my friend George M'Gregor in their own tongue. They said they were going to school, that is to those parts where schoolmasters are placed and appointed, to teach such of the Indian children as their parents choose to send. The master's salaries are paid by government, and the children are clothed and maintained at the expence of government. There is one of these schools at the grand lake behind Majorville, another in the Kanabicaces, and a third higher up the river, behind a captain Artwood's plantation. While the families choose to remain with their children, they are also fed and clothed in the same way. Every Indian gets two suits of clothes, and two blankets *per annum*, a pound of tobacco and a pipe *per* week, and as much provisions, consisting of flour, Indian corn, beans, pulse, and pork, as serves him; yet notwithstanding their being thus amply provided, no sooner does the fall of the year, and the hunting season commence, than off they set, and range the wilderness far and near in quest of game. It is indeed their harvest, on which they wholly rely for support; but when at school, they, like many inconsiderate and idle scholars, do not pay the proper attention, but with this difference, that the latter are made to apply by the birch, but the former are urged by hunger only. I was told that some of the most expert of them at hunting and fishing made shift to draw from twenty to thirty guineas in some seasons for peltry; and as government supply them with clothes, had they common prudence or management, (but of either they have none,) they might live in affluence, and in as much ease as people of their wandering disposition could wish, but their profits mostly go in rum, of which they are immoderately fond.

This morning, and the preceding night, we met about three score of their canoes, loaded with their families and furs, going down the river, as they said, to school. After staying for more than an hour with them, and having got our canoes made tight, we proceeded on our way. The river was here so rapid, and ran with such amazing force, that we were obliged to come out and walk on land, before the canoes could be either dragged or poled up against the stream at the edge of the water ; and if there had been no such necefsity I fhould have deemed it unsafe and dangerous to continue in them. Cold fhowers of snow and sleet came on. We put up at a captain Artwood's, an American gentleman, a facetious little fellow, who gave us a great many songs of his own composing, and repeated many agreeable pafsages of Thomson's Seasons and other poems. Captain Artwood affirmed, what I had been often told by others, that this was the best country of any for grafs, and inferior to none for grain ; that the cattle often preferred pasturing in the woods, to the most luxuriant open fields ; and that he himself had an hundred pounds of tallow from an Ox fed in the woods. This gentleman's farm is situated on a broad point of land, where the river forms an obtuse angle, on which the French had a fort before the Britifh got pofsefsion of this province, and had cleared a considerable space about it. The remains of the pickets and ramparts are still to be easily discovered. The cause of the great rapids already mentioned, I judged to be a rise of one foot in ten, for the space of a mile, which occasioned their immense velocity. In crofsing a large and deep pool at the foot of the rapids, we were very near being overset in the middle of the stream, by inadvertency. In paddling through, I happened to lean too much to one side, which brought the water to edge with the gunnel. My conductor aroused my attention, by hastily calling to me to take care, and very alertly laid his whole weight on the opposite side, otherwise we must have gone to the bottom. Such inadvertencies often prove fatal in those miserable small vessels which float as light as a cork on the surface of the water.

From captain Artwood's we set out by daylight, and had gone but a few miles when the country again became open, the mountains were spread out at a considerable distance, and the river widened. Several islands appeared. We put up and breakfasted at one Sheriff's who kept a public house. Here we were told that the preceding evening three men, crofsing the river in a canoe, were overset and one of them drowned, one swam afhore, and the third held by the canoe, which kept afloat, until a son of Sheriff's, who was the one that had swam afhore, returned with another canoe and relieved him. The poor man that was drowned had left a wife and small family of children, who had not as yet heard of their misfortune, and whose distrefs the people here deplored very much; but said, they had as much crop as would maintain them two years at least. This was a favourable circumstance of a new and little cleared settlement, notwithstanding of its high situation.

This young man, the landlord's son, shewed me the skin of a young Bear which two hardy stout Dogs I had seen him have, had killed a few nights before. He said the Bear had come so close to the house that the Dogs smelled and pursued him; that their barking had brought him, and another person, out with their guns; that before they came up he had betaken to a tree, on which one of them went for an axe and cut it down; that when the tree fell, he ran away and often beat off the Dogs in the chace; that in this way they had continued for half a mile, and got into the woods before the Dogs fixed upon and held him; that his cries, which the young man said he believed could have been heard a mile off, brought him and the other man up; that they stood with their guns cocked, expecting every moment to be attacked by the old Bears, who they were sure would come to the young Bear's relief, were they within hearing; that while the two people faced and looked one way, they were in dread of being seized behind from the other; for this reason they continued facing from side to side, attentive to every quarter, and in full afsurance of being attacked for half an hour, while the Dogs were killing the Bear; they could give no afsistance to the Dogs on account of the darknefs of the night.

After breakfast I proceeded by land a good way on the water side. The habitations continued close, the soil deep and fertile, and I have no doubt, in a little time, that this will become a plentiful and happy settlement, though rather far from market. They seem to regard good soil more than distance and extent in this part of the country.

Towards evening, while the engineer was afhore buying some necefsary provisions, I landed on an opposite island where a number of Indians were settled, and raised a considerable quantity of Indian corn. The day being cold, with a north west wind, I went into a Wigwam to warm me; the owner was a Canadian Indian, who had served under general Burgoyne last war, and had been wounded in that service, but not disabled; he spoke French and a little Englifh; he was an intimate companion and very particular friend of George M'Gregor's, they had been on many hunting excursions together. George afked him where his daughter was, and launched out to me much in her praise. He said fhe was at school in the Kanabicaces and lived in the schoolmaster's house; that she was so saucy as not to speak to him when he went to see her, which is, no doubt, owing to the wretched masters, who teach them to despise their parents; whereas a different conduct might have induced them to send many more of their children to school than they do, which would be the means of civilizing them, and rendering them useful members of society. On my seeing the figures of a Bull and a Cow Moose Deer on the birch walls of his Wigwam, I requested the favour of him to draw the Luservi and Carcaseu. He looked for a bit of charcoal; but on my giving him my black lead pencil, he seemed to understand the use of it, and drew all these very neatly, on the blade of a new and well polished paddle, which I found by me, and reached to him for that purpose. The engineer once shewed me a drawing upon paper, made by an Indian, of two rivers running in different directions, which, he said, he had afterwards found, on a survey he himself had made of them, to be very exact. The genius and mental powers of these people are extremely lively and retentive.

HAVING given two hearty bumpers of rum to this Indian, I left him, and we continued our route, and in the evening encamped in the woods. The night freezed pretty smartly.

N

Next morning we set out early and pafsed several fine islands, on one of which I landed. It had been lately inhabited by Indians, but they had left it and gone to school. They had raised a considerable quantity of Indian corn on it, which they carried along with them. This island, like all the other places I have ever seen the Indians reside on for any time, was rich deep soil, and easily cleared. My servant, who had hitherto walked all along, had fhot several Pheasants; and having wounded a Mink, which is a black amphibious animal, fhaped like a Martin, but much larger and as vicious, the Mink got out on the river, and my Dog pursued him; when the Mink dived the Dog kept swimming about until he rose again to the surface; they had several battles, and afforded us good sport. At length both were much spent, and my servant having compafsion on the Dog, who was smartly bitten in several places, fhot the Mink, which his antagonist brought in triumph afhore to his master.

One of the Pheasants fhot this day was of the Spruce kind, none of which I had ever seen before, and it differs a good deal from the Birch species, and resembles much in fhape and size, and in the roughnefs of its legs, a Grous or Moor Cock; but as they chiefly subsist on the buds of the spruce tree, their flefh tastes very much of it, and does not eat so well as that of the birch Pheasant.

My poor servant being now much fatigued with hard travelling through rugged coarse land for several days, I exchanged situations with him, and walked on shore in my turn.

In the evening we arrived at the military port of Preſkeel. Lieutenant Thong, of the sixth regiment, who commanded at this port, and seems to be a genteel young man, came very politely to wait on us, and aſked us to spend the evening in his apartment. While the engineer was examining the barracks, and settling some accounts with the workmen, I took a stroll around the place to see it. The country, as far as I could discern on both sides of the river, is covered with lofty spruce and pine trees; the soil deep, but incorporated too much with sand; and yet it is cried up as wonderful in the production of pulse of almost all kinds, and vegetables. For my own part I could see nothing deserving such encomiums. The gardens below the banks on which the barracks are built, seem to be deep rich soil, but no other part attracted my particular attention. The troops have cleared a good deal of the ground about the barracks, by using the wood for firing; but as the ground is not kept in tillage, the young growth ſhoot up again, and will become a thicket.

This fort is situated on a point of land, at the junction of the small but rugged river of Preſkeel with that great and spacious one of St John, famous for Trout fiſhing. At this place we paſsed the evening, and breakfasted next morning with Lieutenant Thong and three other subaltern officers of the sixty-fifth regiment, who had come to relieve him.

THE engineer having some directions to give to the workmen, and a report to make to the governor of the condition of the barracks, and the works going on at this place, he remained behind me, and I proceeded, accompanied by my conductor George only, and my servant, who walked on ſhore as formerly. Before our setting out, I was told that the river would become more and more rapid as we advanced; that it was broken with stones and rocks; and was of a wild and gloomy appearance, being hemmed in on both sides by the precipices; that the way became more intricate, and was leſs known; and the next fort distant about eighty miles, and not a living soul to be seen in all that space, unleſs some few savages ſhould be accidentally met with. This I thought bad enough, but deemed no trouble, fatigue, or even disaster, that could befal me, equal to the misfortune of being detained in this province till next May. I therefore puſhed on, but promised to wait a day at the Grand Falls in hopes the engineer would overtake me there.

Towards noon some heavy showers of sleet and rain fell, that made us very wet and cold. We landed and struck a fire to warm us. The evening having cleared up, we continued our journey, and encamped at night at the root of an old cedar tree. The wettest day that is, a large cedar tree will furnish any expert hand with materials for putting up a fire; its bark for lighting, and its decayed lower branches for fuel. The night freezed smartly, and though we had chosen a convenient spot to pafs the night in, we felt it extremely cold. In the morning of the preceding day, I had seen some appearance of good land, but much more of bad.

October 13. A very cold blowing day. The river broken and rapid; the canoe almost constantly in danger of being driven on large stones, rocks, or into strong currents, by the high gusts of wind, and overset. I often exchanged with my servant to ease him, and walked on land, and fhifted from the one side of the river to the other, for the more easy travelling. Towards evening I turned a point of land, and got considerably a-head of the canoe, which at this time was on the opposite side. I sat down to rest myself, and to write my journal, and intended to wait until the canoe came up. Having rested here for double the time I judged the canoe would have taken, I became very uneasy, lest it was overset, and both the men drowned; but still I continued where I was, in hopes that I might have mistaken the distance and the difficulty of getting up the frequent and almost perpetual rapids; until at length I concluded, without a pofsibility of doubt, that some misfortune had befallen them, and that it could be no other than that they were for ever lost. I knew my own servant could not swim, nor did I believe George could.

I now found myself in a very disagreeable situation indeed, without clothes to cover me at night, provisions or amunition but one fhot in my gun, hungry, and much fatigued, having travelled a good deal, and eaten nothing in the morning but one slice of cold frosty meat, and three days journey from any human being or thing that could sustain life. In this desponding condition, I returned to make the best of my way to Prefkeel, and was in great doubt if ever I could reach it, considering the frosty nights, ruggednefs of the woods, and every other impediment that was to fall in my way. I had not returned above half a mile, when, to my no small joy, I espied the canoe coming along on the opposite side of the river. What had detained them

Shoot amongst Rocks, example Rapid Stream

was, that the pole of the canoe broke just as I was getting out of sight. They had to land, cut another pole, put up a fire, toast and peel it, before it was fit for use. This induced me to resolve not to travel more by land without my gun, powder, and fhot, steel, spunge, and flint, for striking a fire, and a piece of bread in my pocket; and I determined to cause my servant have the same when he walked; so that if the canoe fhould be lost, we would at least have some means of supporting ourselves, be the next Indian or white settlement at what distance it would.

WE went some miles further on, and encamped at a pretty little river called Tabick, in an old Wigwam, to which we retired. The floor being dry, I supposed it unnecefsary to put crops of trees as usual under me; but in this I was mistaken, as I found in the morning my great coat frozen and sticking to the ground, and that side next to it cold as ice, and somewhat powerlefs until I walked a little. I always afterwards took care to put bark, where I could find it, or crops of trees under me to prevent the like.

NEXT day, though the frost continued, the sun was warm and revived our spirits. I travelled a good deal on land, and pafsed through an Indian settlement on a spacious plain at the foot of Salmon river. Over all this flat, the grafs, weeds, wild oats, bear or wheat, (I could not say which of the two last,) were breast high, and rendered my pafsage through them very difficult; the Indians had considerable plantations of Indian corn at this place. They fhewed me the fkin of a large Moose Deer, a Buck, lately killed, which was then drying. They admired my double barrelled gun very much, and seemed to be quite unacquainted with guns of that kind. Large logs of spruce, pine, and other timber, amounting to, I suppose, a thousand tons, stuck by some accident while floating in the middle of the river, and admitted of my crofsing over upon them dry.

I PASSED several high mountains this day, and the banks of the river as we advanced, became more rugged, wild, and difficult. When night came on, we encamped as usual at the root of a large cedar, and cut down as much wood as kept up the fire all night. A quantity of snow fell, which covered the ground, and as we were under no sort of fhade, disturbed our rest a good deal, as we were unused to it. Next morning we saw the tracks of several wild animals on the snow, but could not say what they were; these parts are so savage as to be fit for no other living creature. The way was so rugged that my servant was often obliged to walk up to the middle in the water to avoid thickets and fallen trees that obstructed his paſsage. As we came along, my poor Dog was so fatigued, cut, and bruised, that he looked no more for game than we did, and we wiſhed for nothing more than to get on where we might obtain ſhelter and rest. This was the severest day's journey we as yet had had, and a few more such would have cured my paſsion for travelling in the wildernefs.

We arrived in the evening at the Grand Falls, and carried up our canoe and baggage to the engineer's barracks, where we lodged that night. The height of the hill on which the barracks are erected is 130 feet perpendicular above the landing place, and the length of the portage from where you come out of the river below the Falls, to the place you enter it again above, is no more than half a mile, but the ascent is very steep. The barracks erected for the men and officers under the direction and inspection of my friend, are neat and commodious, and sufficient for the accommodation of two companies.

The winter now seemed to be fairly set in with frost and snow, though sooner than usual. We kept on a rousing fire all night, and slept comfortably on a dry deal floor. By the negligence of the engineer's servant a Dog was allowed to carry away my ham and butter; and had not my friend drawn a part of his own rations, and given me half of his pork, I ſhould have been poorly provided in the mountains which I had to paſs. As I did not choose that my faithful servant ſhould suffer such distreſs hereafter as he had hitherto done, though without a murmur on his part, I made inquiry if a canoe could be procured, and had the good fortune to fall in with a little lively Frenchman who spoke some Engliſh, and undertook to carry my servant in his canoe, and conduct me to Canada, at the rate of a dollar *per* day, and being found in provisions.

HAVING now every thing ready for my journey, I rose pretty early, and visited the Grand Falls. It is tremenduous to see an immense body of water falling eighty feet perpendicular on rocks that make it rebound with a noise like thunder, and the spray rising high in the air like a cloud. The rocks all around this place are of lime stone.

OCTOBER 16. I set out from the Grand Falls of St John's river. The preceding night and this day felt very cold; much snow on the ground, and the frost keen; the country level; the hills at a great distance from the river, and the water smooth. Meeting with no interruption, we made great way. We put up at a Frenchman's house, who had a throng family, some lively and gay daughters, much better drefsed than the generality of the common people. On his seeing our canoes making for his port, he and two or three of his sons came very politely to receive us and welcome us to his house. I afked if he would favour us with lodgings for that night; he answered with much civility, if I could put up with such accommodation as his house afforded, I fhould be extremely welcome to it. Here therefore I pafsed that night, and was much captivated with the obliging turn and civility of the family, which formed a perfect contrast to those of the surly common Englifh-Americans; but the landlord, in perfect character of the stock from which he originated, put no value on politenefs, which came easy and cost him nothing; but on every thing else he did, and charged me smartly for every article I had from him, even for lodging and potatoes, which no one else I met with in that country ever did. I bought 20 lb. of Moose meat, and a Muffle, as it is there called; in other words, Moose Deer venison and chops; which last is accounted a great delicacy. I took a turn about the farm conducted by the oldest son, who, as is very common in this country, has a farm of his own, but lives with his father. He fhowed me one small plot of land on which they had sown a single bufhel of wheat laſt May, and requested I would mark the stools and stubble on it, which I did, and found the increase to have exceeded any thing of the kind I had any idea of. He said they were of opinion they had reaped near fifty bufh- els from that one sown.

After paying for my lodgings, and every thing I received, threefold, civility except- ed, I bade the family adieu; and as the day was cold, and the road good by the river side, and the settlements close, I walked much on foot; and as the wind blew smartly a-head, I could in many rapids keep up with the canoes. I put up that night at an old man's house, whose son was married to a daughter of the family I had last left; and from the attention the young couple paid to each other I conceived they had not been long married, and on inquiry found it to be only ten days. Here I bought some loaves of bread; and what my entertainers fell fhort of my former host in politenefs, was made up by a much more moderate charge.

After leaving this man's house, and pro- ceeding, as formerly, on foot by the river side, to where a few miles farther on it branches seemingly into equal streams; the Madawasker comes from the north west, and St John's from the north east. The latter was our course which we followed.

I HAD now paſsed all the settlements of the Madawaſker river, extending I think about fifty miles. The land is deep interval, quite flat, but dry, and of as rich a quality as perhaps any in the world; at least it is accounted most so in this province. But the inhabitants labour under many disadvantages that would be deemed by some unsurmountable; such as a high situation; a distance of one hundred miles from any other settlement, and 200 from market; and a six or seven months severe winter: yet they raise the strongest crops imaginable of wheat, barley, oats, and vegetables of most kinds, (except Indian corn,) in great plenty. Onions, turnip, cabbages, and other garden stuffs, grow here in high perfection in the fields without any manure, which I was told they do not use on any occasion.

FROM the rapidity of the river in many parts, though it glides slowly along in other parts, I ſhould suppose this settlement lies two perpendicular miles above the level of the sea; for I think there must be near one foot in every 100 of rise including the Falls; and the settlement is about 300 miles from the sea. If this in feet, there must be the same proportion in miles. They have magistrates who decide all disputes among themselves. They have very neat plantations, and every thing but money; but where they could get that I am at a lofs to know.

We soon came up to a Fall which obliged us to land and drag our canoes on fhore on the rocks, and enter the river above it. We encamped in the evening in the woods, and lay under the canoes, to fhelter us from a considerable quantity of snow that fell through night.

The river being now much narrower, smooth, and fheltered from the wind by the high wood on each side, we made great way. My Dog having got some days rest in one of the canoes, he went now by land, and seemed by his hard barking to have fallen in with a Bear, Luservi, or Carcaseu, which kept him far behind. I went into an Indian Wigwam to wait for him; the master had been out hunting, and there were only two squaws at home. They had several fine large Trouts drying, which they had speared the preceding night; and they fhowed me a turnip of uncommon size, which they had brought from the Madawafker settlements. My Dog having come up I set out.

I remarked in this day's route the dreadful effects of the thunder on the woods. I had seen in several other places plots of trees said to have been struck down, but at such a distance from me that I could not observe it accurately myself; but I was here within a few yards of the spot it had struck upon, which is a circular space of about twenty yards diameter, where the trees grew very strong, and as close as they well could, but not one was left standing. About two-thirds of them were torn up by the roots, the others broken to fhivers, the stumps split down to the ground, and the splinters driven to a great distance. I fhould imagine the extraordinary force that occasioned this devastation to trees so strong, and to so many of them at once, would have even split rocks, had these come in its way.

In pafsing up the river, we saw large fhoals of fine Trouts of about a pound weight each; they did not seem to be fhy, as they would pafs up and down, quite c.o e to the canoes, without being in the least disturbed, and if we had had spears, or hooks and lines, I suppose we might have killed as many as we pleased.

We now arrived at the lower end of the lake ' Tamisquata, which is supposed to be from thirty to forty :. iles long, and one broad in the straitest part; it is a spacious fheet of water, of many broad and deep bays. As far as my eye could reach on each side, I could see nothing but forests of pines of the loftiest kind, interspersed here and there with clumps of the stateliest birches imaginable, that might supply the Britiſh navy for ever.

HERE I observed a great number of aspen trees, vulgarly called the *quaking aſh*, because of the singular quality of the leaves keeping in almost perpetual motion. The Indian name of it is *woman's tongue*, for they say if one leaf be set in motion all the rest begin, and then there is no such thing as stopping them.

THIS province of New Brunswick is suppoſed to be 300 miles square; and if a bird's eye view were taken of it, it would be seen that the thousandth part of it is not clear, but covered either with wood or water. At the end of this lake we threw away our poles and took to our paddles. We had fifteen miles to go upon the lake before we could get to the Grand Portage; and to ſhorten the way we had to croſs the lake twice, and to paſs from point to point, lest we ſhould be overtaken by any gust of wind, as a gust would soon have overset us. We were all obliged to work hard, so that the paddle was scarcely out of my hand for these fifteen miles. Though we puſhed on for an hour or two of night, in hopes of reaching the Porage, we could not make it out, and the wind having got up we were obliged to land.

We encamped on a very cold point, being so late that we could not see to choose a proper situation to pafs the night in. When day light appeared next morning we saw the Portage, which was not a mile off. Here we landed, drew up our canoes, breakfasted at a house which had been built by one Heginbottom, and in which he resided for the conveniency of trading with the Indians; but having left it some time ago, it is now in a decayed state. We struck up a fire, and after refreshing ourselves, and packing our provisions and little baggage, set out; and on October 20th ascended the Magdalen mountains, which bound the provinces of Lower Canada and New Brunswick; and though they are by no means high from their base, are yet, by my calculation, three miles perpendicular above the level of the sea; and which great height occasions, at this early season of the year, more than their high latitude, their being covered with snow and frost. The distance from this, or the length of the Grand Portage to the foot of the small river De Cop, where it enters the great river St. Laurence, is reckoned to be but forty miles; while that of the city St John, from

P

whence I had come, is about 400; so that the declivity to the north must be ten to one steeper than the slope to the south, and the mountains on the St Laurence side must be piled one above another to this distance; which indeed I found to be the case on my travelling through them.

We had scarcely reached the top of the first mountain, when my Dog, who was not only a staunch and excellent pointer, but had been bred and accustomed to all the kinds of game found in the mountains and woods of Scotland, fell in with the track of some Deer, which he followed so far that he lost his way, and detained us a considerable time waiting for him; but on my recollecting that if he once found our footsteps he would soon overtake us, we proceeded, expecting he would come up with us, until we had gone too far to return for him; especially as we did not know the spot from whence he went off from us, or what course he had taken, and that by that time he might perhaps be ten miles off. My poor Dog, who had been my faithful companion and friend, if I may use the expreſsion, for years in all my hunting excursions and travels, kept me from my usual rest, and when he did not appear next morning I despaired of ever seeing him again. My servant, whose companion he was all that time, and to whom he afforded much sport, was almost crying for him. But when he came up to us, after being twenty-four hours absent, with inexpresible joy at finding us, I believe each of us felt as much pleasure as the Dog himself.

We had gone but a ſhort way from thence when the foremost called out, " The sea, the sea!" We all ran with eagerneſs to see it, when Duncan, which is my servant's name, exclaimed, " What a happy sight the sea is! and now that we know where it is we will make for it, and never part with it again;" and yet when we were at sea he would not give one mile of land for the whole ocean. I rejoiced at the sight as much as I had done at seeing land after being near two months on sea and perfectly unaccustomed to that mode of life: and as our guide steered only by the directions he had received at setting out, and could not tell us distinctly where we were, he having never been farther up than the Madawaſker settlement, I resolved as my friend said, to lose sight of the sea no more. We stepped forward to the brow of a hill, and sat down, the men to rest, and I to contemplate the grand scenes now opened to my view, which the situation I was in afforded; being three miles above the level of the sea, and nothing to obstruct the sight.

Here the eye and imagination had full scope to roam undistur'ed; the bustling of sea port towns or crowded cities never was dreamed of here; no roaring stream to disturb, or purling rills to divert the thought; no warbling of the songsters or feathered tribe, to take up the attention, but every thing still as night. I viewed with astonishment the novelty and grandeur of the prospect before me, which pofsibly very few in the world could equal. The opposite coast of Labrador presented a long range of mountains, the one raised on the other until their towering summits were lost in the clouds. The grand river St Laurence, with its numerous isles, are no lefs striking; whose breadth is said to be 100 miles where it enters the gulf of that name, and its waters supplied along a space of above 2000 miles by the greatest streams, lakes, and bodies of frefh water ever known. Forests of the most stately kind, coeval perhaps with the world, and extensive as the great continent that sustains them, which have never suffered diminution since the creation, and fit to supply the world with fhip timber to the end of time; the gloomy wildernefs in which the traveller is often lost has no end, and is inhabited only by such of the savage tribe as prefer fhade to light.

THESE and a thousand other objects that my pen cannot do justice to, were then under the eye from my commanding station, and such indeed as would give full scope to genius to exercise its descriptive powers, and philosophy grounds for the most profound reflections on the great works of nature, in its rude state.

As the snow was not above a foot deep, and had fallen before the frost came on, we sunk through it in the mud often knee deep, so that we had very bad going, and made but little way. My foot once slipped between two logs; and, but for a sudden jerk I gave round, when I found myself falling, it would have been snapped in two. My servant fell across the stump of a tree, and broke one of his ribs, and the little Cadian Frenchman met with the like accident. We however got through on the evening of the third day after entering the Portage; and though we slept on frost and snow every night, and walked through mud and bogs some part of every day knee deep, we found no bad effects from it, nor did any of us catch the least cold. My servant, who always carried my gun, shot as many Pheasants as we had occasion for; I always preferred a stout stick or staff to help me through. The tracks of wild animals were so numerous in the mountains, that at the root of almost every tree were to be seen the marks of Moose, Rynd, or Keraboo Deer; Wolves, Luservi, Carcaseus, Foxes, Hares, and small vermin innumerable, with which last kind the woods seemed to be swarming.

At the foot of the mountains, in several parts, are extensive Cedar swamps, of a greater growth of timber than any of the kind I had as yet seen, which no doubt was intended by nature for some useful purpose, suitable to its magnitude, and to which it may be applied some time or other.

Having now come to the foot of the little river De Cop, where it disembogues into the river St Laurence 120 miles below Quebec, I pushed on to the first post house, where I discharged my attendants. They were to return acrofs the Portage to New Brunswick, and I to proceed to Quebec. I paid the little French Cadian ten dollars, and four guineas to George M'Gregor, who is one of the most obliging lads I ever was acquainted with. He offered to return me a guinea, but as I knew it was no more than he deserved I did not accept of it. The evening turned very windy, accompanied with cold heavy fhowers of snow. I blefsed my stars for having conducted me in safety out of the wildernefs, and over such tremenduous mountains;—fhook hands with my friend George, and wifhed him and his companion a safe return;—mounted the calafh, which had been provided, and drove on through the long but narrow district of the Camerascas on my way to Quebec.

A CALASH is a two wheeled machine, with an open box, resembling a cart, but having a seat in it like a chaise: it is supported on strong elastic leather straps, which give it a spring, and make it far from being a disagreeable conveyance. The postmasters in general supply every calafh with what the French call a Wild Bull's fkin, and we a Buffalo hyde, which is large enough to cover the greatest part of the box, and keeps all the travellers surprisingly warm, even in the coldest weather. But for these fkins, and the other furs used in this country, there would be no standing the winter's cold in these open carriages. They are drawn by one or two horses as there may be occasion; and as they are made very light, go at a great rate.

THE country is so closely inhabited, that I judge there is a house and family within twenty roods of each other; so that there are from twelve to sixteen families in the course of each mile. The post houses are placed at fhort stages, and obliged to provide vehicles at a call; so that a traveller may post night and day, if he thinks proper, at the low rate of a pistarine, or French shilling, *per* league; so cheap is travelling in this populous country.

In going through this district on a large meadow of some miles extent, I observed a method of securing the hay upon it, which I think might be used to advantage in Britain in the case of meadows and corn fields subject to be flooded with water. Stakes were fixed in the ground in a circular, or rather an octogonal form, over which sticks were laid acrofs, and upon these the hay was made up in cocks, which raised it so high as to secure it from the spring tides which over ood these flat meadows.

All along the coast, fishing wears for catching Salmon were so close to each other, that every f r er seemed to have one on his own property. The number of barrels which are annually exported from these fisheries I have not acquired a sufficient knowledge of, but was told that it was very considerable. About these meadows were the greatest number of Wild Geese, Brants, and Ducks I ever saw; and the principal day of hunting them by the natives was Sunday, which they said was o ing to their being idle from other works; and yet churches and places of worship are here very numerous.

Off the coast of the Cameraſkas, about a mile's distance from shore, lies a long narrow island, where, as well as in several other parts in this river, a great many Porpuſses or Buckers are caught, which from what follows seem to be a timorous sort of animal, and as the manner in which they are caught is somewhat curious, a description of it may here be attempted.

At the head of, and adjoining to this island, is a large bank of sand, which ebbs dry at low water, but when the tide is in, is covered to a considerable depth. On this bank a low circular wear of wattlings is made, the one end of which comes close to the land, and at the other end a small space is left open so as not to obstruct the fish at entering. At considerable spaces or intervals all along this circle long wands are stuck, and so flexible and supple as to yield to the current, which is here so strong as to keep them always in motion. When the flood makes, the Porpuſses, which keep along the coast of the island, enter by the open space, and push directly forward towards the other end, when lo! they see the wand, a long white thing, shaking and bobbing in the water before them, which frightens them much; they turn about in haste, and shift to a different quarter; but a similar appearance is before them there also, shaking and bobbing like the former; and on whatever side they turn, this strange apparition seems to place itself a-head of them. They continue in fright and amazement, going about within the circle, until at last the tide leaves them, so that they cannot get over the low wear, and the bank ebbs dry. In this manner a great many of them are caught, sometimes hundreds at a time, from which considerable quantities of oil are made and exported; and this forms no inconsiderable article of commerce.

Besides these fisheries, there are others about the island of Anticosti, where the river is, from Cape Rosieres on the south, to the coast of Labrador on the north, 100 miles over. Near the middle lies that barren island, which is supposed to be 120 miles long, and thirty broad, inhabited by wild beasts only, chiefly Bears, of which there are a great many, some Foxes, Martins, and small vermin. The Canadians and Indians resort to this island in winter, to kill them for their skins, and are in general very succefsful. From this place to Quebec the river gradually becomes narrower, a distance of 300 miles, so that from that city to Point Levi it is hardly a mile broad. About the island of Anticosti, and many other parts of this spacious channel, are amazing fhoals of white Porpufses, glittering like silver; and lower down, a number of White Seals, and of the Manati or Sea Cow, in all which the fifheries might be carried on to any extent.

When this country was first pofsefsed by the French, the king granted away the land to the *noblefse*, in large tracts from three to twelve miles square, called *Signiories;* such of these as they were able to clear, were feued by the Signiors in perpetuity to small farmers, at the rate of from 3d. to 2s. *per* acre of quit rent conform to its quality. In all these pofsefsions given by the Signiors it was stipulated, that at whatever time the holders were to dispose of their lands, the givers themselves were to have preference upon equal terms; and were to be allowed a year and day to consider whether they fhould buy them or not, so that they had it in their power to keep the lands all that time in the market. The Signiors being poor and extravagant could clear but little land, of course the settlements were but narrow stripes all along the banks of the river; but since this country is become an object worthy the attention of the Britifh government, and that they give grants of the land, the settlements have become numerous, and are extending into the woods, which in some places appeared to me to be at the distance of ten or twelve miles back from the banks of the river.

I ARRIVED in two days and a half at Point Levi from the lower end of the Cameraſkas, a distance of 121 miles, which in this country is deemed but moderate travelling. Croſsed the Ferry in a large log canoe, the common Ferry boat to Quebec.

From Quebec to Montreal.

A DESCRIPTION of this city is here unnecefsary, as it is already well known; I will therefore only observe, that it consists of a higher and lower town; is ill looking, and irregularly built upon an uneven and rugged point of land, formed by the junction of the river St Charles with the great St Laurence. The fortifications, though sufficient to withstand the attack of an irregular army, do not appear to me to be strong; as the rock on the St Laurence side, which forms a part of the walls of the citadel, is easily scaled, and has neither guns or embrasures on it. At the foot of this rock, and between it and the river, is the narrow path, not two feet wide, where General Montgomery was killed last war; and on the opposite and St Charles side was General Arnold wounded. On the latter occasion I was informed of the following circumstance: That a party of the Americans had entered the lower town, and taken pofsefsion of a street and some houses in it. How soon this was discovered, a Captain Law, with a motley party of

British and Canadians, was ordered to attack them in the rear. After giving the necessary orders to his party, Captain Law marched to the attack; and having turned the corner of a street, came suddenly and unawares up to the breast of the Americans; on looking behind him for his men, he found that they had stopped short, and that there were none in view; as it was now too late to return, he stepped boldly on without seeming to be in the least dismayed, saying, " Gentleman, I have come to offer you terms," ' What terms?' replied the others, " Terms of surrender," said he, ' To whom?' " To me," ' Why to you?' " Because my party is just at hand, and I thought it a pity to cut you all to pieces without first offering you terms of surrender." ' But we will not surrender;' and after a good deal of altercation, *pro* and *con*, he told them, as they would not be prevailed upon to accept of honourable terms, not to blame him for the fatal consequence that was waiting them, made his bows, and offered to go away. ' Oh! ho! (said they,) we are not to part with you so.' " Why?" said he, ' Because you are our prisoner,' " That is against the articles of war," said he. ' No', " Yes," ' No,' " Yes." Here another altercation ensued between them, and as neither side could convince the other in this sort of minute warfare, the Americans proposed to put the question to one of their own party who happened to be then in one of the houses hard by, whose knowledge in these matters they deemed far before those then present. On their going in to the house, Captain Law and that gentleman entered on the subject in dispute, and as it was warmly supported on both sides, and a man standing between captain Law and the door with a drawn sword, threatening him, Major Nairn (known in his younger days by the name of Jack Nairn, formerly of Fraser's first regiment of Highlanders, and has, since the reduction of that regiment, settled in that country somewhere near the Falls of Montmorency,) who came up to support Law with another party, entered the house, and seeing the sword drawn to Law's breast, called out in broad Scotch, which he always spoke, " God's marcy maun, are yau gaun to kill the maun!" and instantly ran him through the body. He then threatened to put them all to the sword that instant if they did not surrender, on which they threw down their arms, and the whole party were taken prisoners.

The fhipping of this city, though almost of 200 years standing, amounts at this day, as I am informed, to no more than three vefsels, whereas that of the city St John in New Brunswick, though but of eight years standing, consists of above sixty square rigged vessels. Whether this is owing to the port of Quebec being shut up with the ice for near six months in the year, and the dangerous navigation of the river St Laurence, and the port of St John's being open all the year through, and its vicinity to the West India islands, or to the spirit of the inhabitants, I know not; but so it is that this difference exists between them at this day. The trade of the city of Quebec is carried on in British bottoms. Their exports chiefly consist of wheat, skins or peltry, fish, oil, and some lumber. There is just now in the harbour two ships loaded with skins, bound for England, whose cargoes are said to be worth L.100,000 each, belonging to the North West Fur Company of Montreal. The quantity of wheat annually shipped for Britain is very considerable, and yet no sort of manure is ever used, as formerly observed. The dung is laid upon the ice so as to be carried off by the floods in spring. The Canadians are perhaps the worst farmers in the world. If one of them happens to have a spot in a field that produces nothing, and has industry enough to drop a few carts of dung on it, if the plough and harrow do not spread it, it may lie there for him; he has done his part when he took the trouble of putting it on the land; spreading it is a labour no one would submit to undertake. Their horned cattle are perhaps the worst in the world, and their Horses the best; the former are ill made, big bellied, thin quartered, and poor as carrion, though at this season they ought to have looked best. While the latter are plump, round, well made, stout, and full of spirit. I have seen Horses of many nations, but none in my opinion for common service equal to those of the Cameraſkas in Lower Canada. They have great quantities of vegetables of most kinds. I have seen large strings of onions sold in the streets not far inferior in size to those of Spain or Portugal.

In this town I fell in with a Mr Angus M'Donald who lives in the neighbourhood. This young gentleman seems to have had a chemical turn from his infancy, and by a procefs, the materials for which can be found in any country or place, he informed me that he could make a composition for glafs or soap manufacture, equal to any barilla that ever came from the Mediterranean; that the operation is so simple that any one can make it, and that when he discovers the secret of it, our kelp in the west of Scotland would not be worth the making I answered that if his discovery would, on experience, turn out to his expectation, it would make his fortune, and be of the highest utility to Great Britain, as immense sums of money were annually sent from thence to America for pot and pearl afhes, and to the Mediterranean for barilla; but that I regretted the hurt it would do to many a worthy gentleman in the west of Scotland whose principal income was derived from kelp. He said that was no object to him; that these gentlemen were so opprefsive to their people that they yearly banifhed great numbers of them to American states, and that they deserved a check. He is a very intelligent young man, and is just now concerned in a patent obtained for the discovery of an improvement in the making of pot and pearl afhes. What may be the result of his chemical experiments time only can tell.

I HAVE been informed since I left that country that this gentleman was employed by Colonel Simcoe in making researches in Upper Canada, and that he discovered two fine salt springs fit to supply the whole province with that necefsary article, besides another mineral spring useful in manufactories. Salt cost a dollar the bufhel at Niagara when I was there, but now by this discovery it will become cheap and plenty.

As the winter was now fast approaching, and that I wifhed to pufh on to the south as far as I could before it fhould set in, that I might be enabled to begin my journey the earlier next spring, I staid no longer in this town than to see Wolfe's Cove where he landed, Abraham's Heights where the battle was fought, and every other thing I judged worth seeing about the place.

OCTOBER 28. I set out in a carriole. The post houses and stages from this city to Montreal, a distance of 200 miles, the same as those in the Camerafkas, and by easy stages arrived at *Trois Rivieres*, or Three Rivers.

On the 30th I set out again from the Three Rivers and arrived the 1st of November at Montreal. As I approached towards the latter the land seemed better, and cleared to a greater extent; both sides of the river closely inhabited, so much so that the churches and grist mills were very numerous, which is a sure indication of the population and fertility of the soil. After leaving the Three Rivers I fell in with a Scotchman dignified with the title of *Sieur Forbes*, who kept one of the post houses, an old man, formerly a private soldier in the first seventy-first regiment, or Fraser's Highlanders, married to a Highland girl, who lately emigrated from Morar in Invernefsfhire. Here I dined, and was much pressed to stay all night. She spoke French fluently, but very little English, so that she and I conversed in Gaelic.

Mrs Forbes, when she found I could not stay, directed me to the house of one Mackay, who I believe was also a soldier in the same regiment. There I passed that night. This man has three stout young fellows his sons, who had been for several years employed as clerks in the North West Company of Montreal, and settled at Detroit and Michilimakinac. It is necessary for these clerks to acquire the Indian language as soon as they can; the more intelligent and expert they are at it, and the more of these languages they can speak, the fitter they are for their business; for these reasons they associate much with the Indians, and often have the squaws in keeping. It would seem Mackay's sons were not wanting in that part of their duty, as there were three of their children then living in the house with their grandmother. When these children grow up, and are instructed in the French and English languages, they become very useful to the Company, as the Indians look upon all the progeny of their women to be of the same tribe of which their mothers are; and whatever the father may be, the heritage goes always in the female line, of course they are looked upon as one of themselves and get preference in barter.

The country on both sides of the river between Quebec and Montreal, a stretch of 200 miles as already observed, is flat, or so easy a rise as to be scarcely perceptible, and the hills at a greater distance than the eye will carry. The breadth of this spacious flat is very great even on the south side, and so much so on the north as to be unknown; and were it cleared of wood, and cultivated in the way it will admit of, would maintain as many inhabitants as all Scotland.

In the island of Montreal, of eighteen miles long, are many spacious and fine farms, some of which are pofsefsed by Englifhmen who cultivate and manure their land as is done in that country, and raise crops which astonifh the natives, who now begin to follow their example, and will soon, it is to be hoped, spread over all the populous and extensive province of Lower Canada. The price of wheat this year is 3s. 4d. Halifax currency, about 3s. sterling *per* bufhel; beef 1¼d. *per* pound; Turkies and Geese at from tenpence to one fhilling each; and in the market at this season are to be found numbers of milk white Pheasants; and it is somewhat singular that a white Pheasant never was seen in this country until the last fifteen or twenty years, and from whence they had come is not known, though now to be had in great plenty.

On my arrival at Montreal I waited on Mr Dunlop and Mefsrs Andrew and John M'Gee, brothers, to whom I had letters of introduction, and committed a very uncommon blunder indeed. The former of these gentlemen afked me to dine with him that same day, to which I agreed; this being in the morning I returned home to my quarters to write letters to Scotland. When the hour of dinner came I set out, but in place of going to Mr Dunlop, where I ought to have gone, I dafhed in to Mr M'Gee's without any ceremony, and sat down in the parlour; one of the Mr M'Gee's very politely sat along with me, while the other and some strangers were at dinner. After waiting in this way for about three quarters of an hour, I began to be a good deal surprised that we were not getting a call to dinner, ruminating on this in my own mind, I recollected that it was with Mr Dunlop, and not with the Mefsrs M'Gee that I was to dine, and that the gentleman would suppose I meant to soarn upon him for a dinner. I started up on a sudden, struck my forehead with my hand with such quick emotion and agitation that Mr M'Gee supposed I was out of my judgement, and afked the cause of it seemingly with great concern;

after giving two or three starts on the floor, muttering curses all the while, and paying no regard, while the confusion I was in lasted, to Mr M'Gee's questions, I at last recollected myself, aſked his forgivenefs, and frankly told him the whole story, at which he laughed very heartily, and said I was not as yet too late for Mr Dunlop's dinner. I ran out of the house and in to Mr Dunlop's as fast as I could, who had despaired of me, and was half over with his dinner. I made many aukward apologies and began to pick up the fragments of his dinner. Mr Dunlop very politely said there was nothing uncommon in the mistake, and begged I would think no more of it. In this town I fell in with Mr Alexander M'Donald, priest, formerly from Knodart, a Mr Finlay Fiſher, head schoolmaster, and a Mr John Fiſher merchant, from Breadalbane, and was much obliged to these gentlemen for their friendſhip and attention.

The exports from this place in fur and grain are very considerable. The Fur North West Trading Company in this town have the most lucrative buſinefs known in the mercantile line belonging to Britain, and perhaps of any other country. This concern consists of twenty-two ſhares, and it is said each ſhare will draw this year between L. 2000 and

L. 3000 clear gain. They employ a great number of clerks and domestics to attend and carry their goods to a great distance to trade or barter with the Indians. One of the clerks, a Mr M'Kenzie, who is now a partner, penetrated as far as the south seas where it ebbed and flowed, and from whence he had only returned a few months ago. I wifhed much to have fallen in with this young gentleman, but he was on board a fhip on his way to England when I was in Quebec. He had five Canadians and one Indian along with him, while on this arduous and persevering expedition, and which took him eighteen months to accomplifh. He has gone to qualify himself in London in mathematics and in astronomical observations, and is to undertake the same journey again, and if he succeeds is to publifh his observations on his return.

From Montreal to Kingston.

Having got my little baggage on board one of two battoes going together with merchant goods to Kingston, I set out from Montreal on the 5th of November in a carriole, and pafsed that night at the house of a Mr John Grant, a Scotchman, who has two large storehouses at that place; and though this gentleman, from the situation of his stores and house is under the necefsity of keeping a tavern, and though I dined, supped, and breakfasted, and sat up very late with a Mr Rofs, originally from Rofsfhire in Scotland, and one of the partners of the North West Fur Company of Montreal, and a lieutenant M'Donell from Knoidart, and drank a good deal of Port and Madeira wine, yet he would accept of no payment for either myself or servant, and procured a pafsage for us both *gratis* in these boats to Kingston, a distance of 220 miles,—a point of politenefs and attention to a stranger I have not met with from any gentleman situated as he was, in the course of my travels in that country, and but rarely indeed that I remember in any other.

This gentleman I found to be universally known and well liked, has a most excellent character, and of so active and obliging a turn that it is said he is in a fair way of realizing a fortune, and is allowed on all hands to be deserving of it.

THE river from Montreal to Lafheen is so rapid and rugged with stones and sand banks, that the boats pafsing and repafsing betwixt it and Kingston are generally drawn up at Lafheen, and all the goods stored there; and as this large tract of country is fast settling above to a great extent, Mr Grant's large stores at this place cannot mifs to become a source of independent fortune to him. All the goods that go up the rivers, and the produce that come down, are landed here and carted to and from Lafheen and Montreal; so that it is already a very public station, and must become more and more so as the country advances in population. These large flat bottomed battoes carry in general from two to three tons burden, some more some lefs; they employ five or six hands, and the charges amount to from L. 12 to L. 13 each cargo. Opposite Lafheen is a large Indian village on the south side of the river that will turn out three score of warriors at a call; they are quite civilized, and carry on agriculture and trade in the same manner as the white people.

On the 6th November we set out pretty early, I in one battoe and my servant in another, manned with six Canadians each boat. We had very bad poling, owing to the boat's running foul of large stones and banks under water. Towards evening we crofsed the mouth of the north river which falls into the St Laurence, the opening of which is so broad as to appear more like a lake than a stream of running water, and not inferior in width to the St Laurence itself. I have been informed that this river runs out of Lake Superior; others say that it pafses it to the northward. Be this as it will it has a vast body of water; and the greatest part of the Fur Trade is carried on by it. Mr M'Kay's sons, of whom I have spoken already, and who had been often there, gave me the latter account of it; and added, that it pafses the head of another river which falls into Hudson's Bay; that these two streams pafs within half a mile of each other, and pursue their courses in opposite directions; that the traders could go from sea to sea by water in these two rivers, excepting in the small neck already mentioned, acrofs which they carry their canoes and goods; that the clerks and servants of the Hudson's Bay Company, and those of Montreal, often meet about the heads of these rivers, and encroach on each other's territories so much that it creates great disputes among them; what is more, they encourage the Indians to commit outrages on each other, and strive who buys best. Towards the close of the evening we came up to a small canal cut in a narrow neck of land to avoid the opposite rapids that almost surround it.

The boats stopt at the canal all night, and I and my servant pufhed on for two miles further, and slept at the house of a Yanky loyalist, who had a fine large farm with a considerable deal of flat cleared land about it. I now pafsed all the French settlements, and entered that occupied by Britifh and American loyalists; and though it is but eight years since the first tree was cut down in this district, they do not fall much fhort of having as much of the land cleared as the French who have been more than an hundred years in pofsefsion. The cause of this immense difference in the industry of the people, I suppose to be more owing to the tenure of the land, than to lazinefs on the part of the French and industry on that of the Britifh and American loyalists. The former was given out, as already observed, in large districts, to French nobility, who feued out in small portions such as they could clear of it, and no other would be taken; the latter on their own properties, who could not subsist without using every exertion of industry for the first years, were impelled by a necefsity which the others were not subjected to.

Next morning I proceeded by the river side through a close inhabited country, until I came to a point of land where the boats were obliged to unload, and the goods carted for some miles, to avoid rapids, in which the battoes could not be towed when loaded. Here I found that the Canadians had made free with a bag of biscuit Mr John Fifher merchant in Montreal gave me, and a fine roasted Goose a Mr John M'Arthur had sent with me, so that I had to provide myself in provisions as I went along for the future. I travelled all this day on foot, and slept at a lieutenant Fraser's, who had charge of another fhort canal cut through a point of land like that formerly mentioned. Opposite to this place called the Cedars, is a large island in the river used as a place of confinement for several American prisoners taken last war. From this island some of the prisoners were daring enough to swim down and acrofs this immense rapid to a point of land below it, at three-fourths of a mile's distance: some of them were taken after landing, and others drowned in the attempt.

From lieutenant Fraser's I proceeded to the foot of the river Raifson, where an Italian

Count, on his return from Lake Superior, was encamped. He had three tents, some baggage, provisions, and a crew of ten or twelve Canadians in one birch canoe, the largest I ever saw of the kind. This small river is closely settled for the space of twenty miles, mostly by Highlanders; and in many parts seven conceſsions deep, as they are called here, (*i. e.*) seven farms deep, the one behind the other. This is reckoned a very fine settlement; the soil extremely rich, and the average of the produce in grain twenty fold. I put up at the house of a Mr M'Donald formerly from Ardnabee in Glengary.

On the 10th set out from the Raiſson about two hours before day-light; breakfasted at the reverend Mr Beaton's, also a Scotchman, and from thence went to the house of a Captain John M'Donald who was then fiuniſhing a new house said to have cost him L. 1300 Sterling. Here I fell in with a Captain Archibald M'Donald of the Long Saut. Captain John M'Donald preſsed me much to stay that night, but as the boats were likely to get a-head of me I could not. Captain Archibald M'Donald being upon his way home, he and I travelled in company. We put up that night in the house of Lieutenant Miles M'Donald, at a place formerly called New Johnston, but now Cornwallis. Here the stance of a town is lined out, and the place is very centrical for that purpose, being nearly midway between Kingston and Montreal, situated on a broad level point of land, where the river takes a sweep and forms a bend or an obtuse angle; the country is closely inhabited, and the farms to the eighth or ninth concefsions back; the soil deep, fertile, and not difficult to clear. Mr Miles M'Donald was from home at a new farm he was clearing, and Mrs M'Donald, when I informed her who I was, recollected to have seen me in the house of Captain M'Donald of Morar, her father, with whom and family I had the honour to be on the most friendly footing. This lady received me with every mark of politenefs and attention, which was the more gratifying to me, as fhe was the daughter of my particular friend, and universally allowed to be a most amiable as well as elegant woman. I was further told fhe was allowed to be the most elegant woman that appeared at the afsemblies in Montreal the preceding winter. Mr Beaty, who was then but lately married to a sister-in-law of her's, entertained Captain M'Donald and me with much hospitality with Port and Madeira wines, and kept us up very late or rather early. I have hitherto seen no punch drank in this country.

NEXT morning we bad adieu to the family and proceeded on our journey. Called at several houses on the way; the owner of one of which, Captain M‘Donald said would clear that fall L 200 of his farm, mostly in wheat. This part of the country is improving very fast, and will soon be in a very flourishing state. Dined at a Colonel Gray's, a Scotchman, who had served in his younger days in the Dutch service,—himself a hoary headed little man, and his wife a large fat Dutch American lady. Stopped and drank tea at Captain M‘Donald's, who prefsed me much to stay that night, but having yet some hours of day-light I could not think of waiting; on which he gave me a letter of introduction to a relation of his, a Mrs Huet, who lived four or five miles further on, where I pafsed that night.

When you come to that part of the river called the *Long Saut*, opposite to Captain Archibald M‘Donald's, the attention of the traveller must be particularly arrested by the immense body of water, and the awful rapidity of its current, which some people think nearly as novel and striking as the Great Falls of Niagara. In the middle is a long island, whose stately forests intercept the sight in many parts of the opposite fhore. On each side of this island the branches of the river are about half a mile broad, and that which is now in view tumbles down with a tremendous fury, that makes the surge rise somewhat like the sea in a gale of wind. Here the poor Canadians undergo vast rifk and trouble towing up their broad bottomed and large battoes, which require the strength of four or five men to haul on the painter, which if not sound and well secured, and if it once give way, the lofs of the boat is inevitable; fhe muſt be either filled with water, sunk in the stream, or dafhed againſt the stones and rocks on the fhore. I have been told that all boats and rafts of timber coming down the river hold by the south channel, which is not so rapid and more safe than that which is now described; but in coming up the river it is thought more tedious, and on that account they rarely go by it. Mr Huet was not at home; he is one of the king's surveyors in the province. Mrs Huet and a brother of her's who happened to be then in the house entertained me with much civility, but as the boats were likely to get a-head of me, I set out by day-light, and called at a common farmer's house to get breakfast. They happened to be a German family who scarce underſtood a word of Englifh, and were lately from the States. Here the little German I could speak was of use to me, and sufficed to procure me bread from one house and milk in another. The scarcity of bread is owing to the water's

T

being so low that the mills could not grind the quantity required in the neighbourhood. Some miles further on, I was informed that a Lieutenant Malcolm M'Martin with whom I was formerly acquainted, lived in that neighbourhood. I sent an exprefs for him. He was good enough to come and conduct me to the house of a Captain James Munro who refided some miles farther on. We met Captain Munro at a new grist and saw mill he was finifhing on a point of land that projects a little into the river, the water of which supplies the mill by a cut in that point, and one wheel sets two saws and the grist mill-stone a-going at once. These two mills were contrived and finifhed by a common German architect who was never bred to it or to any mechanic trade whatever.

CAPTAIN MUNRO is originally from the north of Scotland, has been a long time in this country, and joined government in the late rebellion. He now enjoys captain's half pay befides the office of fheriff; and is one of the Members of the Land Board, appointed by government for granting lands to such as he and his colleagues in office find deserving. Captain Munro conducted me to his house, and entertained me with a great deal of politenefs, attention, and hospitality. We sat up pretty late; and his son-in-law Mr Allan Paterson, also a Scotchman, entertained us with many interesting stories and anecdotes of a variety of Indian nations he had traded with for several years. He fhowed me an Indian target made of Buffaloe fkin, proof against dart, arrow, and even a mufket ball when it strikes it obliquely, made in the form of a cuirafse or breast plate, and large enough to cover the whole person when crouching or stooping low. It was tanned to an amazing thicknefs, and rendered tough and hard by some procefs only known to Indians. It was of a light buff colour, very light, and quite portable, with a large plumage of curious feathers on the middle of it. He said that from Lake Superior there is a portage of twenty-seven miles long, where every boatman and servant of the Fur Trading Company of Montreal is obliged to carry two hundred weight of goods on his back; that some of the Canadians were so remarkably good at carrying burdens as to take the whole at once, some at twice, and others at three times. When they crofs this portage they fall in with a river or lake, where they have again water carriage, and go on alternately from land to water to a vast distance. Mr Paterson said, and which I heard from several others, that part of this great continent abounds with large plains, farther than the sight will carry;

that one in particular will take a man fifteen days constant travelling to cross; and for length, neither end of it is known: that when a man enters this plain, he will find the Buffaloes almost as numerous as the trees in the forest, feeding on rich grass near breast high; and if the sight would carry the length, he believes 100,000 of them could be seen at once. The ground is so level, that, like the ocean, the horizon bounds the sight. Every step you travel you meet with heads and carcases of dead Buffaloes. When an Indian has a mind to kill many of them, he mounts his Horse, with his bow and a case containing several scores of arrows: he throws the reins loose about the Horse's neck, who knows by constant practice his rider's intention, and gallops with all his speed through the middle of the herd of Buffaloes. The Indian shoots as he goes along until he expends his last arrow, then returns to pick up his prey, and from such as he finds dead he cuts out the tongue and the lump on the back, which he carries away with him; the rest of the carcase he leaves to Wolves and other ravenous animals. A species of Wolves in these parts are milk white, and are larger than those of any other colour, or any Dog whatever that he had seen. The only fuel a traveller can have in these plains, and with which they dress their victuals, is Buffaloe's dung; and when he is in want of water he endeavours to fall in with a path made by Otters going from one small lake to another, by following which he is sure to find it. The ground is so level that you are just upon the brink of the lake before you see that there is any such thing.

An Indian, when he goes in quest of Otters in winter, makes for these lakes, which are covered with ice and snow. He goes about until he finds out every hole they may have about the lake, all of which he fills up excepting one, two, or three, most suitable for his purpose. To these the Otters must have recourse for air. When he has done this, he sprinkles a little snow on the water, which darkens it; when the Otter is just coming, the sportsman finds the water and the snow agitated; and the animal not seeing what is before him, pops up his head through the snow, on which the Indian strikes him with his tomahawk,—puts down his hand,—pulls him out,—throws him aside, and watches the approach of the next, and serves him in the same manner. In this way sometimes a dozen are killed in one pond. The price of an Otter skin is, like penny pies, a bottle of rum; no more is looked for or ever given; though in Canada they are a guinea, and in England two guineas each. The expence of bringing rum or any sort of merchandize two or three thousand miles back, besides the risk of it, must surely be very great; but the profits, now that the Company are firmly established, are in proportion. Mr Paterson, and a very smart young man his brother, lost, during the first three years they were employed in this trade L. 3000, but in the course of two years cleared this and as much more real profit. But unfortunately his brother and the crew of the boat, with its full loading of merchandize, were drowned and lost on Lake Superior; which induced him to give it up.

When two nations of Indians are at war with each other, the one to the southward burns large tracts of the grass in these immense plains; and when the Buffaloes, who annually emigrate from the south to the north, and return in winter, meet with this burned land, they proceed no further, but return. The northern nations, who trust to the Buffaloe for food and winter stores, are thus deprived of the means of subsistence, and often perish with hunger. Mr Paterson, unfortunately happened to have resided one winter with a nation in this predicament; so that he and those along with him were reduced to the necesfity of eating their own mogazines, and every skin they could find, before the spring opened, and permitted them to proceed to a country where they could get game or provisions.

BEFORE I set out next morning, Captain Munro was good enough to give me a letter of introduction to Colonel Butler, at Niagara; and Lieutenant M'Martin told me that there was a Glenlochy woman whom I remembered to have seen a girl in that country, married to a Captain Thomas Fraser some miles farther up the river, on the way I was to hold. When I came opposite to Captain Fraser's house, which was a little way below the road, my servant said that was the place we had been directed to; but on my looking about, and remarking the good house, but a still larger barn of two stories high, several office houses, barracks, or Dutch barns, the sufficiency and regularity of the rails, and extent of the inclosures, considerable flocks of Turkies, Geese, Ducks, and Fowls, I said it could be no Highlander that owned that place,—that the barracks or Dutch barns were foreign to any Scotchman whatever,—that I had not hitherto seen any of them that had such a thing,—and that he must be a German who lived in that place. Still he affirmed this must be it, agreeable to the directions we had; but I could not be perſuaded, and puſhed on to the next houſe, which was then in sight. When I came up I aſked for Captain Fraſer's, and was told I had left it behind; I therefore had to return. When I came in, they took no ſort of notice of me farther than deſiring me to ſit down. My trowſers being torn with the buſhes, and the reſt of my dreſs being in the like ſituation, they ſuppoſed me to be a Yanky come from the States. After ſitting a while in this way, nobody ſpeaking to me or I to them, Mrs Fraſer happened to ſit by me, I looked full in her face; and clearly recognizing her features, I accoſted her in Gaelic, and aſked her if ſhe had ever seen me before. She could not ſay whether or not. This turned the eyes of every body in the houſe towards us: but on my aſking if ſhe had heard of or known ſuch a perſon, naming myſelf, ſhe said ſhe did, and knew him very well; but could not ſuppoſe that I was him. On my ſaying I was, ſhe turned about to her huſband; "My dear, (ſaid ſhe,) this is the gentleman whom I often told you was so kind to us when he was foreſter of Mam Lorn; and whatever diſputes we and our neighbours had when our cattle treſpaſsed upon the foreſt, he always favoured our family; Captain Fraſer on this instantly welcomed me to his house, ordered dinner and venison stakes to be got ready immediately. While dinner was getting ready, Mrs Fraser fhowed me nine or ten large fat Hogs then lying dead on the floor of her keeping house, and said they, every fall, killed twenty such, and two fat Oxen, besides other provisions, for their winter store. After dinner, Captain Fraser treated me with Port wine until we could drink no more, and prefsed me much to stay that night; but as the boats had pafsed I could not wait. When he found that I would be away, he ordered a couple of Horses to be saddled directly.

I MENTION these circumstances and the reception I met in this place, as it does honour to human nature, and fhews how difficult it is to foresee, when, how, or in what remote place or period, one may meet the reward of a humane or generous action; I little expected when I befriended a poor widow woman, with a family of children, in the north west of Scotland, I fhould meet with any returns for it in Upper Canada. She was but a young girl when I had seen her, and emigrated to America with a brother of her's, who, fhe said, was glad to hear of my being in this country, and would go some hundreds of miles to see me. She was but a fhort time in America when she turned out a tall well looked woman, and her present husband became acquainted with and married her, of which I am convinced he has had no reason to repent. They have a fine family of children, and I have been told there is not a better mother, or more prudent house wife in the province.

AFTER bidding adieu to Mrs Fraser and family, Captain Fraser and I mounted his Horses. This was the first time I had crossed a horse since I came to Canada, and the second or third time since I landed in America;—Called at a tavern, drank more wine, for which he would not allow me to pay one farthing. Arrived two hours after night fall at his brother's house, Captain William Fraser. These two gentlemen, whose father was but poor, and they young, when he emigrated from Straherrick in Scotland, and unable to give them the necessary education, after they landed in America entered into the Royal Cause, and that of their country, when the rebellion broke out; and by their own activity, alertness, and merit, they raised themselves to the rank of Captains, got money and education by it, and are now in very high esteem among all their acquaintances. Captain Thomas said he had six score of acres of cleared land. The soil a clay loam, with three or four inches of rich mold, black as jet on the top; that his average return of grain was twenty fold at least; but said, when the clay underneath and the black mold were incorporated together, and the stumps out of the ground, he would have still a greater encrease. Captain William said that his farm was much of the same quality and extent. These two brothers were, for some years prior to the rebellion, Indian interpreters to the great Sir William Johnston, and had fine farms in his neighbourhood on the Mohauke river.

Next morning I set out before it was clear, and got a-head of the boats,—travelled nine or ten miles before breakfast,—came to a point of land where I was to go aboard, but before the boats had come I went into a little cottage, and enquired if I could get breakfast; they told me I ſhould, if bread and milk would serve me. The owner of this house happened to be one Fraser, a Highlander, who had been a long time a private in the forty-second regiment,—married to a young American woman,—had come from Albany but the fall preceding,—had brought a couple of Cows with him, and put up a little cabin and barn in this place, where he got a lot of land. In the course of our conversation I aſked him what he had done since he came here. He said he had cleared nine or ten acres of land, but that the wood was not thick upon it; and that he raised, (to be within the mark as he exprefsed it,) ninety bufhels of wheat, between sixty and seventy of Indian corn, besides potatoes, and other things on which he did not count. " And what afsistance had you to all that?" said I; 'None (answered he) but a hoe and axe, and what that woman could give me,' meaning his wife; but added as he had not a boat to send it to market he could get no sale for it. On my afking him what I had to pay for my breakfast, he said nothing for the bread; that he had more of it than would serve him for three years; and that I might settle with the wife for the milk, as fhe and I pleased. I gave her half a dollar, and but for the scarcity of money in the place, I am convinced none would have been accepted.

The boats arriving, I stepped on board, and the water now becoming smooth, and more like a lake than a running stream, the wind favourable, we put up sails, and made great way, till late at night, when we put up at a poor lame ragged man's house with a numerous family of small children; but the wife buxom and well drefsed. I and my Canadian crew threw ourselves down upon the floor opposite to the fire, and slept soundly till four o'clock next morning, when we got up and set off in the usual way. The wind still favoured us, an we soon entered the thousand islands, which never were, nor do I suppose ever can be counted, by reason of their numbers, and for which reason they were formerly called by the French, and now by the British the *Mille isles*. They are of very little value, and produce but scraggy wood of useless pine. Here are innumerable flocks of water Fowl, mostly of the Teal kind. Such a diversity of creeks, bays, channels, and harbours, I suppose are to be rarely met with in the world; and if a crew be not well acquainted with the direct course, and if they once miss it, they may chance to be bewildered, and for days may not find it again.

AFTER passing these islands we entered upon the lower end of Lake Ontario, and about night fall arrived at Frontinac, or Catrauquey, now called *Kingston* and put up at the coffee house. On hearing that an Indian of considerable consequence lodged then in the house, whose name was Captain Thomas, I sent him my compliments, and if agreeable made offer to join him; his answer was that he would be happy at it. After I joined him, he asked me very politely what I would choose to drink; I answered whatever was agreeable to him. He then called for a small bowl of punch, of which he took but very little, excused himself by saying he had dined in a private family, and drank too freely after dinner. We slept in the same room. He was a tall handsome man, extremely well drefsed in the Englifh fafhion, and had nothing particular about him but a string of small silver buckles hung down on his breaſt, fastened to his long lank black hair, from each side of his head. He spoke French fluently, but not Englifh enough to enable us to converse freely in that language; however he understood it better than he could speak, and enough to make me enjoy his company very much; his place of residence is eight or ten miles above Montreal, in the village already mentioned opposite Lafheen. In this village there are about 170 houses, and an elegant stone church. What is singular in that place I am informed is that several of these houses, covered with bark of water afh, and bafs wood, have stood so for three score of years, and are now so close covered with mofs as to be perfectly water tight. Captain Thomas is the principal man in that place, has a fine house, and a squaw every day elegantly drefsed; he deals much in the mercantile line, mostly in furs; and can get on his credit at a call in any of the principal mercantile houses at Montreal, two thousand pound's worth of goods. I saw him pick up all the fkins worth buying from the merchants in this place. I was informed there were twelve hundred pound's worth of skins of his property seized last year, which he had hid in the woods, and meant to smuggle into the States dominions, where they give a better price than at Montreal. White people practise smuggling of this kind as well as Indians, and when detected, the goods are confiscated in the same manner.

KINGSTON is situated upon a broad point of land, the Grand Lake Ontario on the south, and a creek on the east and north east runs three or four miles into the country, so that it is surrounded with water on three sides. At the foot of this creek is a fine safe anchorage, and on the shore quays and wharfs are beginning to be built. The whole point of about two or three miles broad is clay lying on limestone, not high, but with an easy slop descending to the water. The limestone in this place lies in curious strata level with the surface of the ground, and cut short; some in square pieces, others in pentagons, hexagons, and polygons, and many different flat sides; and is the finest and most easily quarried perhaps in the world, and so fit for building as not to require the stroke of a hammer. The very beach on the shore is limestone, and so pounded that if a kiln were made close by it might be shovelled in and burnt into lime without any further trouble; yet notwithstanding the materials for building with stone are so easy to be had here, even on the very stance of the houses, they prefer building them all with timber. I never saw a prettier situation for an inland town than this place. The country along the coast, and about the Bay of Kenty, for fifty or sixty miles is closely inhabited, and in some parts three or four concessions deep. The timber on this flat, but not low point, is mostly of hard wood of a fine growth and very stately, and useful for most purposes. The town is in its infancy as yet, but fast encreasing. It is well supplied with provisions of all kinds from the fertile country behind it. It is a little surprising the stir of trade that is in it already. I have been told that above 6000 bushels of wheat were bought up and stored here the preceding year, and that at least a fourth more would have been so this one; and so on in proportion every succeeding year. This is a very extraordinary circumstance in a country not above eight years settled. I have been also informed that six score of Deer have been sold in this town this same year. I see venison every day in the market and prefsed upon the inhabitants to buy; but the best only is bought.

HERE I fell in with Lieutenant William M'Kay, originally from the north of Scotland, and Lieutenant Daniel of the twenty-sixth regiment, an Irishman, both going for Niagara, with whom I lived in strict intimacy and friendship afterwards while I continued in Canada. In this town there are two companies of foot and some artillery men, kept for guarding the king's stores for supplying the troops of the forts on the Upper lakes; the troops were commanded by Captains Porter and Ingram. I met with a great deal of politeness and attention from them both; with the latter I dined every day at the mess, when I was not otherwise engaged; and the like civility from Mr Joseph Forsyth, merchant, and Mr Neil M'Lean, commissary. Here I staid for several days, waiting a fair wind to proceed in one of the king's sloops to Niagara.

NOVEMBER 23. I took a ride into the country along with Captain Ingram who furnished me with a Horse, and Lieutenant Daniel. We went through a thick wood for about six miles, passed several settlements newly begun in the middle of the wood, every one of which was on limestone: I saw neither stone nor rock in this neighbourhood of any other quality. We returned by another road. The wood mostly hickory, streight, and almost of equal thickneſs for forty feet to the branches. The hickory nuts are very sweet, and very much resemble the walnut, but are not so large, and much thicker in the ſhell. Here are great quantities of chesnuts also, and some butt nuts. On our return, we rode about a mile up the side of the Grand Lake,—paſsed Parson Stewart's house and farm, who has L. 200 sterling salary, from the Britiſh government, and a fine farm of 200 acres, which lies on the side of the lake, and large tracts of it clear. We croſsed again from Parson Stewart's along the summit of this flat and charming point, to the house of Sir John Johnston, which is situated above the town and harbour of Kingston, and commands a beautiful prospect. Near this place, but a little more in view of the Grand Lake, it is supposed the new governor of Upper Canada will erect his place of residence and fix the seat of government. If so, surely none can be more suitable; every thing is inviting, and it seems by nature intended for the emporium of this new country, capable of being extended to a considerable empire.

November 24. We got on board the Colville, sloop, mounting two six pounders and two swivels, Captain Baker, bound to Niagara; Lieutenant Daniel, Lieutenant M'Kay, and myself pafsengers. The day was hazy, the wind fair, but promised no continuance. We pafsed several large woody uninhabited islands. About nightfall the wind changed to streight a-head,—the captain, quite drunk, went to bed, the crew, little better, went to rest, and indeed were almost uselefs when sober, as they seemed to know scarce any thing at all of their businefs; no watch or reckoning kept, but by an ignorant wretch at the helm. The wind increased, and now became a storm. In this way, beating to windward, the night dark, and surrounded by land fhoals and islands, our situation could not be very agreeable. None of us knew where we were, and in fear of being a-ground every moment. A man was ordered to sound, and once sung out of a sudden, " Five fathoms." I expected the next moment to hear her strike.

The ship was put about, and the mistake in the sounding discovered to be owing to the ignorance of the sailor, and the lines having been entangled in the rails, as at the next sounding no bottom was found; from these circumstances I clearly saw, that if we escaped being wrecked it would be a mere chance, and it appeared that there was at least five to one against us. I could not help contrasting this wretched drunken captain and his crew, with the sober, cautious, and attentive Captain Wylie, who never went to bed any night that had the least appearance of a gale of wind. But drunk as this man was, before he went to bed he ordered the main-sail to be double reefed, and the fore-sail to be handed, a precaution I was very glad to see. About midnight a severe blast or hurricane was heard coming on. The man at the helm sung out, which brought the captain and all the crew on deck, who got all the sails handed, and we now went under bare poles; that done, he again returned to bed, eternally bawling out, "Oh! my poor family!" and with the next breath, "Let us all go to hell together." Thus we continued till day-light. The surge ran very high, but not equal to that I have seen on sea; and as the wind blew very fresh and hard against us, we had nothing for it but to return back, and anchored about two o'clock p. m. at the head of Carleton island opposite to Kingston; but as several large islands were between us and the town, they could not see us, or know what had become of us. The 25th, 26th, and 27th, we lay here without stirring, the wind continuing a-head, or calm.

On the 28th I went on fhore on Carleton island where the Britifh had a garrison last war; the barracks, dry ditch, and rampart, are still remaining, but in a decayed state. A serjeant and twelve men are kept here to preserve the barracks from being burnt by the Indians, and the Americans from taking pofsefsion of it, and the dismounted guns thereon. The cause afsigned for our forsaking this post, is said to be because it is doubtful whether these islands be within the Britifh or American lines.

Early in the morning of the 29th, a fine clear day, and a small breeze in our favour, we weighed anchor, hoisted sail, and steered for the lake; but had gone but a fhort way when the wind again veering about a-head obliged us to return and anchor in our former station.

On the 30th, Lieutenant Daniel, myself, and some of the crew, went on fhore on the main and south side of the lake, part of the province of New York, to look for Deer,

Pheasants, or game of any kind; but not venturing to go far into the woods, met with nothing worth mentioning. Returned on board with a quantity of fire wood only. Next day went on ſhore on one of the islands, where my servant ſhot two Pheasants and a Hare, which helped our meſs. The day following we returned to the same island and ſhot seven Hares, saw some Muſk Rats, which I at first supposed to be Beavers, and had a great deal of trouble in stalking them, for which there was no occasion, as they are a stupid small animal of the amphibious kind. Duncan wounded one, but it escaped among thick reeds, where we could not find him. A day or two after this we killed three Racoons, which we found in the trunk of an old log. Lieutenant M'Kay, who was well acquainted with the kind, traced them to the place of concealment. This animal is very fat, and too luscious for my palate, and resembles much the Badger in Scotland, but has a longer and more buſhy tail.

December 7. The evening preceding, the wind veered about by the west to the north, accompanied with heavy ſhowers of snow, which indicated a continuance from that quarter, for which we were all night very anxious, but durſt not venture to set out till day-light, as there were a number of islands and banks in our way. The wind having kept steady, next morning hoisted sail, and steered for the lake under a smart breeze from the north; all sails were up; went at the rate of five or six knots an hour. No sooner night came on than our good captain, in the usual way, filled himself stupidly drunk with grog, and retired to bed, leaving the vefsel to be directed by as stupid a crew. Mr M'Kay, who had most to say with him, sat up all night, in hopes of having it in his power to keep him sober, but it defied him, as not an hour pafsed during the whole night but he must have a tumbler of grog.

The 8. Last night continued to freeze very hard, and this morning the smoke of the hoar frost, when the sun got up, involved us in fog, and drove away in thick columns with the wind, which much obscured the sight. One of the seamen got up to the topmast head, and swore we had outrun our course twenty miles at least,—that we were embayed,—that he could see land a-head and on each side of us. This kept us in great doubt for the most part of the morning, and made us fhorten our sail, until the sun about mid-day dispersed the fog. We steered for the south fhore, and soon discovered land, when we found, that in place of outrunning our reckoning twenty miles, that we fell short of Niagara thirty or forty miles. We had now no dread but that the wind would shift to the westward, which, if it did, would drive us back to Kingston, and oblige us to continue there for the winter and spring; but fortunately for us it still kept fair; and more by good luck than any thing else, we landed at the quay of Niagara about four o'clock p. m. I must not here omit, that when the day cleared up, we could see the spray arising from the Falls of Niagara at the distance of thirty or forty miles, like a cloud in the air, and driving before the wind to an immense distance. Captain Baker told me that he had often seen it at the distance of sixty miles. On my landing, the day being very cold, I went into Captain Baker's house to warm me, and there found a decent looking young woman his wife, with five beautiful children, of whom the father seemed uncommonly fond; and though their whole support, and in a manner their existence, depend upon his life and industry, yet such is his love for grog, that it would seem he would forsake them and every other consideration in the world, for its sake; at least that he would not forsake it for them.

I crossed the river from the north to the south, and put up at the only public house in the place which is near the fort.

The fort of Niagara is built on the south side, and within the American lines, on a point of land at the foot of the river of that name, where it disembogues itself into Lake Ontario, and has the sole command of the entry to that river. It is a pretty strong stuccade fort with regular bastions, pallisades, pickets, and dry ditch, sufficient against the attack of any irregular army. On that side the river there are no settlements nearer than the Genesee country, which is distant about 100 miles. I crossed the river to the north side to see the fishing, and saw 1008 caught at one hawl of a Seine net, mostly what is called here *White Fish*, and a few Herrings; the former weighs at an average above two pounds, the latter has the exact shape, scales, and colour of our Herring on the coast of Scotland, but is considerably larger and fatter in appearance, yet has neither the taste nor flavour of our's, and is deemed inferior in quality to the White fish. I saw several other kinds caught here, particularly the Sturgeon, which is a bad useless sort of fish, excepting for isinglass, of which it is said a deal might be made here; many of them weigh from thirty to forty pounds each. It may be thought somewhat worthy of remark, that they eat nothing, and subsist wholly by suction, and have not a bone but in the head. In place of a back-bone, in common with other fish, they have only a large sinew full of gristle, of which the best isinglafs may be made; and yet this is a strong active fifh, and often jumps high out of the water. They are so numerous in Hudson's river in the State of New York, that they are called in derision, *Albany beef.* The fifhing here continues from the middle of October to the middle of May, and I have been told that 6000 have been caught in a day. This is of great benefit to the troops and inhabitants, who have stated days in the week to fifh, during the season.

OPPOSITE the fort of Niagara, on a large flat point, on the Canadian side of the river, is a town lined out, and lots given *gratis* to such as will undertake to build on it, agreeably to a plan laid down by government, which to me seems to be a good one; half an acre is allotted for the stance of each house and garden, and eight acres at a distance, for inclosures, besides a large commonty reserved for the use of the town. Several people have taken lots here already; and no doubt as the country advances in population, so will the town in building. In the event of the fort on the opposite side being given up, it is said there is one to be erected on this side, and the ground is already marked out for that purpose.

ON the opposite side of the lake, t a lace called *Torento*, fifteen miles acrofs from Niagara, is a fine bay and safe anchorage, where some people suppose the seat of the new governor will be erected. From thence, round about the head of the lake, westward to Niagara, is all settled, and in some parts several concefsions deep. The land low;--the soil a deep sandy clay upon the coast, but farther back, clay and loam mixed, with a few inches of rich black mold a-top, owing to the falling leaves enriching the soil annually since the creation. The wood lofty, and chiefly oak of different kinds, interspersed with wild vines, walnut, chesnut, hickory, mapple or sugar tree, afh, pine, a few cedar, and a variety of others. The point on which the fort of Niagara is built is between twenty and thirty feet deep solid earth and clay mixed, which is easily seen and ascertained from the perpendicular banks of th river and lake, adjoining to the fort, and for a considerable way along the coast on both sides of the river. No wonder then that such an amazing deepnefs of soil, when afsisted by the powerful rays of a clear and unclouded sun in latitude 43°, fhould bring to maturity every vegetable common to temperate climates, sown or planted therein which is really the case, not only here, but in general all over this extensive tract of the country.

WHEAT is rarely left here above a day on the ground after reaping, and often carried home to the barn on the very day it is cut; the ground is no sooner cleared of one crop, than it may be, and often is immediately plowed down and sown with another, and so on alternately without using any sort of manure. The richnefs of the soil and salubrity of the air, make all sort of stimulus totally unnecefsary.

By arriving at this place I so far succeeded in fulfilling my original plan of exploring all I could of New Brunswick, Lower and Upper Canada; and when the traversed course I took, to and from the foot of the Merrimafhee river, is taken in account, may be fairly reckoned 1400 miles. My further intention was to have gone from this place to Detroit, from thence to Fort Pitt down the Ohio, Kentucky, the back settlements of North Carolina, and fall down on the sea at Wilmington or Charlestown in South Carolina, and embark for Britain. But here my course was stopped. On Colonel Gordon's being told of my intention, he sent me notice that I would not be permitted to go from Detroit to the States, but might from this place; and if I wifhed to see Detroit, he would give me a pafs, but that I must come back here again. On hearing this, I thought it too much to travel 300 miles, which distance Detroit is from this, and as many back again in the same course, which would make 600 miles in all, for the sake of seeing one settlement. I thought of continuing here all winter, and how soon the spring should open to go by the Genesee country, and from thence to proceed by the Monongohela river to Fort Pitt, and if that should be found too hazardous, to go from the Genesee by the Susquehana river through Pensylvania to Philadelphia, from whence there is a sort of post road on which I could ride to Fort Pitt. I soon found that there was no way of going from Detroit to Fort Pitt, or to any part of the States, but through the middle of the seat of war, where no white man or unknown Indian dared venture. Some time after this my good friend Captain Brant was kind enough to make me an offer of some of his people, acquainted with the way, to conduct me to Fort Pitt. Even this would be attended with fatigue, and too great a risk, improper for me to take, on account of total ignorance of walking on snow shoes, for above 300 miles of a wilderness, through the skirts of the seat of war, where I and my party might be knocked on the head while asleep;—the like had often happened before; our track would discover us, and the course we must take would be suspicious. These and many such reasons against this expedition occurred; so that I had nothing now for it but to content myself in this place until the spring should open, and then pursue the course already mentioned; and sure enough I could not have pafsed my time in a place more agreeable.

I HAD hardly put up at the public house here, as already observed, when Captain Colin M'Nab, and Captain Campbell of the twenty-sixth regiment, though unacquainted with either, came to call on me, and invited me to their respective houses, with whom, and their genteel families, I had the honour of being on an intimate footing during my stay at Niagara. Some fhort time thereafter Mr Robert Hamilton, a gentleman of the first rank and property in this neighbourhood, and now one of the governor's council, came also to wait on me, and invite me to his house,—an honour I readily embraced. He and Mrs Hamilton were so very obliging, as to go along with me in their own slea, to see the Grand Falls of Niagara. Mr Hamilton gave me the following statement of the Falls, made a year or two since by the geographers of the Fœderal States, which I suppose to be exact, and now give to the public.

Measurement of the Falls of Niagara.

THE perpendicular height of the rapids above the Great Falls, with the height of the perpendicular Fall, is as follows, taken by the geographer of the United States afsistants.

	Feet	Inches
Perpendicular height of the rapids above the Great Falls, - - - - - -	57	11
Distance of the beginning of the rapids above the pitch, is, on the island side, 148 paces.		
Perpendicular height of the Great Falls is by true measurement, -	149	9
Total,	207	8
Projection of the extreme part of the table rock is, - - - - - - -	50	4

Measured 8th December 1789.

A DESCRIPTION of these tremendous Falls has been so often attempted by preceding travellers, without giving the least idea adequate to the grandeur of the scene, that, lest I split on the same rock, I will not efsay it here; I fhall therefore only remark, that there is an island of a mile or two long, and about a quarter broad, which divides the stream about two-thirds over. This island is clad with poor spruce pine, and so overrun with Rattlesnakes, that it was dangerous for any person to walk through it, until a parcel of Swine were put on it, which nearly rooted them out. Hogs are so fond of Snakes, that if once they get a hold, fhould they be so hard bitten by a strong Rattlesnake as to make them squeel, which sometimes happens, yet they hold fast until the Snake is devoured. It is said a Hog sometimes swells when severely bitten by a Rattlesnake, but that a crevice bursts open between the hoofs, through which the venom is discharged, the swelling subsides, and the Hog soon becomes as well as formerly.

In this neighbourhood live a set of religionists called *Moravians*, with long beards, originally from Germany; they emigrated to this place from Pensylvania. They are a very innocent, inoffensive, and industrious people, that have many peculiarities in their manner of worſhip and mode of living, though of the Lutheran persuasion. In one settlement in that province they have all sorts of trades and manufactures, and have every thing in common. There is a large house or hall for the young women, apart, in which they work, and another for the young men in which they do the same. The sexes are never allowed to see one another. When a young man signifies a desire to marry, he and the first girl on the list are put into a private room together, and continue in it for an hour. If he agrees to marry her after this meeting, good and well; if not, he will not get another, and ſhe is put the last on the list; so that all before her must go off before ſhe gets any other offer. And though the parties had never seen one another before this meeting, which is rarely otherwise, they have no alternative, and must make up their minds and acquaintances in that ſhort intercourse. If the parties are satisfied, and they marry, a house is built for them in the village where they live, and carry on buſineſs for the good of the community at large. There are as yet not above a score of them in this neighbourhood, but many more are expected; I have heard several people say that they would like them well as neighbours, and the Quakers are particularly fond of them on account of their mild and inoffensive dispositions.

From Niagara *to the* Grand River *and back again.*

On the 9th of February I set out with a party of gentlemen in two sleas, on an excursion to the Grand River. Put up the first night at Squire M'Nab's, and next day dined at the house of one Henry, who had only been here for six years; and though he had no subject to begin with, by great attention and industry has acquired a considerable property, and now afsociates with the first people in the district. He has cleared seventy-five acres of land of the first quality, and has stock and cattle in proportion. Put up at night in the house of one Smith, who came from the colonies two years ago, from whence he brought a good stock of cattle, which all perifhed the following winter for want of provender, the general scarcity that prevailed all over America that year having affected this quarter, though one of the most fertile in it. He told me that he regretted the lofs of his team of Oxen, and two fine breeding Mares, more than all the rest of his stock; and said, that poor as he was, he hoped to become richer and happier on his own property, than ever he was or could be on that of another. When he resided in the colonies he pofsefsed 200 acres, twenty-five of which only were cleared, at L. 11 rent, and L. 3 taxes, and could only procure a lease of two years endurance, which obliged him to remove every third year; this, joined with the heavy rent and taxation, induced him to look out for lands where he knew he would meet with no such incumbrances. The lands as we came along, seemed extremely good, heavy timbered, consisting of oak, walnut, chesnut, buttnut, hickory, mapple or sugar wood, afh, pine, and a variety of others, all lofty of their kind, particularly in that space which lies between the long stretch of precipices, called the *Mountain*, and the *Side of the Lake*. This space is from one to four miles broad, and from fifty to sixty miles long, from Niagara to Lake Geneva; it is in general a deep clay soil, with black and fat mold of some inches on the top. The lands on the top of the stretch of precipices called the *Mountain*, is of a much lighter soil, intermixed with sand, thinly timbered, and all of oak, but produces heartier wheat than the lands below, though not in such quantities. I remarked that the top of the Mountain would make good pasture for cattle in its present state, particularly for Sheep, could they be preserved from the Wolves. The Foxes here are of various colours, black, red, and grey; I have seen ſkins of each kind. They are caught in traps, and I have been told of one man who since laſt fall had taken about sixty in that manner. This Mountain begins in the Geneſee country, and stretches along until it croſses the river Niagara at the Grand Falls: from thence in a serpentine form to the head of the small lake, called by the Indians, *Ouilqueton*, and known to the white people by that of Geneva, and from thence to the Bay of Torento, opposite to the Fort of Niagara, on the north side of Lake Ontario, a stretch of between two and three hundred miles long. Though it is called the Mountain it is no more than a ridge of rising ground about 300 feet higher than the flat lands below it. The lands on the Mountain appear to me to be the fittest I have as yet seen for a poor man to begin upon, as it requires scarce any clearing, there being no more wood upon it than a sufficiency for rails, inclosures, and the necefsary purposes of farming; so that if he chooses he may plough down the land the moment he acquires pofsefsion of it. Clearing land of heavy timber is both expensive and tedious; but if one has sufficient stock and patience to go through with it, he may be afsured of being amply repaid in the end.

On the 10th we set out early from Smith's house, and pafsed through many fine farms and rich land, keeping all along close by the foot of the Mountain; the timber the same as the day before, extremely lofty and of e-qual variety. A little before we came to the head of the Grand Lake, we met a man with a slea and team of Oxen. I afked him if he had come from the head of the Lake; he answered in a twang peculiar to the New Englanders, " I viow niew you may depen I's juſt a-comin ;" ' And what distance may it be from hence ?' said I; " I viow niew I guefs I do'no,-- I guefs niew I do'no,--I swear niew I guefs it is three miles ;" he swore, vowed, and guefsed alternately; and was never like to come to the point, though he had but that instant come from it. Mr M'Nab damned him for an old Yanky rascal, that never gave a direct answer in his lifetime, and was sure he had only come from New England but that or the preceding year at farthest. They rarely answer in any other way.

We proceeded on our journey, and in about half an hour we fell down on the Grand Lake, and drove along a fine beach until we came to the neck of land which separates the two lakes, the Grand Ontario from the Geneva.

This neck is a fine dry beach, five miles long, and from two to three hundred yards broad; on this neck there grows very long grafs, which the neighbouring inhabitants cut down for hay, and it is extremely useful to them.

We now entered upon the Lake Geneva, and drove along it on the ice. This lake is a fine small sheet of water, of a triangular form, six miles one way and five the other. The snow was about ten inches deep on the ice. Here I saw several Indians of the Mefsefsagoe nation fifhing for Pickerel, Mafkanongy, Pike, and other kinds of fifh, inhabitants of, and peculiar to this and other Canadian waters. The Mefsefsagoe nation of Indians rarely cultivate any land, and wholly subsist by fifhing and hunting, at which they are more expert than their neighbours, with whom they frequently, as well as with the white inhabitants, barter fifh and venison for other provisions. How soon I saw them I requested of Mr M'Nab, in whose slea I was, to drive towards them. Their manner of fifhing appeared to me somewhat curious. The Indian provides himself with a small spear, of two prongs each prong about six inches long, with a fhaft of light wood, about ten feet long. A little false or artificial fifh made of wood, so exactly formed and coloured, that it is impofsible to conceive it to be any other thing than a real fish, without handling it; when in the water the deception is not to be discovered. A little lead is put into the body of this image to make it sink; a hole is made in the ice, into which the fisherman drops the image, suspended by a small piece of twine, of about a fathom or two long, so exactly fitted in the middle as to make it balance; he then lays himself flat on his face at the side of the hole, which, as well as himself, he covers with his blanket so close that no light can get in from above; holding the twine in one hand and his spear in the other he tugs and works the thread to make his little fish play, as if alive in the water, which being observed by a ravenous fish, he makes at it to snap it up, and the others who are not so, come from curiosity to see what it is that makes this little fish so sportive and playful, and continue for some time swimming about, which gives a fair opportunity to the Indian, who is ever watchful, to strike them with his spear. In this way they catch a great many fish of different kinds. I saw one man with about a score lying by the side of his hole, of whom we bought or bartered a few of the largest kind for a loaf of bread; they seemed to weigh from two to eight pounds each, and were as delicious in taste and flavour as any I have met with. I looked through one of these holes, and when closely covered with the blanket could easily perceive the bottom, where I supposed it to be twenty feet deep.

On the borders of Lake Ontario, and I suppose on all the other great lakes in Canada, a great deal of different kinds of fish are caught in freshets in the spring of the year, which the frost in winter confine to the body of the lake, and from which they seem anxious to be relieved: how soon the small brooks are open from ice for their reception, they push out in such numbers that one would be apt to suppose, that none of certain kinds stay behind, the one striving to get a-head of the other. The inhabitants in the neighbourhood are provided with small nets, such as we call in Scotland *bag* or *hose nets*, with three or four hoops in the body of each to keep them open; the small end, which is close, is fixed to a stake uppermost in the middle of the stream, the wider end, stretched down in the water, is open with a wing extended from each side to the opposite banks, which prevents the fish from passing any way but through the hoops and body of the net; a contrivance is made within that allows the fish to pass easily through to the upper end, out of which they cannot find their way back. The nets are generally set at night.

and raised in the morning often full of fish. I am of opinion that nets of the same construction, but on a larger scale, might be used to advantage in Scotland for catching Salmon on small rivers.

How soon the Indian got the loaf of bread, as before mentioned, he sliced the greatest part of it down with his knife, and shared it with his neighbours. Here for the first time, I tried on snow shoes, and found I could walk on them with great ease, so much so that I am determined to have them, if ever I live in a country subject to deep snow. After satisfying myself with every thing worth remarking of this Indian method of fishing, we mounted our sleas and drove on to the house of a Mr Baisley, who keeps a shop at the head of the Lake Geneva, and trades much with the Indians in peltry. He showed me a great many skins of different kinds, among the rest that of a black Fox whose fur was extremely soft and beautiful, and of high value, supposed to be worth five guineas. The Foxes in Lower Canada, Nova Scotia, and New Brunswick, are chiefly red, few black or grey to be found among them; but in this part of the country they are of all these colours. I have seen some speckled red and grey. The real black is very rare. We staid that night with Mr Baisley who entertained us with the highest hospitality. Here I was told of a phenomenon that surprises every body in that neighbourhood supposed to be a vulcano, which makes at certain times a loud report, resembling that of a great gun at a distance.

THE Indians only know the spot in which it is, and from a foolish notion or tradition among them will not discover it; they suppose it is occasioned by the great spirit, and how soon the white people find it out, that they are to be extirpated the land, if not from the face of the earth, and an end put to their race. As this opinion prevails among them, no inducement will make them discover it. Dr Kerr of the Indian department, told me he meant to search for it next summer, and flattered himself he would find it out. Whatever is the cause of this singular phenomenon, it must be very deep in the bowels of the earth, as no smoke issues from it, or any crevice or opening to be seen about it.

FEBRUARY 11. We set out from Mr Baisley's. For several miles on the way towards the Grand River, the lands are so open as to have scarce a sufficiency of wood for inclosures and the necessary purposes of farming; but towards the mountain, the wood becomes thick and lofty, as is common in this country, for several miles along the mountain. The wood again thinned like that which we entered in the morning. I however observed by the girding of the trees in several parts as we went along, that the land was granted away, though few settlements were to be seen, and as we had plenty of provisions along with us, we stopped and dined at a mill, the water of which was supplied from a fountain in the hill, its source but a short space from thence. This mill was built at the foot of a small precipice, over which the water poured on the head of the wheel, which was greatly admired by my fellow travellers, who protested it to be one of the finest contrivances they had ever seen, and worth going 100 miles to see it, requested I should take particular notice of it in my journal, but I told them it was not new to me, though so to them, as scarce a mill in my country but was served with water in the same way. Here we saw a beautiful young woman seemingly of exquisite shape and form, going on crutches, occasioned by rheumatic pains in her haunches. After refreshing ourselves and horses we proceeded on our journey through the mountain. The snow was deep and no beaten tract; our carriages dragged heavily on. Towards evening we fell down on a gentleman's farm, where we stopped to warm ourselves, and bait our Horses. The weather being windy, accompanied with cold showers of snow, we no sooner entered the house and standing by the fire side, than our travelling companion, a little French captain looked up and swore it was the finest place for smoked meat he had ever seen in all his life, and that he was sure that piece which he now held in his hand must eat very well, at the same time he handled several pieces which hung near it. Our honest landlord instantly took the hint, and told us if we would have a little patience he would order venison stakes, (of which he and every body in that neighbourhood had plenty). We apologized for what our friend said, to no purpose, the hint was too broad to be parried. The stakes came, on which we feasted most sumptuously, and dined for the second time that day. No sooner our repast was over than we bade adieu to the family, mounted our sleas, and drove on to the Indian village, alighted about nightfall at the house of the famous Indian cheif and warrior, Captain Joseph Brant. This renowned warrior is not of any royal or conspicuous progenitors, but by his ability in war, and political conduct in peace, has raised himself to the highest dignity of his nation, and his alliance and friendship is now courted by sovereign and foreign states. Of this there are recent instances, as he has had within the last three weeks several private letters and public dispatches from Congrefs, soliciting his attendance at Philadelphia on matters of high importance; but after consulting Colonel Gordon, commandant of the Britifh troops in this place, and all Upper Canada, he excused himself and declined to accept of the invitation. He just now enjoys a pension and captain's half pay, from the Britifh government, and seems to keep quite staunch by it; but a person of his great political talents ought to be cautiously looked after; at the same time I am convinced he bears no good will to the American States, and seems to be much rejoiced at the drubbing their troops got from the Indians on the 4th of last November, when, by the Indian account, 1300 of them were killed on the spot, but by the American, only 800, including the wounded; the former is nearest the truth, and gains most credit here. By comparing the numbers brought to the field, with those that remained after the action, which is the surest way to judge, their lofs must have exceeded 1600; I saw a muster roll and returns of some of the companies, and examined if there were any Scotch names among them, and could find none but one Campbell, which it would appear by their Orderly Book was among those that deserted, of whom there were a great many. My reason for examining this so particularly was, that I was informed the American army were mostly made up of Scotch and Irish emigrants, to whom Congrefs promised free lands at the close of the Indian war, in the event they would engage in it. Captain Green of the twenty-sixth regiment, who held the Orderly Book, made the same remark in regard to names, so that I am happy that report was ill founded.

CAPTAIN BRANT who is well acquainted with European manners, received us with much politenefs and hospitality. Here we found two young married ladies, with their hufbands, on a visit to the family, both of them very fair complexioned and well looking women. But when Mrs Brant appeared superbly drefsed in the Indian fafhion, the elegance of her person, grandeur of her looks and deportment, her large mild black eyes, symmetry and harmony of her exprefsive features, though much darker in the complexion, so far surpafsed them, as not to admit of the smallest comparison between the Indian and the fair European ladies; I could not in her presence so much as look at them without marking the difference. Her blanket was made up of silk, and the finest

English cloth, bordered with a narrow stripe of embroidered lace, her sort of jacket and scanty petticoat of the same stuff, which came down only to her knees; her gaiters or leggans of the finest scarlet, fitted close as a stocking, which fhowed to advantage her stout but remarkably well formed limbs; her mogazines [Indian fhoes] ornamented with silk ribbons and beads. Her person about five feet nine or ten inches high, as streight and proportionable as can be, but inclined to be jolly or lusty. She understands, but does not speak Englifh. I have often addrefsed her in that language, but fhe always answered in the Indian tongue

THEY have a fine family of children; I remarked of one fine looking boy, about eight years old, that he was very like his mother; his father said he was so, and that he was glad of it; that he was a good scholar and a good hunter; that he had already fhot several Pheasants and other birds; that he and two other boys of the same age had been lately in the woods with their guns, that they supposed they had found the track of a Deer, which they followed too far, got wet and turned cold; that, however, young as they were, they put up a fire and warmed themselves, and returned home; that before they arrived their toes were frost bitten, of which he was not then quite recovered. I mention this circumstance to shew how early the young Indians are bred to the chace. Another instance of their being early bred to war is, that I myself saw a riffled barrelled gun taken by an Indian boy from an American whom he shot dead in the action of the 4th of November last, and allowed to keep on account of his gallant behaviour. Tea was on the table when we came in, served up in the handsomest China plate and every other furniture in proportion. After tea was over, we were entertained with the music of an elegant hand organ, on which a young Indian gentleman and Mr Clinch played alternately. Supper was served up in the same genteel stile. Our beverage, rum, brandy, Port and Madeira wines. Captain Brant made several apologies for his not being able to sit up with us so long as he wished, being a little out of order, and we being fatigued after our journey went timeously to rest; our beds, sheets, and English blankets, equally fine and comfortable.

Next day being Sunday, we the visitors went to church. The service was given out by an Indian in the absence of the minister, who was indisposed, and I never saw more decorum or attention paid in any church in all my life. The Indian squaws sung most charmingly, with a musical voice I think peculiar to themselves. After sermon I went to the school house to converse with the master, an old Yanky. As it was Sunday, the scholars were not convened, so that I had not the pleasure of seeing them. He teaches Englifh and arithmetic only. He told me he had sixty-six on his list, some of whom had excellent capacities for learning, and read distinctly and fluently. After this I visited several houses in the village, and found the inhabitants had abundance of the necefsaries of life to supply their wants, and are better and more comfortably lodged than the generality of the poor farmers in my country. Few of the houses I saw but had two apartments, deal floors, and glafs windows. They have a deal of crop, and excellent cattle, inferior to none I have seen in the province. The old people attend farming, while the young men range the woods for different sorts of game, and supply the family with venison, of which they generally have more than suffices; the overplus they sell to the white inhabitants in the neighbourhood. I have seen many loads of venison come in to the market of Niagara, and it is rare to find in the season a house without some. Here I fell in with Mr Aaron Hill, a young Indian gentleman, of very agreeable looks and mild manners; he is eldest son of the renowned chief, Captain

David, whom every one that knew him allowed to be the handsomest and most agreeable Indian they had ever seen; he died about two years ago, and, what would be deemed very hard by many, the son does not succeed to the honours and titles of the family, but they go in the female line to his aunt's son. Captain Brant did all he could to get the son, who seems worthy of his gallant and amiable father, to enjoy the titles, but it would not do; the ancient laws, customs, and manners of the nation could not be departed from. This young Indian was the best scholar at the university of Cambridge, in New England, when he was there. He writes a remarkably fine hand, both in the Roman characters and German text, a specimen of which he gave me, and I now have in my custody. I remarked of the Indians in this part of the Continent, that they never speak in a hasty or rapid manner, but in a soft, musical, and harmonious voice. I am charmed with the mildnefs of their manners when friendly, but when enemies their ferocity has no bounds. Dinner was just going on the table in the same elegant stile as the preceding night, when I returned to Captain Brant's house, the servants drefsed in their best apparel. Two slaves attended the table, the one in scarlet, the other in coloured clothes, with silver buckles in their fhoes, and ruffles, and every other part of their apparel in proportion. We drank pretty freely after dinner, Port and Madeira wines, as already observed; but were not prefsed to more than we chose. Our first toasts were, King, Queen, Prince of Wales, and all the royal family of England; and next, to the brave fellows who drubbed the Yankies on the 4th of last November; all given by the landlord in regular progrefsion.

AFTER dinner Captain Brant, that he might not be wanting in doing me the honours of his nation, directed all the young warriors to afsemble in a certain large house, to fhow me the war dance, to which we all adjourned about nightfall. Such as were at home of the Indians appeared superbly drefsed in their most fhowy apparel, glittering with silver, in all the variety, fhapes, and forms, of their fancies, which made a dazzling appearance; the pipe of peace with long white feathers, and that of war with red feathers, equally long, were exhibited in their first war dance, with fhouts and war hoops resounding to the fkies. The chief himself held the drum, beat time, and often joined in the song, with a certain cadence to which they kept time. The variety of forms into which they put their bodies, and agility with which they changed from one strange posture to another, was really curious to an European eye not accustomed to such a sight. Several warlike dances were performed, which the chief was at particular pains to explain to me; but still I could not understand or see any affinity, excepting in the eagle attack, which indeed had some resemblance. After the war dances were over, which took up about two hours, as the whole exhibition was performed in honour of me, being the only stranger, who they were told by my fellow travellers meant to publish my travels on my return home, which they judged of by the notes I took of every thing I saw, though in reality I had no such thing then in view, I was desired by Mr Clinch to make a speech, and thank them for their handsome performances. As this could not be declined without giving offence, I was obliged to get up, and told them that I would address them in the Indian language of my country, and said in Gaelic, " That I had fought in many " parts of Europe, killed many men, and be- " ing now in America, I did not doubt but I " would fight with them yet, particularly if " the Yankies attacked us." My worthy friend Captain M'Nab explained in English my speech, as did Captain Clinch in the Indian tongue; at which they laughed very heartily.

No sooner the war dances were over, than they began their own native and civil ones, in which Captain Brant and I joined; he placed me between two handsome young squaws, and himself between other two; in this way we continued for two hours more, without coming off the floor, dancing and singing. He himself sang to keep time all along, which all the rest followed in the same cadence.

THE serpentine dance is admirably curious: one takes the lead representing the head, and the others follow, one after another, joined hand in hand, and before the close of the dance we were put in all the folds and forms a Serpent can be in. After this, and every other dance peculiar to their nation was over, we began to Scotch reels, and I was much surprised to see how neatly they danced them. Their persons are perfectly formed for such exercise. The men, from the severity of their hunting excursions, are rather thin, but tall, streight, and well proportioned, extremely agile and supple. The women much fairer in the complexion, plump, and inclined to be lusty.

HERE we continued until near day-light. I told Captain Brant that in my country at all country weddings and frolics, it was customary to kifs both before and after every dance. He said it was a strange though agreeable custom, but that it would never do here; I suppose owing to the jealousy of the men. I had brought two gallons of rum to entertain them, and he had ordered six bottles of Madeira wine from his own house, and would hardly allow the other gentlemen and myself to taste any other liquor. By my being in a manner under the necefsity of often drinking grog with the young Indians and squaws, I got tipsy, though I and one young Indian were the only persons present in the least affected. As for the squaws, I could hardly get them to taste, however warm they might be with dancing.

WHENEVER Captain Brant observed the young Indian affected with what he had drank, he requested I fhould give him no more, taxed him with being drunk, and said he must turn out of the company if he did not take better care of what he was about. On the whole, I do not remember I ever pafsed a night in all my life I enjoyed more; every thing was new to me and striking in its manner; the old chief entered into all the frolics of the young people, in which I was also obliged to join; but the other gentlemen, to whom none of these things were new, looked on, and only engaged now and then in the reels. After paſsing the night in this agreeable manner, and I being a good deal fatigued with drinking and dancing, we retired to rest.

CAPTAIN BRANT ſhowed me a brace of double barrelled pistols, a curious gun, and a silver hilted dagger, he had got in presents from noblemen and gentlemen in England, when he was in that country on an embaſsy from his own and other Indian nations. Each of the double barrelled pistols had but one lock, the hammer of which was so broad as to cover the two pans and two touch holes, so that both ſhots would go off at once; and when he had a mind to fire but one barrel at a time, there was a slip of iron which by a slight touch covered one of the pans, so as that one only which was not covered would go off.

THE gun, being once sufficiently charged, would fire fifteen ſhots in the space of half a minute. The construction of this curious piece was, as nearly as I can describe it, as follows. There was a powder chamber, or magazine, adjoining to the lock, which would hold fifteen charges, another cavity for as many balls, and a third for the priming, and by giving one twist round to a sort of handle on the left hand side, opposite the lock, the gun would be loaded from these magazines, primed, and cocked; so that the fifteen charges could be fired one after another in the space of half a minute, at the same time he might fire but one or two ſhots, leſs or more of them as he chose. He said that there was something of the work within wrong, so that he could not get it to fire more than eight ſhots without stopping. He tried it at a mark, and said it ſhot very well. Of the dagger, he said it was the most useful weapon in action he knew; that it was far better than a tomahawk; that he was once obliged to strike a man four or five times with a tomahawk before he killed him, owing to hurry, and not striking him with a fair edge, whereas he never miſsed a stroke with the dagger. Others told me that they knew him to be not over scrupulous or sparing on these occasions. Another instance, he said, was, that he had seen two Indians with spears or lances attack a man, one on each side; that just as they puſhed to pierce him through the body, he seized on the spears, one in each hand; they tugged and pulled to no purpose, until a third person came and dispatched him. This could not be done to a dagger, of course it was by odds the better weapon.

Mr Clinch, who is a young man of liberal education, had served all last war in the Indian department, and was on many expeditions along with Captain **Brant**; they put one another in mind of many strange adventures, among others that of their having once brought boys, and a **number-of** women and girls, prisoners to Detroit, and so served the whole settlement, which was much in want of females. Their description of the consequences gave me a lively idea of the rape of the Sabine women by the first settlers of Rome; but the difference was great, for here the former huſbands and lovers had been killed. A taylor in this place told me he was one of the boys captured on that occasion; that his eldest brother and father had been killed; the latter after he had been taken prisoner and brought a great part of the way, had got fatigued and could not travel, on which he was tomahawked by the Indians.

I CANNOT see how the necefsities of war can warrant such barbarity to women and children, independent of the cruelty ſhown to men and prisoners. Another story of Captain Brant's relating to hunting was, that he, Captain Brant, and another, being on an expedition with a large party to the south, and nearly run out of provisions, and dreading the consequences, had gone a-hunting on horseback; that they preferred small to large game, as the small would be the exclusive property of him who killed it, whereas the great game must be equally divided among the party. That they rode on through the woods, and at last fell in with a large flock of Turkies, and galloped after them as hard as they could, until they obliged the Turkies to take wing and get upon trees, when the party alighted off their horses, and ſhot seventeen fine Turkies, with which they returned to camp. They all ſhot with rifles. Lieutenant Turner, of the first regiment of Continental troops, was the only officer taken prisoner by the Indians in the action of the 4th November 1791, who survived the slaughter of his countrymen. He told me that when he was prisoner among the Indians, he was one day permitted to go along with them to the woods on a ſhooting party; that how soon they fell in with Turkies, the Indians pursued on foot as fast as they could run, bawling and hallowing all the time to frighten the birds, and when they had thus got them upon trees, that they ſhot many of them. Several other persons told me that this was the surest way to get them. They are so tame or stupid when they are in the trees, as to stand perhaps till the last of them be killed; whereas, on the ground, they are so quick-sighted and fleet, that in an instant they are out of sight. An old Turkey Cock can outrun any man on the ground. Another method practised, is that of watching them on the ground until they get up to roost in the trees in the evening, when the sportsmen may fhoot on until the last in the flock be killed.

With Captain Brant I had a conversation upon religion, introduced by him, indeed, and not by me. He said, that we were told every one that was not a Christian would go to hell; if so, what would become of the miserable souls of many Indians who never heard of Christ? afked, if I believed so, and what I thought of it? I told him very frankly, that if all the saints and priests on earth were to tell me so, I would not believe them. With such as were instructed in the Christian religion, and did not conform to its precepts, I did not doubt but it would fare the worse; that I believed it might be so with those of every other religion; but that I supposed it was a matter of no moment in the omnipotent eye of the Creator of the universe, whether he was worfhipped on Sundays in the church, or on Saturdays in the mosque; and that the grateful tribute of every one would be received, however different the mode of offering might be; that every man has only to account for those actions which he knew to be wrong at the time of committing them; but for these, that surely a time of reckoning would come. He spoke of the Virgin Mary, and her hufband Joseph, and even of our Saviour, in a way that induced me to wave the subject. It however fhowed the difficulty of converting these people from the early prejudice of education; but his discourses brought to mind a conversation on traditionary record, that pafsed between Ofsian the son of Fingal, and Patrick, the first Chriftian mifsionary he had seen. In regard to this Patrick, I suspect the literary world are in a mistake, as they suppose he could be no other than the saint of that name who flourifhed a century or more later than Ofsian, of course what is said to have pafsed between them must be considered as fictitious and false, whereas neither Ofsian himself, nor any Gaelic tradition or poem on record, ever yet hinted at his being the Patrick who converted Ireland, or the saint of that name. I therefore see no improbability in supposing that a Culdee, named Patrick, might have known a little of Christianity, and have preceded the saint, and fallen in with Ofsian. The very exprefsions that are said to have pafsed between them are obsolete, and evidently belong to a very remote period. The questions put by Ofsian were natural for a deist, and are quite in his own stile. I myself can repeat them in the original language, and I never yet heard a translation of them into any other. Since I am upon this subject, I cannot help saying a word or two on that of Ofsian's poems, which has given such subject matter of controversy to the literary world. The reproach, malice, and envy, they brought on Mr M'Pherson on the one hand, and the laurels with which he was crowned on the other, are both unmerited. To say that he was the sole fabricator and author of these poems is grofs calumny, and a glaring falsehood. That Mr M'Pherson has a deal of merit in the translation, every one must acknowledge; but that he has done it such justice as to equal the original, I flatly deny; and if it is true what I have heard afserted of Pope's Homer, that the translation exceeds the original, the Greek will not, as a poet, come up to the Celtic Bard, no more than M'Pherson does to Pope in their translations of the same Greek author. Of the two translators M'Pherson surely had the hardest tafk. To follow Ofsian in the sublimity of his style; his beautiful rounded periods on the one hand, his plaintive melancholy strains, and the smoothnefs of his poetic language for the lofs of his friends, on the other, I do not suppose it to have been in the power of the first genius ever the world produced, unlefs his heart felt (like Ofsian himself,) as he went along. These poems are repeated with a plaintive air peculiar to themselves, that cannot be transfused into the Englifh tongue; and I can most solemnly say, that I never was in all my life so charmed as with hearing them repeated with a musical tone. To suppose that these poems were wholly fabricated by M'Pherson, and that he was indebted to his own genius alone, as many pretend to do, is strange scepticism indeed, when the contrary has been so often affirmed by gentlemen of the first respectability, not only in this nation, but in all corners of the world that understand that language.

It would suppose a man to have the front of the very devil himself, to say what I am now about to afsert, were it not a fact, when thousands and thousands are still extant to confront him with falsehood. From my earliest youth I remember to have heard these poems repeated in their original language, and I vow to God and the world, that I never saw or heard a retranslation of any one of them from M'Pherson's into Gaelic, to my knowledge; and I am fully persuaded there has no such thing transpired in the world. It was customary in the corner of the country where I was born, when the people assembled on any public occasion, particularly at late-wakes, to place their best historian in some conspicuous and centrical place, where he could best be heard in the house, but more frequently in a barn, where the corpse was kept; and after they were tired playing games and tricks peculiar to that country, in which all the strength, agility, alertnefs, and dexterity, were exerted to their utmost, the best orator began and continued till day-light, repeating Ofsian's poems, and recounting the atchievements of his race, which exalted their minds and ideas to perfect enthusiasm. I myself, when a boy, was present on many of these occasions, and I well remember that I never observed a sermon by the greatest devotee, or any other discourse, picked up with half the avidity that the young people did these poems; and I have different times gone on a Saturday evening from school eight or ten miles off, to a friend's house to hear them repeated, and to learn them. Not many years ago I sent a servant of my own forty miles to learn them, from a man, who, for all I know, never spoke a word of Englifh in his life; at least my servant did not. That in this way, I am fully persuaded, these poems were handed down from a very remote period, and from generation to generation, till the present time. And with the gradual decline of these manly exercises and heroic poems, so did the spirit of the people, which the rebellion in the year 1745 much abated, and now the oppreſsion of their landlords and chiefs has crowned, and put beyond all poſsibility of recovery, excepting by leaving the country to their oppreſsors, lords, and masters, and setting out for the Britiſh dominions in America, where alone they will find an asylum, free lands, a fine climate, and the best government in the world, superior to that of Old England, on which the new Canadian law is founded, and an amendment.

" What may we not live to see!"

THE man to whom I sent my servant to learn Oſsian's Poems, as already mentioned, whose name was John M‘Nicol, lived in Glenorchy, the property of the earl of Breadalbane, was the most conversant on that subject I ever met with, told me that there were two Fingals, and gave a long string of patronimics to each of them. But that the son of Comhall, and father of Oſsian, and grandfather of Oscar, was by far the most renowned, which partly accounts for a Fingal being claimed by both the Scotch and Iriſh, as the hero of their respective countries. And as the Caledonian Fingal made several excursions into

Ireland, it is very possible that the Irish bards might have blended the mild actions and heroic deeds of that prince with those of their own nation, and ascribe them to the latter. I the more readily fall into this opinion, as I have heard poems in imitation of Ossian's in the Irish dialogue, but they were more full of bombast than those of the Gaelic. Whether Mr M'Pherson fell in with this man in the course of his researches in the Highlands, I know not; but I am convinced he could not find a greater antiquarian in the language, traditional history, and poems of those times. I appeal to the reverend Mr M'Nicol, the opponent of the northern luminary, called the *Bear*, of whose partiality and prejudice, now that he has dropt into the grave, we shall take no farther notice, for this assertion of his namesake's knowledge and information, with whom he was well acquainted.

But before I take leave of this charming country, and the honours done by this renowned chief, and his warlike tribe of handsome young warriors, all of the Mohawke nation, I must not omit saying, that it appears to me to be the finest country I have as yet seen; and by every information I have had, none are more so in all America. The plains are very extensive, with a few trees here and there interspersed, and so thinly scattered as not to require any clearing, and hardly sufficient for the necefsaries of the farmer ;---the soil rich, and a deep clay mold. The river is about 100 yards broad, and navigable for large battoes to Lake Erie, a space of sixty miles, excepting for about two miles of what is called here rapids, but in Scotland would be termed fords, and in which the battoes are easily poled up against any little stream there may be. Abundance of fifh are caught here in certain seasons, particularly in spring; such as Sturgeon, Pike, Pickerel, Mafkanongy, and others peculiar to this country; and the woods abound with game. The habitations of the Indians are pretty close on each side of the river as far as I could see, with a very few white people interspersed among them, married to squaws and others of half blood, their offspring. The church in the village is elegant, the school house commodious, both built by the Britifh government, who annually order a great many presents to be distributed among the natives; ammunition and warlike stores of all the necefsary kinds; saddles, bridles, kettles, cloth, blankets, tomahawks, with tobacco pipes in the end of them; other things, and trinkets innumerable, provisions and stores; so that they may live, and really be, as the saying is, as happy as the day is long.

FEBRUARY 13. When Captain Brant found that we would be away, he ordered his slea to be got ready, and after breakfast he and Mrs. Brant accompanied us the length of ten or twelve miles, to the house of an Indian, who had a kitchen and stove room, deal floors, and glafs windows, crop and cattle in proportion, where we put up to warm ourselves. Captain Brant brought some wine, rum, and cold meat for the company; after refrefhing ourselves, we bade adieu to our hospitable and renowned host, and elegant squaw, and proceeded on our journey along the banks of the Grand River. The land seemed extremely good as we came along,---the first village of Indians, the next of white people, and so on, alternately, as far as I have been, and, for all I know, to the side of the Lake. The Indians in this part of the country, seem to be of different nations, Mohawkes, Cherokees, Tufkaroras, and Mefsefsagoes.

I CALLED at different villages or castles, as they are called here, and saw the inhabitants have large quantities of Indian corn in every house a-drying, and suspended in the roofs, and every corner of them. We put up at the house of a Mr Ellis, who treated us very

February 14. We went a visiting for several miles down the river side, and dined at the house of a half-pay officer, a Mr Young, who had served last war as a lieutenant in the Indian department, married to a squaw, sister to one of the chiefs of the Mohawke nation who succeeded Captain David. This gentleman, of Dutch extraction, used me with marked attention and hospitality. Mefsrs Clinch, Forsyth and I, staid with him that night, playing whist, cribbage, and other games.

Here I for the first time played cards with a squaw. Next morning he conducted us in his own slea the length of Mr Allises. He told us that a few days ago a Wolf killed a Deer on the ice near his house, and fhowed us the remains of a tree, which before it was burnt measured twenty-eight feet in circumference.

February 15. We set out from Mr Young's; crofsed a forest of about twenty miles without any settlements, fell in with Mr and Mrs Andrew Butler, a Mr Henry and his wife, and some sleas loaded with grain going to mills. Here we all stopped to bait our Horses at the side of a stream or creek, put up a fire, and dined on such victuals as we brought along with us, in a fhade put up by some travelling Indians. I saw the track of Deer as we came along, and where one of them was dragged in a hand slea, or tobagan, on the snow. Mr and Mrs Butler invited our company to their house, to which we chearfully agreed. Mrs Butler is a very well looking agreeable young lady, and he himself a good plain sort of man.

We arrived about nightfall, and after refreſhing ourselves with some tea, and some glaſses of Port and Madeira wines, two card tables were produced, on which we played till supper time. In this, as indeed in every place we had been in, we were very genteelly and hospitably entertained.

The woods through which we paſsed for the last three days, much the same with that formerly described, thick and lofty in the valleys, but thin, ſhort, and scattered, along the mountain. The land also the same, clay, with a black mold on the surface. The only way to judge of the land in snow, and the surest without any snow, is by looking at the soil that sticks to the roots of new fallen trees, which can be seen every where, and will clearly discover the quality.

This gentleman's farm lies on a spacious broad point, bordering on the Grand Lake, about thirty miles from Niagara. A creek runs along one side of it, which in the spring and fall is swarming with wild fowls, Geese, and

Ducks innumerable. The wood Duck, which is the most beautiful of the aquatic kind, is frequently to be met with here; they are so called from their perching on trees.

My friend Captain Colin M'Nab, on whose veracity I can depend, told me that he and others had once in the spring of the year gone a-fhooting to this creek and the head of the lake, where they staid ten or fourteen days; that notwithstanding their living mostly on wild fowl, they brought home about 100; each of them had two fowling pieces, which they fired away as fast as they could be charged.

FEBRUARY 16. After breakfast, we set out from Mr Andrew Butler's, and bade adieu to him and his amiable wife. Called at major Tinbrook's, and dined at Squire John M'Nab's. Here we were told that a party of pleasure had gone from Niagara and the barracks to meet us on our return from the Grand River, at a place called the *Cheapway*, three miles above the Grand Falls, and have a dance there that night, which would disappoint them much in the event we did not appear. Captain M'Nab insisted on my being there in particular, for reasons, he said, I could not well dispense with. I therefore agreed, and my particular friend, the Squire, was good enough to furnifh me with his carriole, and a couple of good horses. This Mr John M'Nab is a gentleman of genteel and independent property,—is a Justice of the Peace, which gives him the title of Squire, and a Member of the Land Board. After dinner we all set out, I with Mr Johnston Butler, called at his father's the Colonel of that name, from thence to Captain Clinch's on Mefsefsagoe Point, opposite Niagara fort, from thence again in one carriage to the Cheapway, where we arrived about eight o'clock at night, two or three and twenty miles from the place we had dined in. Here we drank tea, supped, played cards, and danced until day-light. In the morning I took Mr Forsyth, Lieutenants Daniel and M'Kenzie, of the twenty-sixth regiment, into my slea. Breakfasted at a Mr Birch's house, who has some saw and grist mills on a small stream cut out from the side of the great river. Stopped at the Grand Falls, and saw them for the second time. Called at Mr Hamilton's, and arrived in the evening at Niagara.

From Niagara *to the* Genesee Country.

March 4. 1792. The weather now becoming fine, and the snow fast wearing away by the heat of the sun, in all exposed places, and the fields and open ground totally clear of it, I prepared for my journey through the Genesee country, bought a couple of Horses, and every thing I judged necefsary for the occasion.

On the 10th of March, I set out from this place, after bidding farewell, and thanking my good friends on each side of the river.

Before I take leave of Niagara, I must not omit to exprefs my obligations and acknowledgements to my very particular friends, the Mefsrs M'Nab; Mr Hamilton and family; Mr Dickson, merchant; Drs More and Kerr; Mefsrs Crookes and Forsyth; Mr Clerk, storekeeper; Mr Farquarson, commifsary; Mr Johnston, Indian interpreter; Mr Clinch, Captain Law, and his son, and young Mr Alexander M'Nab. Did I particularize every mark of attention and hospitality of these gentlemen to strangers, which I myself experienced to a very high degree, and how many happy nights I spent with them in that place, at afsemblies, entertainments, and card parties, I fhould make a diffuse narration of it; let it therefore suffice to say, that I am extremely sensible of their politenefs, and will always make grateful acknowledgements.

I must also exprefs my obligations to Captain Campbell of the twenty-sixth regiment and family, Colonel Gordon, Captains Bygrave and Hope, Lieutenants Daniel, Doyres, Duke, and to my travelling companion, and fellow sufferer on the Lakes, Lieutenant William M'Kay.

I arrived at an Indian village after night fall, and put up at the house of one Hoff, who (as the people here exprefs it,) keeps a tavern, which is no more than what we call in other places, a dram house; he lives with a squaw, who it is said a little time before then had on a quarrel between them wounded him with a knife

The 11th, set out from Hoff's house; my guide one David Ramsay, a native of Scotland, who was well acquainted with the way we were to hold; and as the thaw had come on some days before we set out, the brooks and creeks were full of water, we had very bad going, and often sunk in water, mud, and snow, knee deep. Pafsed through two Indian villages, about four miles from that which we had left. After pafsing the last of these villages the snow was very deep. We mifsed our way, and had to return two miles before we came on the right line, and from the faintnefs of the few prints of footsteps, we had the utmost difficulty to make it out. When night came on, we stopped, put up a fire, and slept on the snow. Next day proceeding on our journey, the thaw stopped, and some frost had come on, a good deal of snow had fallen the preceding night, so that our going was as bad as formerly. We crofsed several bad creeks, ourselves and Horses up to the middle in water, in all muddy bottoms, were obliged to wade through, as the Horses sunk in it. Towards evening we came opposite to the Indian village of Tonowanto, inhabited by the Senekees. I meant to put up at this village, but the creek was so high that we could not crofs it. It is a considerable broad stream, which discharges itself into Lake Erie above the Grand Falls. The land on the banks of this river, seemed very good; and from the appearance of the houses in the village, the inhabitants seem to live comfortably. We had the utmost difficulty in making out the way as we came along, but here met two men driving a parcel of oxen to Niagara, which marked the way, so that we were no longer at a lofs for the course we were to hold; also met a Dr Allan, whom I had seen at Niagara, going with a letter from Congrefs to captain Brant, requesting him to go to Philadelphia on matters of considerable importance regarding the Indian war. It freezed now very hard, and being wet up to the haunches, we were much afraid of being frost bitten, and as we could not crofs to the village, we found ourselves much at a lofs where to encamp at night. Going on in this way for an hour or two of night, looking for some place of fhelter, we saw a spark of fire before us; at which we rejoiced very much indeed. We made for it, and found a small fhade of bark, and two squaws and a boy, who had put up the fire, and taken pofsefsion of the best side of the fhade. Ramsay said, that we could not dispute it with them, first come first served; so that we were obliged to put up with the windy side, which was then really cold. But as the squaws were better lodged, and had more room, I was permitted to join them, and slept along with them that night, they rolled up in their blankets, and I in my great coat; and as we kept on a rousing fire, and had some bafs wood bark betwixt us and the snow, we slept very soundly. I offered them a dram, but they would not take it.

Rámsay said the women of several Indian nations would not taste spirits; though there are other nations that will, and even get drunk, but this does not in general prevail among them. The night freezed very hard, and a deal of snow fell. Next morning, after boiling a kettle of water, and infusing some tea and sugar in it, we drank it out of the kettle, and proceeded on our journey. The frost and snow that came on the preceding day and night, dried up the brooks and creeks, and made them more pafsable. We had gone but a few miles on, when we entered a plain of considerable extent, the trees so thin and distant from each other, that we could see half a mile on all sides. Driving the Horses before us on this plain, the one that had the bag of corn on, having taken some fright, ran off, tore the bag, and before we got hold of him, the greatest part of the corn was lost, so that we had now to keep them upon half allowance. Proceeding on our journey, we came up to an Indian hunting wigwam. A deal of Deer and Racoon venison a-drying, and hanging about this house. It continued to lay on snow most of the day. Crofsing a deep swamp, ourselves on Racoon bridges*, the portmantua Horse, on wading through, fell acrofs a log, tumbled on his back, and wet all our provisions and

* Trees fallen acrofs the stream.

clothes. We pushed on to a shade that we were told was about eight miles a-head of us; but before we reached it, an hour or two of night had come on, which fatigued us very much, and me in particular, as I had walked almost the whole way. The Horse could not carry me except in very hard dry ground; through swamps and bogs I was obliged to walk. We at length made out the shade, put up a fire, and got our clothes and provisions dried; cut crops of trees for the Horses to brouse on, and slept soundly. We set out next morning after boiling our kettle as usual, came to the banks of a large creek, called the *Butter Milk Falls*, where we had to unsaddle our Horses, crossed ourselves on the ice, and made the Horses ford it. Continued our route to the skirts of the thick wood in the Genesee country; stopped at an Indian wigwam, who had killed a Deer the preceding day, the skin of which he had then stretched to dry upon the side of his wigwam. Here I got a little corn for my Horses, which I had bartered for a loaf of bread, being wholly run out of that article, and the Horses almost laid up. We now entered what is called here, a plain, of six miles extent; that is, where the wood is so thin that you can see half a mile through it. We came to a village of the Senekee Indians.

Ramsay could not make himself intelligible to them, as he only spoke the Mefsefsagoe tongue, which they did not understand. It is rare, that the one nation understand the language of the other. After pafsing this village, we came down on a perfect flat, covered with rank natural grafs, and not a tree on it. In a link of the Genesee river at the end of this plain, when we came to the side of the river, my baggage Horse being well acquainted, entered the river, to swim acrofs, when fortunately old Ramsay got hold of him and turned him back, otherwise he and my whole baggage would have been totally lost, which would have distrefsed me very much. We crofsed the river in a canoe, and swam the Horses. In the evening arrived at the house of Gilbert Berry, an Indian trader, who keeps the tavern at Cananagas; here I stayed that night and next day to refrefh myself and Horses.

On my arrival here, I found that the course I meant to have gone up this river, and acrofs the mountains, and down the Susquehana to Philadelphia, impracticable thus early in the season, on account of the snow in the mountains, and the overflowing of the rivers and creeks; or to go by the Mongahela river to Fort Pitt, as the Indians at war would be out in scouts scouring the country the way I should hold; and to wait here for two or three weeks, until the snow should be off the mountains and the rivers subside, I thought too much, and therefore resolved to proceed by the Mohawke, Albany, and New York. This was unfortunately the worst time of the year for travelling. Had I set out from Niagara ten days sooner, before the snow began to difsolve, or two weeks later, when it would have been totally off the ground, I would have found the matter much easier. By the round about way I took from Niagara to avoid swamps, I am convinced it could be no lefs than 100 miles, yet were there a streight road made, it is believed it would not exceed sixty miles: the country flat, and fit to be inhabited all the way.

This large tract of country extends to some hundred miles on each side the Genesee river, and belonged to several nations of Indians, until of late that they sold all that lies on the east side of the river to the Honourable Mr Robert Morris, and other merchants in Philadelphia. Mr Morris sold about a million and a half of acres of it to Mr Pultney of London at, it is said, 72000l profit. Mr Pultney committed the sale and management of it to a Captain Williamson, a Scotchman, and the latter has advertised the sale of it in lots and townfhips. Hundreds flock from the New England States and different parts of the coast to see it and purchase parts of it, so that it is now fast settling. Some of those that purchased lands here last year are now desirous to sell them again and go for Canada, totally owing to its great distance from market. Captain Williamson hearing that I had come to Niagara with a view of purchasing a large tract of lands, wrote me a letter from the Genesee, acquainting me that he had such a quantity of land to dispose of, and launched out very much in praise of the country; but I wrote him back, that if I fhould be inclined to buy lands I would have no occasion to purchase from him, while I could get lands from the Britifh Government in Canada for nothing.

THE west side of the river Genesee is still pofsefsed by the Indians, so that the water only divides them and Mr Pultney's settlers.

BEING desirous of seeing this country, Mr Berry was good enough to take a ride with me for a considerable way up the country. We called at several houses as we went along, and at one in particular, where there was a distillery, at which was made the worst spirits I ever tasted. Here are large stocks of cattle, and many farmers of considerable property; and on each side of the river large and extensive flats without a tree or fhrub upon them, and of the richest soil I think I ever saw, but is every spring flooded by the freshes. The up'land on each side of these flats is thinly timbered, with small crabs of black and white oak, chesnut, and poplar; the soil thin and sandy.

FROM a hill which commanded a great prospect as far as my sight could carry on the Indian side of the river, the lands were flat, and not so much as a hillock in the whole view, all covered with stately hard wood. For some days that I staid at Mr Berry's house, and while I was exploring the country above, David Ramsay gave me the following sketches of his life, which I here offer to the public.

The Story of David Ramsay.

DAVID RAMSAY was a native of Scotland, born in the town of Leven in Fife. He was my guide through the wilderneſs, from Upper Canada through the Genesee country to the settled parts of the province of New York. His story, as given me by himself, was nearly in the following words. It was and authenticated and confirmed by numbers of people of my acquaintance in Canada, New York, and most other parts of America through which I travelled.

"I LEFT my native country in the early part of my life, and entered on board a transport bound for Quebec in the capacity of a ſhip's boy, and served the Britiſh till the close of the French war in 1763, when I settled upon the Mohawke River, in the province of New York; I afterwards engaged with the Fur North West Company of Montreal, to trade with the Indians upon the upper lakes of Canada. After serving them for some time I returned to the Mohawke country, where I resided until a boy, a brother of mine, named George, arrived from Scotland; and having the aſsistance of this lad, I thought of trading with the Indians on my own account, and for that purpose purchased a large battoe at Skennecktity, and procured credit to the amount of 150l. York currency's worth of goods, and proceeded with these up the Mohawke river to Fort Stanix. Crossed the portage down Wood Creek, to Lake Canowagas, from thence down the river that empties itself into Lake Ontario, at Oswego; and proceeded up that lake, the river Niagara, to the Falls of that name. Carried my battoe and goods across the portage to Lake Erie; from thence to the river Sold Year, or Kettel Creek, and proceeded up that river for sixty miles, where we met tribes of different nations of Indians encamped for the purpose of hunting; and informed them of my intention of residing among them during the winter, and erected a sufficient house of logs which I divided in the middle by a partition; the one end I used as a kitchen, or place for dressing our victuals, and in the other I kept my goods, and placed our bed. I continued bartering my goods for furs till towards January 1772, when two Ibawa Indians came down express from Detroit to Niagara, carrying with them a war belt, and publishing, as they went along, that it was the intention of the Ibawas, Otowas, Potervatomies, and other western Indians, next spring to wage war against the British and the Six Nations. There was an

Otowa Indian from Detroit that hunted close by the place where I lived, and upon the return of the Ibawa men from Niagara, they remained two or three days with me. They all visited me frequently, and behaved to me with the greatest civility. Upon the departure of the Ibawa men, the Otowa Indian came often to my house and boasted of the great feats he had performed, particularly of his having killed three Englishmen like me, and said he would think nothing of killing me and my brother also. I told him that if any Indian should offer to trouble me, I would kill one and hurt another. The Otowa Indian came frequently to my house for rum, which he as frequently received, I always repeating my former threat to him of killing one and hurting another, should I be mollested. About the 20th of February some families of Ibawa Indians, and one family of the Mefsefsagoe Indians, came and resided in the neighbourhood of my house. The Otowa Indian formerly mentioned, accompanied by the other Indians, used to come to my house and demand rum, ammunition, clothes, &c. &c. which I did not think prudent to refuse them as their number then amounted to forty. The Mefsefsagoe Indian was a poor infirm old man, and had a family of ten children to provide for, and I having compassion for him gave him snow fhoes and other necefsaries for the support of his family, and also used to afsist him to carry home the venison he killed. The whole Indians were in use to afsemble to the house of the Otowa Indian and send for rum to me. One night the Otowa Indian and his companion came to my house for rum. I suspecting they had a design upon my life, searched them and took three knives from them, and sent them away without giving them any. A few nights thereafter the Otowa came to me for the loan of a gun to fhoot a Deer he said he observed near the house; I suspecting him as formerly, immediately got up out of bed, and pretending to be intoxicated, made a great noise, at which the Otowa went out of the house, and I followed him as far as his hut, carrying with me a large knife. I found there the whole other Indians, and among the rest the old Mefsefsagoe Indian, who upon perceiving me hung down his head, and pretended to be asleep. I frequently afked them what they intended to make of a gun, as there was no Deer to be seen, but never received a satisfactory answer; I then returned to my own house, as did all the Indians to their respective huts. The old Mefsefsagoe Indian fearing the other Indians meant to kill him, and having cause to suspect they would make an attempt upon him that night, carried with him two Deer fkins, his gun, and ammunition, and placed himself upon the road which led to his dwelling, so as to intercept them if they fhould come. He did not continue long in this situation when he fell asleep, and the other Indians coming upon him, took his gun from him, and demanded the cause of his being there. The Mefsefsagoe, afraid to acknowledge the truth, pretended that he had dreamed that the Senekee nation of Indians that night were to kill all the Indians that were there hunting, and that he had placed himself where they found him to intercept them. Soon afterwards the old Mefsefsagoe, his family, and all the families of the Ibawa Indians, left the place; there only remained the Otowa Indian, his companion, a woman, and two children, the one of whom was nine, and the other thirteen years of age. And being tired of giving away my goods and rum for nothing, and being also much exasperated with the many insults I met with, resolved to refuse them every thing they demanded, and to repel force by force, while I was able, whatever the consequences might be.

"Upon the night of the 15th of February, the Otawa Indian came to my house, and easily entered the outer apartment, where he alighted a fire with straw, and as I knew tha he could come with no other intention at that time of night than to kill me, for which cause alone he and the others staid behind the rest, I stood with my spear ready to receive him. The Indian sought admittance into the inner apartment, where I slept and kept my goods, which being refused him, he broke in the door with an axe, and on his entering, I who was ready waiting for him, struck him with a spear on the breast, and following my blow from the inner to the outer apartment, threw him down on the floor, and rammed him through; on this he called out that he was killed. At this instant I received a violent blow from behind, which nearly brought me to the ground, on which I turned about, and struck that person with the fhaft of my spear. By the light of the moon which fhone bright, I saw another Indian coming to the door with a long knife drawn in his hand. I sprung out and struck him with my spear in the breast, and killed him also, I then returned and killed the one who struck me in the dark. After this, I waited in expectation that the whole tribe had returned, but after some time, and seeing none come, I understood that it was only the family that staid behind, who had a design upon me, that I had then killed. These I scalped according to the Indian custom, and having dug a grave for them in the snow at the gable of my house, put them all in together; at the same time repeating, that they should never more quarrel with me nor any other person. The Indian children still remained, and being from their youth unable to provide for themselves, would have inevitably perished, had not I sent for them*.

"I still dreading that the Indians who were formerly encamped in the neighbourhood might return, and being unwilling that my brother should be hurt, and being also assured, that if any Indians discovered the children with him, that they would conclude what really had happened, I therefore removed them and my brother to a small valley, about a mile distant from the house, where I erected a sort of shade for them, and carried provisions to them as they required. From the top of one of the hills that formed the valley, my brother could easily see my house, and from its smoking, or otherwise, discover whether or not I was in life; and if I happened to be killed, I gave him directions to pro-

---

* Had not David been humane and generous enough to send his brother for them to his own house, his conduct and behaviour to the children, clearly evince, that in killing the Indians he was actuated by motives of self defence, and not from a thirst of blood.

ceed with the children to Detroit, a distance of 150 miles*.

In about twenty days, the ice in the river broke up, and I judging it high time for me to leave my present comfortlefs situation, went for my brother and the children, and having put my furs and other goods, consisting of five Christian packs, chiefly Deer fkins aboard of my boat, proceeded with them for Niagara, it being unsafe for us to go to Detroit as the war then raged there. We proceeded down the river, as far as Long Point, and the drift or floating ice having choaked up the entrance to the Lake, we were forced to go afhore and encamp at that place.

Some days after this, being out in the creek with my boat, I discovered two men in a canoe coming towards me. On their coming near, I challenged them, and bade them keep off; but they laughed at me, and still came on, saying, that they came in a peaceable manner, upon which we went to my Wigwam. I afked where they staid, and if there were any other Indians in the neighbourhood.

---

* After these attempts on his life, and what ensued in consequence of it, no man but David himself would think of staying alone in the place; but it would seem that David would have faced all the Indians of America, and devils in hell, before he would abandon his property, which he could not then carry away. He therefore slept in the house, and killed venison for his brother, the children, and himself during the day.

They answered none but them, and pointed to a large pine tree, upon a height, nine or ten miles off, and that there they resided. After giving them a little rum, they went off, saying they would return next day to trade with me. The wind blew very hard at south west, which scattered all the ice in the bay, and the day following I went out in the morning to shoot Ducks. When I came a-shore, being wet, I stripped all off excepting my shirt and breech cloth, and hung them up to dry. After breakfast my brother and the two children went to gather juniper berries; I desired my brother to take his gun, and to allow no Indian to come nigh him, but to stand behind a tree, and shoot any one that would offer to approach him; for that there was no dependance to be placed in an Indian. In his absence, about eleven o'clock, came the two forementioned Indians, and sate down in the Wigwam with me, (the Wigwam, or encampment, was a few poles set up and covered with matts of flags, which the Indians in that country make, and carry about with them in winter.) They asked me for rum, I told them that it belonged to my comerade, and that I could not give any till he came. I observed two canoes coming along the lake, and asked to whom they belonged, they said that they were Milechiwack and

Renauge's canoes, (the names of two Indians.) I then aſked them why they told me the day before that there were none but them in the neighbourhood; they anſwered that the woods were full of them. The canoes landed; the two men came into the Wigwam, sat down, and aſked for rum. I anſwered as before. The two women, as customary, went into the wood and put up a fire, cut some wood, and carried up their things to the fire, and laid their canoes bottom upwards. Then they came into my Wigwam, and the young chief of one of the tribes, took my pot, that was boiling for dinner, off the fire, and gave it to the women to take to their fire and eat. I begged of him to leave some for the children that were with me against they came home, but in an angry manner he told me that I had victuals enough, and might cook more. I then judged what they would be at, and put on my leggans and mogazines, and other clothing, and took the large knife, I had formerly taken from the Indians I killed, and put it in my girdle. They aſked me what I meant by that, I told them I always wore it among Indians. Soon after my brother and the two children came home, I took them to the boat, and gave them some biscuit and dried venison, and aſked them if they wiſhed to see what they had seen three weeks before. They afked me what that was. I answered, " Blood." They said, 'No.' Then I told them not to tell that I had killed their people. They said they would not. My brother gave the Indians some rum, and I returned with the children. The chief afked whose children they were. I answered, that they were the children of white people, going to Niagara with me. He afked who they were again; then I stood up and pulled out the knife and struck it into one of the poles of the house, and told them how I had been used, and what I had done, and afked them if they were angry. They said they were not; that those I had killed were not Ibawas, but that they were Pannees, *i. e.* prisoner slaves, taken from other nations. They then afked for more rum, which I gave them; then two of them went over to their own fire, and two of them staid by me, and in a fhort time the other two come back, and these that were with me went over to the fire in the wood, and carried the children with them, by which fhifting, it would appear they were laying the plot they afterwards very nearly effected. They demanded my arms, and said that I had been drunk and mad all winter. I told them that I thought myself always fit to take care of my own arms, and putting myself in a posture of defence, laid hold of my gun, ammunition, and hatchet. After killing the first Indians, I cut lead, and chewed above thirty balls, and above three pound of Goose shot, for I thought it a pity to shoot an Indian with a smooth ball. I then desired my brother to carry the things down to the water side, to be put into the boat; but he being but twelve months from his father's house in Scotland, but seventeen years of age, and unacquainted with the manners of Indians was dilatory. I went to afsist him, and the Indians, under pretence of taking leave of, and shaking hands with me, seized upon me, threw me down, and tied me neck and heels. One of them took up my hatchet, and would have killed me with it, had he not been prevented by another of them. He then struck me with his fist upon the face, which hurt me much, and put an end to my great talking. They then set me up, pinioned my arms behind me, and caused me go and sit down by the fire. One of them watched, and took care of me, and drank only one dram during the night, it being customary among Indians, that one of a party shall always refrain from drinking, to take care of the rest. My brother coming to look for me, they seized upon him also; and I fearing they would kill him, called out, " That he was a boy; that it was me killed the

Otawas, and that they might aſk the children if it was not so." They only tied him, and placed him upon the other side of the fire, under the care of another of them who did not drink any. They used frequently to untie my brother, and send him and the Indian who had him in charge, for rum, which they brought in a braſs kettle that would contain about three Engliſh gallons. The chief and his companion drank freely, and also made me drink some out of a large wooden spoon that would hold a pint. As I sat by the fire tied, having only the Indian dreſs on, I complained much of cold, my ſhirt being tore down, and laid open; my leggans were also tore in the struggle, and my blood ran down my belly and thighs from the stroke I received from the Indian on the face, I therefore requested of them to put a pair of my own blankets about my ſhoulders to keep me warm; but the Indian that had the care of me did not approve of this measure, Renauge's wife used to paſs by me, and raise the blanket upon my ſhoulders to keep me warm. She also gave me a drink of water when I was first tied; and if the Indian that had the care of me happened to be out of the way, ſhe used to touch me on the back with her knee, and tell me to pray;— that my time was ſhort. She and all the children went to sleep under the tree where all the guns, hatchets, and other things stood. Nican, Equom's wife, kept walking about all night. They had tied my hands up to my neck, as well as pinioned my arms behind me, and some of them accused me of things I knew nothing of. I always appealed to one or other of themselves, that what they alleged was not true. As my hands were tied to my neck, it gave me great pain, and I requested to loose them, saying, that while my arms were pinioned behind, I could make no use of them. Though I was sure they were to kill me, I did not think much about it, as I believed it was as good for me to be dead as alive. What I regretted most was, that I could not be revenged of them. I then desired my brother in broad Scotch, so as not to be understood by one of the Indians who could talk a little Englifh, to bring me one of the clasp knives from the boat, and drop it by me, in order that I might get the cords cut; but Nican, Equom's wife, seeing him go off for the boat, called out, " To kill me directly, that my companion had gone for arms to the boat." On this I called him back, so that I did not get the knife. The Indian who had charge of me, told me, that Johnston, meaning Sir William Johnston, superintendant of Indian affairs, would forgive an

Indian for killing a white man; but not me for killing an Indian. He then drew out the big knife, and turning up the coals of the fire, afked me how I fhould like to be roasted there to-morrow. I answered, " Very well." They then gave me the spoon half full of rum, of which I drank a little. The Indian putting the knife to my breast, afked, " If I wifhed to see vermilion ?" (meaning blood;) which was saying as much, as that he meant to kill me unlefs I drunk it off, which I therefore did. He made me drink two spoonfuls more in a very fhort space, but it did not affect me. This rum was one-third water, mixed for trading with. The Indian who had me in charge and I, entered on a hot argument; upon which I stood up, and as I would not yield, he seized me, and threw me down. In the struggle, I grappled him by the breast, so that he fell upon me; I made a grasp at the large knife, which he held drawn in his hand, and by a sudden jerk wrested it from him, gave him a brog, and wounded him in the head and breast, upon which he ran off, as I did also. Another Indian pursued me, seized and threw me down. I called to my brother, who struck the Indian that was upon me, relieved me, and cut the cord that pinioned my arms behind me. The Indian was foundered by the stroke he received, and disabled from running off. I killed him, returned, and killed the other two, one by one, as they were coming to his afsistance. At this time the women and children ran away, excepting one boy, who seized upon a gun to fhoot me. I struck and killed him also. What I drank did not disable me, but rather made me more furious and alert than I otherwise would have been. My left hand being severely wounded in wresting the knife from the Indian, my brother bound it up with a rag; and on our way to the boat, I broke the canoes to pieces, to put it out of their power to follow me. I looked about, (the moon was just then descending down over the wood,) and I saw the wounded Indian coming as hard as he could in quest of me. I sculked by the canoe, and just as he was running by, I sprung up, grappled him, threw him down, and put my knee upon his breast. He then begged his life; but I, remembering what he told me a fhort time before, that he would roast me upon the fire, struck him with the knife, and killed him upon the spot. I proposed to return to carry the few things we had afhore with us, but my brother opposed it, as I was lame of the left hand, and could give no afsistance. We therefore made for the boat, which was a piece off the land, and wading through the water to it, I fell and wet all my clothes; when I got into the boat, I wraped myself in a Bear skin. Then, and not till then, did the rum I had drank operate upon me. I fell asleep, and when I awoke I was all over ice. We rowed till we got out of sight of land, and then put up sail, and made for Niagara; but the wind having got up a-head, drove us back. I then steered for the south shore of Lake Erie, judging it safest, and that the Indians on that side would not hear what I had done, till the lake would open, and be free of ice. The wind drove us upon a bank, and the sea washed over us, and wet every thing in the boat excepting the guns and ammunition, which I took care to preserve dry. Next day we got the things ashore unpacked, to dry them, but not so much so as not to serve as ballast for the boat. Here we made a Wigwam, to serve us until such time as the lake should be totally free of ice, in a place where we supposed the remotest from such as the Indians frequent, and were in hopes they would not find us out; and if any of them came near us we determined to kill them. I however was here but a few days when two Indians came; and as I supposed they had not heard of what had happened on the other side of the lake, I treated them in a friendly manner. They asked me if I had rum and ammunition; and when I answered that I had, they said they would come next day, bring fkins, and trade with me. I told them not to let any other body know that I was there; and that if any more than them two were to come, that I would not deal with or allow them to come near me. They solemnly promised that they would not, and that they would come alone. However, as I did not choose to trust them, I got every thing on board, and kept at some distance from the fhore. The two Indians accordingly came, and requested I would land and trade with them; but upon obferving other Indians sculking in the wood, I refused to comply. On this the whole party appeared, and threatened to fire at me in the event I did not trade with them. By this time I was pretty much out of reach of their fhot, and proceeded down the lake, and some days thereafter reached Fort Erie. I told the commanding officer of the Indians I had killed; upon which he confined me, and sent me with a party prisoner to Niagara, where I was again imprisoned."

HERE ends the information given me by David in writing, our time not allowing him to proceed any farther. My information from others was, that though my friend David acknowledged to have killed but eight Indians, yet that he really killed eleven; but as I give ample faith to his own narrative, and as he in every other respect seemed to be a man of strict veracity, honesty, and integrity, I disregard what others say, and trust to his own account. On the Indians hearing that David was at Niagara, they afsembled in great numbers, and insisted upon his being given up to them; and on the Governor's refusal, threatened to set fire to the fort. They became at last so clamorous, that the Governor sent a party, unknown to the Indians, to Montreal with David, where he was fifteen months in prison; and as no proof could be brought against him in a regular trial, and that every body knew he acted in self defence only, he was liberated. And what is strange, and what the like never was known before, is, that he now lives in intimacy and friendfhip with that very tribe, and the sons and daughters of the very people he had killed. They gave him a grant, regularly extended upon stamped paper, of four miles square of as good lands as any in Upper Canada.

In the Genesee country, when with me, I saw him write a letter in the Indian tongue, to some chiefs then afsembled in Philadelphia, at the request of Congrefs, directing them how to act in the matter under deliberation. I told him that it was in vain, as nobody there could read it. He said that any body could read the words, and that the Indians would know the meaning of them. On another occasion I told him that I was informed, as I really was, that when the Indians got drunk, but only when drunk, that they still threatened to kill him; at which he seemed extremely displeased, and swore that if he knew any one of them that dared threaten him, he would be about with them yet; that it was he that was ill used, and not them; that his goods were taken from him, and himself threatened to be roasted.

DAVID never was married; nor do I think he ever will. Skins to the amount of 150l. being seized upon him, which he, in common with many others, was smuggling into the States, has reduced him; and at present he has no other employment than that of carrying dispatches and money for gentlemen of the fort and district of Nafsa, to and from any place they may have occasion. His honesty and fidelity is so well known, that he is entrusted with sums of money to any amount, without requiring any token or receipt for the same; and I was told, when with me on his way to New York, that he had seven or eight score of pounds belonging to different people, sent for articles which he was to bring them from that city.

David was a staunch friend to the British during the last war; and was well known to those who were in high command, and had ample recommendations and certificates of his services from them. Scarce a corner of the British Colonies or United States but he is acquainted in.

The strange adventures of his life are so well known, that I was told that he was offered 200l. for a detail of them from a printer in Albany. I put the question to himself. He only acknowledged 100l. from a printer in New York; but he declined to accept of it, as he thought it too troublesome. Yet I know that he would have given it to me, had we had time and leisure; as he sat up a whole night, when we were travelling, to give me what I have already inserted, for which I consider myself much obliged to him.

David told me that he never was in Britain since he left it young but once, when he landed in England, on his way to Scotland to see his relations; and knowing that a sister of his was married and settled there in a respectable line, he waited on her; but as he was in the Indian dress, though excellent of its kind, she refused to acknowledge him for her brother; and as he did not know but his friends in Scotland might do the same, he returned to America, where he means to end his days: and as the country is now fast settling in the neighbourhood of the grant of lands he got from the Indians, he is in hopes it will yet turn out to good account for him.

From the GENESEE COUNTRY *to* NEW JOHNSTON *on the* MOHAWKE RIVER.

MARCH 18. 1792, I set out from Gilbert Berry's house in Canawagas. Crossed a deep creek called *Honia river,* but fordable. The Horses my servant rode, were almost at the swiming; he got a tumble just as he was landing, fell back in the water, and wet my little baggage. Passed through several tracts of open woodland, very easily cleared, but sandy and light soil; and other tracts of close woodland of deep and rich soil. Crossed one swampy creek of about sixty yards broad, where we were obliged to wade through up to the middle, lead the Horses, and break the ice with heavy sticks at every step as we went along. In this situation I travelled the most of that day on foot through the bad parts of the road, and on horseback on the best parts of it only. Toward evening came to the settlement of Conondacway, and put up at the house of Anthony Sanburgh, who keeps (to express it in their own words) a tavern. Such as keep what are called in Scotland small tippling houses, would be said here to keep taverns. Here I fell in with

General Chepin or Shepin, an agreeable facetious man who lives in that place, was good enough to come and spend the evening with me; himself plain, homely, as any farmer, with clouted mogazines, breeches, and clothes, but his wife and two daughters extremely handsome and genteelly dressed. Among several stories the General told me of the Indians, one was, that in a conversation he lately had with an old Indian, he said, "What great things do you suppose the white people are now about to do for us? they are to give us a smith to mend our guns, tomahawks, and hows; that is a good thing; and to make us ploughs, but I am against that; for if we have ploughs we must work, and if we work our squaws will turn lazy; whereas they raise as much bread for us at present as serves us; and to send us a man to teach us to pray; but I swear I'll pray none; but if they send us a man to teach us to make rum, we'll attend him, and thank those that sent him."

Another was, that on his once asking an old Indian what was it that made them so fond of war which the white people hated, he answered, "That when he was a little Baboose*, that their fathers had taught them to keep their breasts always to the east; that he, and one and all of them, teaches the same thing to their Babooses; that from the east the white

---
* Baboose is a child.

people came; that the first sight that ever was seen of them on these coasts, was so many winters ago; that they stopped in a bay with a large canoe, came afhore in a smaller one, and fhowed them some sick people they had on board which they wifhed to get afhore for the recovery of their health; we had compafsion on them, said he, and permitted them. They then sought liberty to gather herbs in the fields to be given them, which was also permitted; then to build a house for them; and after this was granted, they sought a small spot to plant some corn; and from that to more, until at last he extended both his arms, and said, they must have the full of all; which signified that they must have all they could grasp, and at length all America." In other respects he gave quite a similar account of that recorded in history of the first landing, and the most material proceedings since.

It is customary with the Indians where any one of them has been killed, not to allow any grafs to grow on that spot; for that reason every one that pafses by the place, tramples and treads down the ground, to prevent the grafs from growing; and if any does grow, they pull it out by the root, so as to keep it always bare. I have seen a spot where an Indian was killed used in this manner.*

* A similar custom prevailed in the Highlands of Scotland, by erecting cairns of stones on the spot where a person had been

MARCH 19. Set out from Conondacway, in company with General Chepin, who had come four miles of the way to see a saw mill of his. Paſsed by the head of Conondacway Lake, said to be thirty miles long, and between one and two miles broad. This lake does not abound much in fiſh. In this neighbourhood are many Deer; and when the snow is deep, with a hard crust upon it, any Dog could, in the space of 200 yards, overtake and detain one; so that they are sometimes taken alive without receiving any injury. Arrived in the evening at a Captain Paterson's, on the head of Lake Geneva, said to be thirty-six miles long, and as broad as the other.

HERE I was told that the carriage of 100 w^t. of any article from Albany to this place would cost two dollars; but that there is a piece of a canal talked of to be cut next summer, of two miles long, which when finiſhed will bring down the freight to half what it is at present; and when the country is properly settled, there is no doubt but that and several other things will be done for their accommodation.

THE 20th set out pretty early from Mr Paterson's house. Croſsed a river which comes out of Lake Geneva, and after a course of twelve miles, falls into Lake Kieuga; and from thence,

killed. I myself added many a stone to a cairn of this kind where a friend of mine had been killed.

by another river of that name, discharges itself into Lake Ontario. In the evening we crofsed Kieuga Lake, a mile and a quarter broad, on the ice. These three lakes run parallel to each other, south and north, and are said to be much of a length and breadth. After crofsing this lake, I put up at the house of a gunsmith, one Harris, who kept a tavern, and who afsured me he could make a riffled barrelled gun of iron to his liking, that would hit an egg at a hundred and thirty paces, could so small an object be seen at so great a distance, and fhowed me the apparatus by which the riffles were made in the barrel. This man kept me up till very late reading Paine's Rights of Man, of which he seemed very fond, arguing, and making commentaries on every pafsage as we went along.

The 21st, from Kieuga, set out pretty early. Crofsed through a close wooded country of about twenty miles extent, without a hut in that space but two, then newly put up. The land as I went along seemed to be the best I have seen in the Genesee country, excepting the links of the river of that name. Crofsed a creek of about 100 yards over, in which I was obliged to wade through up to near the middle. Put up at the house of one Burke, lately come from New England. Congrefs has reserved in this neighbourhood, purchased from the Indians themselves, a tract of land nine miles by twelve, for the Unindagoe Indians, and the like space for the Kieugas, as a place of settlement and hunting ground for them. General Sulivan, when sent here last war against the Indians, had cut down several hundred fruit trees they had in their gardens and about their houses, which is now very much regretted by the late purchasers.

THE 22d, set out from Burke's house. Crossed about twenty miles of a forest without a single hut or habitation in all the way.

HERE many tons of sugar could be made, i do not remember to have seen so many mapple or sugar trees in all my travels since I left the province of New Brunswick, none of which seemed ever to have been tapped. The wood in this day's journey is interspersed with much hemlock spruce and cedar. Towards evening I fell down on the Unindagoe creek, a remarkable fine and spacious valley belonging to the Indians, and part of the lands they reserved for themselves. On seeing a hut on the plain, I directed my course towards it, and having come up, I called at the window to some Indians whom I heard talking within. A gentleman put out his head, and afked me if I was going for the German Flats; when I anwered in the affirmative he came out, requested

I would walk in, and take the trouble of carrying a couple of letters to that place; that he resided there, and that his name was Patrick Campbell; I answered that that was my name also; at which he seemed very much surprised, and said he never saw one of the name before. He said he was born in this country; that his father had come last from Ireland, but formerly from Scotland, and always passed as an Irishman. He had been only on a start here to trade with the Indians, who, on hearing that I was a Britainner, and had just then come from Canada, immediately came up, shook hands with me, and welcomed me to the country in the most cordial manner; but while they supposed me to be an American, took no sort of notice of me. This gentleman was a captain in the American army last war, now a colonel of militia, a justice of the peace, and keeps taverns at the Mohawke Flats. Here I staid that night with my namesake, and was hospitably entertained. The owner of the house, one Brown, farmed the place from the Indians for 130 bushels of Indian corn *per annum*.

One of my Horses being nearly knocked up by the scarcity of provender and badness of the way I had come through, I gave them the next day's rest to refresh them. Borrowed one of my landlord's Horses and set out with Colonel Campbell, who was good enough to go along with me to see the salt works at the head of the Unindagoe Lake.

There are many salt springs at the head and round about this lake, which is a beautiful sheet of brakish water, of about six miles long and two broad. The land all around this lake lies well, with an easy slope towards the water; the soil rich and productive. About three hundred yards from the head of it, the salt springs, of which the salt is made, issues out of the foot of a steep bank thirty feet high. Here are several other springs whose waters are said to be twice as salt as that of the ocean. Here are twelve kettles, of forty gallons each, constantly kept boiling, and make at the rate of twenty bushels a day of beautiful small white salt. The water is pumped out of the well, and conveyed by a trough into the works and kettles; and I suppose there is water in one well sufficient to supply 100 kettles. There was 200 cord of wood lying by the works; and yet one of the managers told me, it would not last them above six weeks, so that they must consume much wood, and clear a deal of land in the course of time. As the country is fast settling this will become a considerable work, and can easily supply the whole back settlements of the extensive province of New York.

When the spring opens, and the ice off the lake, it swarms with Geese, Brants, and Wild Ducks and Swans, which the inhabitants kill in great numbers.

A SORT of Salmon Trout, Pickerel, and Maſkanongy, are so numerous, that with a spear and torch in a canoe at night, they sometimes catch a barrel of fiſh in one night. The woods on the banks of the lake abound with Deer and other sorts of game; so that this part would make one of the most agreeable places I have seen in this country for a settlement.

ON the Unindagoe river, a great many Salmon are speared in the fall of the year, and the cedar swamps abound with Pheasants. I this morning heard them drumming on old logs. The manner this is done is a little curious, and peculiar to that beautiful bird. When the cock Pheasant happens by any accident to separate from the Hen, and wiſhes to call her to him, he perches on a large hollow log of wood, of which there are many every where lying on the ground; he then beats a ruff with his wings, resembling that of a drum, which is heard at a considerable distance, and apprises the hen of the place of his abode, to which ſhe presently resorts. This they practise in the spring and fall of the year, and is called *drumming*.

We staid that night at the salt works, in the house of one of the managers. The water of these springs is perfectly clear, and only discoverable from any other by the taste. While boiling the water, they hold a pretty long iron ladle in the bottom of each kettle, into which all the sediments fall, which they now and then throw out, otherwise, if left in the kettle, it would discolour the salt, and make it look brownish, and not so fair as when it is turned out. By constant use, the ladle gets a hard crust of this stuff on it, which will require to be burnt out every twelfth day, by putting the ladle in the fire, and when properly heated the crust falls off in scales, and leaves the iron as clear as ever.

The 24th, returned from the salt pans with Colonel Campbell, to my former quarters at Brown's house, where I had left my Horses. The Colonel paid for our night's quarters at the salt springs, and would not allow me to be a sixpence out of pocket, and treated me while I staid with him at Brown's; so that I had only to pay for my Horses. This gentleman seems not to be a niggard of any thing he has, and treated me with much civility and friendship.

Method of finding out BEES *in the Woods.*

IN autumn, a man sets out to a distance from any habitations, takes with him his Dog for a companion, and his gun, as no man is safe in the woods without both; a blanket to lie on at night, a tomahawk, Bees wax, vermilion, a pocket compaſs, a watch, and a little honey. He proceeds in the woods until he comes to the largest growth of timber he can find; there he stops and puts up a little fire; on a flat stone in this fire, he puts a little Bees wax, and on another stone hard by, he drops a little honey; around this honey he sprinkles vermilion; he then takes his stand at a little distance, and is sure if there are any Bees in the neighbourhood, the smell of burnt Bees wax will attract them. As soon as they come, they begin to drink of the honey, and on their approach, they unavoidably tinge themselves with some particles of the vermilion, which adheres a long time to their bodies and wings. He next fixes his compaſs to find out their course, which they keep invariably streight when they are returning home loaded. By the afsistance of his watch, he observes how long those who are marked with vermilion are of returning. Thus pofsefsed of the course, and in some measure the distance, which he can easily guefs at, he then follows the first that comes, and seldom fails of coming to the tree where they are lodged; this he marks, and takes his own time to cut it down. It is astonifhing what a quantity of honey some of those trees will contain.

By this patient method, near a dozen of hives have been discovered in a season by one person.

It is said, Bees never cast or swarm until there be not room enough for them in the body of the tree. Bears are very destructive to the hives, where they can come at them. The trees are for the most part cut down with a saw, to prevent the Bees from being disturbed by the chopping of the axe. In the house in which I now am, there is a large trunk of a tree, said to contain as much as half a dozen of ordinary hives, standing by the side of the wall within.

The 25th, I set out from Onandago. Crofsed this fine valley of about a mile broad, and fell in with a man going the same route all the way to Albany, who was somewhat acquainted in the way. Ascended a hill thinly clad with wood, mostly white oak, which I observed is light timber, and thinly scattered every where. It grows on light soils. There were some new habitations here and there in the hill as we came along; and for the first eighteen miles, I hardly saw a stone that was not of the lime kind. Here for the first eight miles, fine grazing farms could be made at very little expence, as the wood is so thin as to require very little clearing. In the remainder of the way to Canowaga, the wood was close, abounding with maple. Stopped at the house of an Indian who keeps a tavern. This man, how soon he understood I had come from Canada, made no hesitation, when the American, my travelling companion, was not present, to disclose his mind to me. Made many inquiries about the Canadian Indians; and if any of them were going to the southward next summer; meaning if they were going to war, along with the southern Indians, against the Americans; and added, whether they did or not, that many Indians from this part of the country would; which shows how ill disposed they are towards the Americans, notwithstanding of their living in their territories, and their attachment and good wishes towards the British. This Indian was a smart handsome fellow, spoke good English, kept a good house and accommodation for the public. With an Indian in this village I saw a beautiful Peacock. Proceeded on our journey,—crofsed the Onido river, and arrived after nightfall at the Indian village of that name, situated on a spacious flat plain, and put up at the house of an Indian who kept a tavern. Here there was a beautiful young woman, half blood. Her hair, eyes, and eyebrows jet black, and fkin milk white. She and her hufband slept in the far end of the house. An old squaw slept in a bed near the fire, where I and my servant were stretched on the bare floor, with our soles to the fire. After we had lain down to rest, a drunken Indian came in, made a hideous noise, leaping and capering about, which made me fear he would fall down or trample on my head. After continuing a while in this way, he sprung into bed with the old squaw, who did not seem to feel so warm as he did; made a noise, got out of bed, and sat by us at the fire side. Her gallant soon followed; on which fhe returned to bed, where he still pursued her; and in this way the farce was kept up for some time, alternately leaping in and out of bed, until the Indian in the other end of the house got up and turned him out of the house, and freed us all of this disagreeable guest.

Here I got good hay for my Horses. A little Canadian Frenchman, who lives always with this family, served as an interpreter.

March 25. Set out from Onido; breakfasted at Whitestown, a new settlement; from thence to Fort Scouler; from that to German Flats town, where we put up that night. In the country about Fort Scouler and German Flats town, the Mohawkes and six Indian nations lived prior to the last war.

The 26th, after riding a few miles farther on, I came up to the head of the German Flats, a spacious plain, of a triangular form, two miles broad, through which the Mohawke river slowly glides, principally inhabited by Germans, who still retain their primitive language. I heard a great deal of the industry of these people, but saw little of it, as the plains and flats on each side of the river are only cultivated, and not an acre of the rising ground adjoining these flats to be seen clear; whereas, with a little attention, the woods behind their houses, if cleared, would make good pasture for their cattle; but they seemed to be contented with what their grandfathers had done, and will not be at the trouble to clear more. And yet their stock is but small; I have not seen above half a dozen of milk Cows about any one house as I came along.

I called at Colonel Campbell's house, and delivered my letters, and understood that if I was to stay a week, I should have free quarters; but as it was pretty early in the morning, and I did not choose to lose time, set out on my journey. Lodged that night at a ferry. The ice came so thick down the river, that it could not be crossed. The land thin and stony, particularly on the east side of the road.

The 27th, crossed the river early in the morning. Breakfasted at Captain ———'s house, who kept a tavern, and where I got remarkably fine oats for my Horses; I do not know that ever I saw any to exceed, and rarely to equal them. He said the seed was but twice sown since it came from England, and that when standing it was about six feet high; that, but for a storm that happened two or three weeks before it was cut, which battered it to the ground, he supposed he would have forty bushels for every one sown; and notwithstanding of that, and what it suffered, he hoped it would turn out twenty fold. The plains on each side of the river are but small, and the land back from that thin, stony, and mountainous. The thaw having come on, with a little rain and south wind, the ice gave way in some parts of the river; in other parts it stopped and dammed up the water, which overflowed the whole flats, and when it subsided, left the lands covered with large junks and flakes of ice, which obstructed our way, and made it tedious and disagreeable to get through. My fellow traveller said that the road led through a certain field, then covered with water; and as we supposed it not deep, we pushed on to the far end of it, when we found a creek in front which we could not get over; but before we got back to where we entered the field, the flood made so fast that my Horse had to swim two or three strokes before we got to dry land; and after getting through a rugged woody precipice, we made out a public house, kept by a German, where we put up to refresh ourselves and feed our Horses. The landlady, a young, chearful, well looking woman, hearing from my fellow traveller, and judging by mine and servant's language, that we were Scotch, accosted me in Gaelic, and asked if I understood that language; when I answered in the affirmative, she seemed very happy. The whole family and other strangers that were there, all Dutch, looked with amazement on hearing her and me converse in an unknown language.

She was born in this country, of Scotch Highland parents, of the name of Fraser, from Straherrick. I knew two uncles of her's

Captains of that name in Canada who were extremely obliging to me when there.

AFTER leaving this place, I encountered still greater rifks, crofsing small log bridges over ditches, that were afloat with the flood. In one of these my horse fell twice through, and I had to wade up to the middle, alternately in snow and water; and endeavouring to return, night came on before we could extricate ourselves out of this difficulty; and had not a farmer seen us, who lived hard by, and had the humanity to come down to the water side to direct us what way to hold, it is hard to say how we might have fared. We at length made out this man's house, where we staid that night. He entertained us very hospitably, and with much civility, and charged but moderately, though he was a Dutchman. He said he had only come two years ago from the Jersies,—held his farm on fhares, that is to give the landlord half the produce, deliverable on the ground where it grew. The landlord is obliged to furnifh half the seed, and to manufacture his own quota, *viz.* the one half. He told me he sowed about forty bufhels of wheat and rye last year, and that the return would be about fifteen seeds.

THE up-land in this neighbourhood is poor, and but from the great salubrity of the climate the produce must be in proportion. It is but drofs in comparison to the soil of Canada. Here the land, both high and low, is thin soil, sandy, stony, and hilly.

MARCH 29. Set out from the farmer's house who relieved us the preceding night from the swamps and creeks, occasioned by the overflowing of the river, and breakfasted at a miller's house, a jolly Dutchman, who directed me to Albany-Bufh, near New Johnstone, where many of my countrymen resided, eight miles north of the Mohawke river. I was sorry I could not conveniently go to Cherry Valley, but was fhown where it lies, twelve miles south of the Mohawke; which I could easily see from a rising ground as I went along to New Johnstone. In this village I dined and baited my Horses, and called on a Mr John Grant, who keeps a store, and has a potafh work, and explained the whole apparatus of it. From this place I proceeded to the house of a John M'Vean, with whom I had been well acquainted in Scotland before he left that country, and was much trusted and employed by myself; at first sight he thought he knew me, but I addrefsed him in the German language, which if not spoken, is partly understood by every one in this neighbourhood; this disconcerted him much, and made him suppose that he had been mistaken; I afked him in that language if his name was M'Vean, and if he understood German; he answered in Englifh, that his name was M'Vean, but the devil a word of German he could speak. I then afked him in the same language, if Mr M'Vean could speak Gaelic, he understood me well, and said he could speak Gaelic; and instantly turned about to his wife, and said in that tongue, seemingly with a great deal of surprise in his countenance, that he never saw any one so like the head forester of Mamlorn, (by which appellation I was well known in that country,) as that Dutchman was. At length, after some conversation in this way, with a great deal of surprise on his part, and amusement on mine, I discovered myself, by afking " What would you say if it was the forester himself?" 'In troth I believe it is,' said he; of which discovery we were both equally happy. I staid that night with my friend M'Vean; and next morning, his wife often reminded the children to look after the Cows, and take care they fhould not steal into the bufh; even the endlefs forests are here termed the bufh. I afked why fhe was so anxious about the Cows getting into the bufh; and if fhe was afraid they would stray and could not be got. " By no means, (said fhe,) but they are so fond of the sap of the sugar tree, that one drunk out of the trough that held it, until she died of it.

MARCH 30. Hearing that a daughter of my friend Mr M'Intyre of Glenoe, the chief of that name, resided in the neighbourhood, I directed my course towards her house, and found that she and her husband, a smart decent young man of the same name, lived very happily on a fine farm he had lately purchased. Here I took up my head quarters while I staid in these parts, and was entertained with a great deal of friendship and hospitality by both. Mr M'Intyre is to erect a grist mill, on a creek well adapted for that purpose, that intersects his farm. He has entered into partnership with a merchant of New York, by whose asistance he is also to commence a potash work. Great quantities of pot and pearl ashes are made in this district, much to the advantage both of the farmer and manufacturer, as it pays the farmer the whole expence of cutting, gathering, clearing, and burning the woods, in his land, and the latter has the profit of the making and the sale. These are advantages they do not enjoy in upper Canada, as the merchants do not deal in that article; so that the farmers get no sale for their ashes, of course they gather none excepting for making soap for family use. Among my countrymen here, I have seen many acres of newly cleared land, of which they told me the afhes paid the whole expences. The soil is pretty good, but stony, the situation high, and the ground uneven, full of knolls, with very few level spots to be found in it. The farmers seem to be at more pains to clear and cultivate the knolls, than the dales, the former being more productive for the first years, whereas the latter are too rich, and fhoot out more rank in straw than in grain; but in progrefs of time, there is little doubt but they will change their system of farming, and give a preference to the latter. The knolls, they say, are better adapted for wheat, peas, and potatoes; the dales for Indian corn, hemp, and hay. They scarce make any use of dung, but leave it in heaps about their doors. Barn, stable, and Cow house are under the same roof. The wood is neither thick nor leafy, and chiefly consists of maple, pine, hemlock, and beech. The Wolves were here very troublesome, but now that the inhabitants have got Slow Hounds, the Wolves are banifhed.

The Scotch inhabitants in this neighbourhood, hearing that I had come to Mr M'Intyre's house, came from all quarters to welcome me, and invite me to their houses. I accepted many of their invitations, and found the people in general well lodged and pofsefs. ed of every necefsary accommodation. They live in intimacy and friendfhip with each other; and in every political afsembly carry any point they can agree about, and elect one of their own number to afsefs them with the taxes necefsary for supporting the State. The manner of raising these taxes is as equitable as can be. Congrefs afsefses every province with a proportional quantum; the legislative council of the province lays a stated proportion on every district; the people of the district on a certain day afsemble, and one man, well acquainted with the ability of every inhabitant, is elected to subdivide the quota among them; these afsefsors are put upon oath to do justice between man and man, and to proportion the burden according to their abilities and stock. Tax gatherers are next appointed to collect the money, who are accountable to the Treasury of the province for their intromifsions. I was present at one of their meetings; their proceedings were regular, but took up more time than was necefsary. Near the village of New Johnstone is the seat of the late famous Sir William Johnstone, Baronet, of whom the inhabitants speak to this day with the highest gratitude and respect. He died a year or two before the breaking out of the war. He was a man of unbounded power in this part of the country. Affability and generosity were his distinguished qualities. He had a large property in land, and was to the Indians, as well as to the Scotch inhabitants, a father and a friend. To him they looked up for relief in all their distrefses and wants. He kept a squaw*, sister to the famous Captain Joseph Brant, by whom he had several children, male and female, now in life, to each of whom he bequeathed at his death 1500l. besides leaving a large sum to the mother, who now lives at Niagara. It is said the sons are somewhat wild, savour a little of the Indians, but that the daughters have the mild dispositions and manners of the Europeans. One of them is well married. I have often been in her house, and very genteelly entertained. She is the best dancer I think I have ever seen perform. Her hufband, a particular friend and countryman of my own, is surgeon to the Indian Department in the district of Nafsa, with a salary of about 200l. a-year from Government. To crofs the breed of every species of creatures is deemed an advantage, but I am convinced it can be to none more than to the human species; as I do not remember to have seen an instance where a white man and an Indian woman did not produce handsome

* Now called old Mifs Molly.

and well looking children: thousands of examples of this kind might be given. The famous and handsome Captain David, and the present Mr Brant, afford striking instances of this kind, and of whom I have spoken already in another place*.

THEY retain the exprefsive features, the fine large black eyes, hair, and eyebrows of the Indian, with a much fairer tint of fkin, which are easily discernible to the third generation, if not longer.

SIR WILLIAM lived in great splendour in this place. In his family were slaughtered 100 fat Hogs and twenty-four Oxen annually, and every thing else was in proportion.

SIR WILLIAM was wont to say that he was born in Ireland, but that his father, when a boy, came from Glencoe, in Scotland; and that he deemed himself of that country. The Johnstones, or as they are called in the Gaelic language, the M'Ians of Glencoe, now M'Donalds, were anciently a very warlike race, and in times of barbarism not the least so of their neighbours; but it is somewhat singular that scarce a one of them who left their country early in life, and ifsued out into the world to pufh their fortunes, but made a distinguifhed figure in it. Their vein of poetry was such

* The greatest warriors, and most conspicuous characters among the southern Indians, now at war with the Americans, are half blood.

that any one of them who could not compose extempore in rhyme, was deemed a bye leap; but that practice, which was then much in use, and shone very conspicuous in them, is now discontinued, and their genius in that line is no better than others.

Sir William had the distribution of the king's gratuities and stores to the Indians, and his manner of issuing them was very different from what is now practised.

When an Indian came for his presents, he was carried into the store, and allowed to choose for himself, which pleased him mightily, and he often went off with a few trinkets of little value. At present I have seen saddles, bridles, &c. given to Indians, who never had crossed a Horse, and many other things given in the same way of as little utility to them; and the first use the possessers made of them, was to dispose of them to the first bidder at half value.

Sir William was so remarkably beloved, that if he had been in life when the war broke out, it was supposed the whole inhabitants of the back parts of the province of New York would have risen in arms along with him.

His son, Sir John, was more distant, and not so affable in his manners, and of course was not so well liked; however, the greatest

[274]

part of the young Scotch settlers, besides some Irish and Germans, adhered to his fortunes; and he raised a corps of the smartest, liveliest, and most useful troops in the British service. Their sufferings were very great: they were often obliged to eat Horses, Dogs, and Cats, and yet were never heard to complain, if they could distress their enemies. They and the Indians went hand in hand; the former led on by a son of Colonel Butler, a gallant young officer, who was killed in the war; and the latter by the intrepid Captain Brant.

[margin note: *Captain Butler did not belong to that corps*]

This chosen corps,—this band of brothers, was rarely known to be worsted in any skirmish or action, though often obliged to retire, and betake themselves to the wilderness, when superior force came against them.

Sir John's corps and Butler's rangers were very distressing to the back settlers: their advances and retreats were equally sudden and astonishing; and to this day the Americans say, they might as easily have found out a parcel of Wolves in the woods, as them, if they once entered it. That the first notice of their approach, was them in sight; and of their retreat, their being out of reach. These two bodies were chiefly made up of Indians and Scotch Highlanders, who adhered closely to their country's cause, and such of them as survived the war, are now settled in Upper Canada. I have known many of them, both officers and soldiers; and the account they gave of the fatigue and sufferings they underwent, is hardly credible, were it not confirmed by one and all of them.

MARCH 31. Here I was informed that my old friend Angus Cameron, who had served me for several years in the capacity of under forester, when I had the charge of the fine Deer forest of Mamlorn, was living in that neighbourhood. He was a very smart lively young fellow when with me, and for whom I had a particular regard; and I well knew that he always entertained the same sentiments for me; I therefore resolved to set out for his house before he fhould hear of my being in this country, in order to enjoy the pleasure of taking him by surprise. As he had not seen me for near twenty years, I judged he would not know me at first sight.

He pofsefses a farm of about 150 acres of very good land, all his own property, with grain, utensils, and cattle in proportion. Mr M'Intyre was good enough to go along with me, and to tell Cameron that I was a Dutchman from the Mohawke Flats, come to inquire if he had any Oxen to dispose of.

A LARGE fur cap I had brought from Canada, and had on at the time, disguised me so much in the eyes of my friend, that he supposed me to be a Frenchman or a Dutchman. I accosted him in German, and afked him if he had any oxen to dispose of. He said, that I must change my tongue, and speak to him in Englifh or Lochaber German, otherwise he would give me no answer. Mr M'Intyre afked him in Gaelic, if he knew me; he answered, not; "Why then, (says the other,) he says he knows you." 'The fellow is a d------d liar, (says Cameron,) he never saw me in his life; but let him be what he will, he speaks more languages than one.' On saying this he put on such a curious inquiring face, that I could not help smiling, which he observed, and then came up to me and examined my clothes and took off my cap, and knew me; a discovery at which we both exprefsed equal pleasure.

HERE I staid that night, and talked over our adventures in the forest of Mamlorn, and how many fatiguing days and nights we had spent in the bare mountains and fhealings of Scotland, where we slept wrapped up in our plaids; the chaces we had with two fine large Deer Gray Hounds I kept, and the Deer we had killed; at which my friend sighed deeply, and said, he wifhed he had been still in these hills. It is not a little singular that this man, who, while in Scotland, never handled an axe, spade, plough, or had done any sort o work, but go about with his gun, fhould totally lay it aside, and betake himself to the necefsary occupations of a farmer when he came to this country; and notwithstanding game being plenty about him, never fired a fhot at a Deer but one since he came to America. Very fortunate for him he did so; for he now makes out very well, and enjoys abundance of the comforts of life on his own property, from which, he says, no other can dispofsefs him. His wife and children told me, that he often cursed the country, because there was no rain in it; that when a plump fhower happened to fall, he would run out of the house, stand under it until he would get drenched to the fkin, and say what a pleasant thing rain was. Among other old stories, he reminded me of a time we had been in the forest, and night coming on, we retired to an uninhabited hut, where we were in use of keeping a small chest of provisions, for the benefit of such of us as fhould be under the necefsity of pafsing the night in the mountains, and rising before day, to intercept the Deer before they fhould get into the nursery or sanctuary, to which they always retired early every morning during the hunting season. At this time there happened to be no provision in our little magazine, excepting a small portion of oat meal; and as we had not ſhot any thing that day, we had recourse to it. I desired Cameron to bake a couple of oaten cakes for us to eat; he swore he never baked one in his life, notwithstanding his being bred from his cradle in the wildest forest and mountains of Lochaber. I insisted on his trying it, as otherwise we must fast. He at length with much reluctance did, but to no purpose; he went so aukwardly to work, that I thought I could do better myself; I therefore begun, but could not make it out. We alternately set to work, but with no better succeſs; so that we were, after all our endeavours, obliged to eat our meal in dough, without ever being put to a fire. It however served us for the time, and when our repast was over, we threw ourselves down on a sort of bed of heath, and slept as soundly as if on down. Got up by the dawn, ascended the hills before it was clear day, and at sun rise each had ſhot a fine Hart; Cameron wounded another, which our Gray Hounds run down and caught. The best of these was sent to my constituent, the Lord of the Manor, the second to his factor or steward, and the third I reserved for myself. In this way I spent seven years of my youth, and prime of my life, void of all care but that of my charge, which indeed was more a pleasure than a trouble to me. On the eighth I gave it up, on a slight misunderstanding with the factor, who I am very far from suggesting was more to blame than myself; and from his high honour and worth, great understanding and personal qualifications, I have been always more apt to think the fault must have been more on mine than his side of the question; but a few years thereafter, the same thing happened to himself, on some misunderstanding with his noble constituent, of whose ancestors he was lineally descended, and whose family he had served through a long period of fifty years in the same station, with equal honour to himself and benefit to his employers, and to the regret of his numerous acquaintances, many of whom were of the first rank and character, excepting one lady, which tempts me to use the words of the poet*.

It, however, was fortunate for me that I removed. The change of situation made me alter my idle mode of life. I betook myself to farming, traded a little by sea and land, by which I made out so well as now to be enabled to give up all business, and gratify a passion for travelling, and seeing as much of the world as my little finances will admit of.

* Mankind, since Adam, have been woman's fools,
Women, since Eve, are still the devil's tools.

April 2. This being the day appointed for electing their afsefsors and tax gatherers, I went along with them to New Johnstone, where I saw between fifty and sixty Scotchmen afsembled there on that occasion. They were happy to see one so lately come from their native country; brought me along with them to a public house, where we spent the evening. Some were drefsed in their Highland plaids and bonnets. They were much surprised at the account they heard of the rise of rents in their mother country; and afked why the people had not come over here rather than submit to be over-rated. They blefsed their stars that they had left Scotland, while they had something left to pay their way. Even my friend Cameron, who was with us, regretted only that he wanted the beautiful sight of the Highland hills, considering the happy days he had spent among them in his youth. There was scarcely any one of them who did not invite me to their houses, to some of which I went and spent five or six days among them very agreeably. They in general pofsefs lands of their own, and live comfortably and happy. As the soil is inferior to that of Upper Canada, I recommended to them to go to that country, and told them they would be much happier there under the Britifh government. Many of them said they had heard so from almost every person; and that they had a mind to go and see it, as they could get their farms here disposed of, and could get lands there for nothing. Some of them had very fine orchards, and made a great deal of cyder. Here it was that I first saw a cyder mill in this country.

N N

From the MOHAWKE RIVER *to* NEW YORK.

APRIL 6. I set out from Mr M'Intyre's house in Albany-Bush, within two miles of New Johnstone, and proceeded by the north side of the Mohawke river, through much barren, sandy, and stony soil, in which, however, there were many orchards. I saw one large spot of about six acres, planted with young fruit trees, so sandy and barren to appearance, that I was surprised it could answer the purpose. I put up at a house on that side the river, about twenty-five miles from that I had left in the morning. The country here is hilly on both sides, a little way out from the river.

APRIL 7. Crossed the river in a flat bottomed boat to Skenectedy, a small town built on the south banks of the Mohawke river, seventeen miles higher up than Albany. The town consists of several hundred houses, some of wood, and others of brick, with some regular streets, merchants and tradesmens shops, and but little trade. The country close to it as barren as can well be, and producing little besides a few stinted fir and pine trees. From this town to the half way house, a stretch of ten miles, all a poor sandy bottom.

Here I fell in with General Peter Ganswarth, and rode in company with him to Albany; a stout handsome man, who is High Sheriff of the place. He told me that the land on each side the sandy ridge we had come along from Skenectedy is good, and the country well settled. I put up at the city tavern, the sign of the Arms of the United States.

I staid here two days. The city of Albany is about a mile long, stretched on the west side of Hudson's river, a few miles below where the Mohawke falls into it. The houses are mostly of brick, many of them very neat, but not high built. They have a new built goal, that is handsome, and even elegant, and strong; it is the most fhowy building about the place.

From this city are exported to New York, annually, a great deal of grain, lumber, pot, and pearl afhes.

The flats on the banks of the river are about a mile over, and are now overflowed with frefhets, which is the case every spring.

They have about thirty sloops belonging to the town, and some scows with sails, that will carry each two thousand bushels of wheat. On the river side, there are several wharfs, where vessels of upwards of 100 tons may load and unload. The whole inhabitants of the back parts of the wide and extensive province of New York, and part of the new State of Vermont, send the produce of their land to this town, where they are supplied with merchant goods, and all the necessaries they want; and as these countries are fast settling, this city in a little time must be a place of considerable export and import.

THE city is built very irregularly on the side of a sloping hill, in some parts steep, and full of gullets. It has one fine broad street well paved, that runs about half way through the middle of the town, but the buildings on each side have not the least uniformity.

THE soil sandy, and thinly timbered with poor pine and miserable oak. At the city tavern I fell in with a Mr John M'Intyre, a Scotchman, lately married to the daughter of a rich merchant in New York, who owns some salt springs, and a large tract of land in the Genesee country.

THIS gentleman invited me to his house, which was on my way to New York, and I chearfully accepted of his invitation.

APRIL 9. I went along with Mr M'Intyre from Albany to his house, twenty-five miles below that place. The land as we came along was in most parts barren, thin, and sandy, excepting one small valley, through which a small river glided slowly along, like what we call the strath of a glen in Scotland, with low hills on each side. This is a beautiful spot, and abounds with fruit trees and orchards. After paſsing this valley, we ascended a high hill, of a thin and stony soil, partly clear and inhabited, and which commands a fine prospect of the country all around. Near the summit of this hill, where four roads meet, is Mr M'Intyre's house, with his store and potaſh work. The farmers carry their aſhes to the store, for which they are paid at the rate of one ſhilling, York currency, *per* buſhel. Here I staid two or three days, and Mr M'Intyre was good enough to go along with me to the town of Hudson. On our way thither, I was surprised to see a good deal of new cleared land, so thin of soil, stony, and barren, as not to seem worth the clearing, and yet he said it would yield good crops for the first years. It however ſhowed, that all the good land in the neighbourhood had been formerly taken up, and that none now remained but this kind, which in any other place I had been in, would not have fetched one shilling the hundred acres for cultivation; but here land is not to be got without purchase, at a pretty smart rate. Came through one beautiful valley of old cleared land, mostly laid out for hay. From this valley to the river side, opposite to the town of Hudson, is all grafs land, cleared for some time back.

CROSSED the Ferry to Hudson; this town is now inhabited mostly by New Englandmen.

THE Catfkill mountains were in view to the westward all this day. They appeared to be high and rugged, and covered to the top with wood. In the town there are some good new brick and timber houses, and several wharfs; and some vefsels of considerable burden are built here annually. The plains on the river side are narrow, being little more than half a mile over, and are just now overflowed by the frefhets. I put up at the principal inn kept by one Gordon.

THERE are numbers of Quakers in this neighbourhood. The women of this religion can be easily discovered by the plainnefs of their drefs,---much the same as in Britain. They use nothing gaudy, such as ribbons, lace, &c. to ornament their persons, whereas those of any other persuasion drefs very gay. If a Quaker contracts debt that he is unable to pay, if he is a liar, a drunkard, a cheat, or guilty of any midsemeanour whatever, he is turned out of the community, and no longer deemed a brother, which he considers as the highest punifhment that could have been inflicted on him. A merchant here told me if a Quaker took goods on credit, and did not pay them about the time he promised, that by a complaint to the Rector, Intendant, or Head of the Society at the place, he would be forced to pay, if it fhould be with his last penny, and that he would be turned out of the community in the event he did not. I suppose their religious tenets, in point of morality and decency, to be the best in the world, and they in that respect come nearer the Scotch Presbyterians, than any other clafs of men whatever.

As my Horses were much fatigued, I agreed with Captain Hatchway, master of the packet to New York, a distance of 130 miles, to carry myself, my servant, and Horses, at a dollar for each Horse, another dollar for myself, and half a one for my servant, I finding forage and provisions. And as the vefsel was not to set off till next day, I took a walk to a neighbouring hill, from whence I had a prospect of the country around me, as far as my eye could carry. On the east side I could see the country to be pretty closely inhabited, each farm having a clump of wood by it for fuel. The wood appeared to me to take up three-fourths of the ground, though it is an old settled country; and I could discover ten times as much wood on the west side, towards the Catſkill mountains. They have a conſiderable fiſhery here, of a sort of Herring, called *Ellwives,* for two or three weeks in May or June, and they exported this last year to the West Indies, 4000 barrels, all caught in seines.

This little town flouriſhes fast; and though but of eight years standing, they have regular streets and some genteel houses; and belonging to the place there are four ſhips, fifteen brigantines, and twelve sloops. I could not find that New York had double that number of square rigged veſsels. The trade of this little town to the West Indies is conſiderable; they export lumber, Horses, hay, and grain; and import molaſses, of which they make a good deal of Yanky rum. I have seen a veſsel here loaded with hay, bound for Charlestown in South Carolina. I am told the southern provinces are not productive in that article.

The 15th we set sail very early with a quarterly wind. Paſsed several stores said to be full of grain,---Newburgh and New Windsor, small villages, where General Waſhington had his head quarters during a part of last war. Nine miles below the latter, the high lands commence, and they continue for fifteen or twenty miles more. Here the river enters between high rocks, and precipitate mountains, that are bold and rugged to the water's edge, and to a person in sailing through, forms a wild, romantic, and picturesque scene. After pafsing three or four of these mountains, you come to West Point, where the remains of several small forts are still to be seen, and the old barracks, occupied by a few invalids. These forts were built on pointed knolls and rocks, of difficult accefs for cannon to be brought against them.

THE river here is hardly 100 yards broad, but said to be extremely deep. After pafsing West Point, you come to Fort Montgomery, rendered memorable by the death of the brave Colonel Mungo Campbell; and (as the Americans say,) by the fall of 1100 Britifh troops along with him. When you pafs Fort Montgomery, you arrive at Stony Point, and leave the high lands behind you. A little farther down, the river becomes a mile broad. The country closely inhabited upon the east side. Pafsed Fort Wafhington, and all the other forts on this celebrated river. Opposite to Fort Wafhington, is a ridge of a long rugged and precipitate mountain. On our course down this river, we pafsed several fine vefsels, principally sloops, and saw one large scow loaded with grain coming down. We outsailed all the vefsels we fell in with on our pafsage. The captain told us none on the river could keep up with the packet, that fhe sailed within four and one half points of the wind. Had a fine view of the country, better it is said than if we had come along the road on either side of the river, and arrived at New York, a little before daylight on the morning of the 18th April.

From NEW YORK *to the* JERSIES *and back again.*

To offer a description of this town would be idle; I shall therefore only say the wharfs were crowded with vessels, mostly small craft, the markets extremely well supplied with every necessary of life, and the inhabitants seemed to be doing well, excepting such as suffered by the late great failures occasioned by the speculation of Colonel Dewar and Mr M'Comb, said to have failed for three millions of dollars.

HERE I was told that the Indians, how soon the spring opened, were daily committing depredations about Fort Pitt, and the banks of the Ohio; that they had driven so many of those that settled in that part of the country towards the coast, that the lands had risen to an unusual height by the concourse of people that flocked from the back settlements to it; that by the last accounts they had killed, even that early, 350 of the peaceable inhabitants, including men, women, and children; that two families in particular, which they named, consisting of ten each family, were all killed, not one escaped the slaughter.

ANOTHER gentleman told me that a brother of his was attacked, wounded, and some of his party killed, in a boat going down that river; but that they had kept up such a well directed fire against the Indians, as to beat them off and get quit of them; that for these, and many such reasons, it would be in vain for me to think of going by the Ohio; but as I knew I would be better informed at Philadelphia, I staid but four or five days in this place; and after seeing every thing about it, said to be worth while, I set out for Philadelphia. Crofsed at Poul's Hook, and pafsed through the Jersies to Elizabeth Town. Such parts of this province as I have seen, is an old settled close inhabited country, but the soil thin and poor in comparison to that of the back countries.

HERE I fell in with a Mr Donald Stewart from Appin, who had gone the preceding year, with a fhip load of emigrants from Scotland to North Carolina, where he resided all that winter. He had been for some time in Philadelphia, and afsured me that the accounts there of the depredations of the Indians in the back countries were every day increasing, and that it was in vain for me to think of going by that route;

my hopes and expectations of exploring the back settlements on the Ohio, which my mind was much bent upon, being now frustrated by the Indian war, was a great disappointment; but as I could not now help it, and having no pafsion for going coastwise, and a vefsel being next day at New York, ready to sail for Britain, in which he was to take his pafsage for Scotland, I resolved to change my route, and return with him to New York.

WHILE at Elizabeth Town, in the house of Mr Robertson merchant, a Scotchman, his clerk, Mr Mitchel, informed me, that a man who lived a little out from the town, had the fkin of an immense large Serpent; that he was acquainted with him, and would go along with me to see it. We accordingly went, and the man who had it was one Pit, a poor carpenter, who had got the fkin by his wife. Her father bought it for twenty dollars, and very few in the neighbourhood knew of their having such a curiosity. The wife having got it from her father, would part with it on no account; and said they kept it always concealed, in hopes that some time or other it would be the means of procuring them a livelihood, by going about with it as a fhow, in the event they turned poor and reduced to make use of that fhift for maintenance.

Mr Mitchel could not prevail on them to show us the skin, until he told them that I and Mr Stewart, who was along with me, were not natives of this country, and that we were going off that very day for Scotland, and that it would not be heard in this country what we would say of it; for that reason he produced the skin, and he and his wife, whose property she deemed it to be, gave the following account of it. " That some time after General Bradock's defeat near Fort Pitt, at the commencement of the last French war in this country, when he himself, and seven or eight hundred men were killed, or rather slaughtered by the French and Indians, (General Washington was in this action, and is said to have given his opinion decidedly against the mode of procedure,) seven soldiers were hunting in the woods, and heard a rustling noise descending down a sort of hill hard by them; they waited to see what it was, as it seemed coming towards them; at the moment it came in view, it raised its head seven feet from the ground, on which four of them fired, and disabled it from proceeding any farther; the other three fired afterwards and killed it. When they came up to it, it proved to be an immense large Serpent, of the horn kind. They cut it along the back and skinned it; that it was then twenty-four feet four inches long, and four feet four inches broad; that the horn was ten inches long; but when I saw it it was so shrunk in as not to be above twenty-two feet long, and about as many inches broad; the scales on the lower part of the belly were very broad, but those on the sides and back not larger than a sixpence. It was dark coloured on the back, and light or yellow on the belly, and much resembled in shape and colour that of another horn Snake I had seen of about seven feet long. The wife told us that it was said an Indian child and Dog were found in its belly."

I HAVE not seen any body that ever heard of a Serpent of its size having been seen in this country. It is possible that by living on the carcases of the dead bodies slain in that action it became overgrown, and the monster it was when killed. It had the marks of the balls in the skin.

Here I sold one of my Horses at twenty-five dollars, just the one half of what he cost me. The other I sold on my return to New York in the same way.

From NEW YORK *to* FREDERICK TOWN.

HERE I staid a few days, and as it was earlier in the season than I wished to return to Scotland, as already said, I proposed to go in the stage to Boston, but was told I might remain there some months before an opportunity would offer from Boston to either St John or Halifax; and a vessel being just then at New York ready to sail for St John, I embraced that opportunity as the surest way for me, agreed with the master for my passage, and on the 30th April stepped on board, and arrived at St John the 12th of May. I remained there but a few days, when I proceeded up the river St John's to Frederick Town, and staid at the engineer's house for a month, waiting a vessel that was to sail for Britain.

WHILE in this place I made the following remarks on what I observed while in the States.

THERE is reason to suppose that the inhabitants of New York are more attached to Great Britain, than those of any other part of the American States. A gentleman in that town told me the following instance, of which he was an eye witness. Two years ago, a French frigate had put in there, the officers of which waited on the late General

Malcolm, and signified a desire of going to see a play. The General went along with them, and out of complaisance to the officers, requested the manager that the musicians should play Malbrook, a lively French tune, before the play began. Accordingly the band was desired to play that tune. On the galleries hearing this, they called out for God Save the King. The General desired the musicians to go on; but in an instant, God Save the King resounded from all parts of the house; but the General still persisted, which put the house in an uproar, and the musicians were so pelted with apples, oranges, and other things, that their instruments were like to be broken to pieces about their ears. One of them, a German, who got a cut on the brow, went up to the General, and told him in half English half German, "*That his cop had been slachen*, (that is his head broke;) *and swear nout*, (d————d himself,) *if he would play any more Malbrooks, for all the Yenerals in Amerique.*" The band were compelled to desist, and play God Save the King, which they had no sooner done than the house resumed its tranquillity, and were told, they might now play Malbrook, or any tune they pleased. I observed to him, that it must have been you Tories that began that business; "By no means, (said he,) we would not have taken it upon us; it all proceeded from themselves;" meaning the Whigs, and old friends of the late rebellion. This was but a sorry instance of their attachment to their French allies.

I FELL in with several well informed gentlemen in that city, who did not hesitate to say, that they never would be right or easy until connected with Great Britain, in some shape or other, and the sooner that was brought about the better.

IN this province, and I believe over all the United States, they have more canvasing in the election of Members to the Provincial Assemblies, and Congress, than prevails in the choice of Members to the House of Commons, in any part of Britain, with political publications, letters, answers, replies, and rejoinders, couched in severe terms against the opposite party. On these occasions the successful candidates who enjoy the emoluments of office, extol their independence; while the opposite faction reprobate it, particularly the measures pursued; but on account of the share they themselves bore in attaining the former, they are more severe on the latter. If the act of parliament referred to in the declaration lately published in the American Gazette by Sir John Temple, the British Consul General, takes effect, by putting the old navigation act in force, which prohibits any produce of America to be imported into British ports, excepting in British bottoms, owned by British subjects, navigated by a British Captain, and two-thirds of the seamen to be British, under the penalty of confiscation of ship and cargo, it will disconcert them much, and increase the discontent. The interest of the Southern States are so diametrically opposite to that of the Northern ones, that it is not likely their union will be of any long duration.

The foreign commerce of the Southern Provinces, is already carried on in British bottoms; they have no shipping of their own excepting small craft; so that this act, though put in force, will not affect them in the least; while the New England States, who may be justly called *maritime*, and are the coasting carriers of the Northern Provinces, and much interested in foreign commerce, will complain much of such a measure, and probably aim at retaliation, by imposing a duty on goods carried in British ships, equal to a prohibition.

This matter, like most others, will no doubt be warmly contested in Congress; and if the Northern States carry the point, it will be very distressing to the Southern ones; but, on the contrary, if they lose it, they may burn their capital ships, or let them rot in their docks, and there will be an end, in all probability, of ever America having a navy. It will be extremely difficult to enact a law congenial to the whole, or strike a medium between them; so that it is probable, ere long, this great empire will be divided into two separate Governments and Independent States. If Britain should foment a misunderstanding of this sort, then would she be umpire between them, and have no cause to regret the loss of her American colonies; and be soon reimbursed by their commerce, in the treasure she expended in attempting to subdue them; each state would then court her alliance and friendship, and be emulous who should enjoy it most.

This matter is not so difficult to bring about as some may suppose. If Britain but gives the proper encouragement to the settlement in Upper Canada, by cutting a canal, to avoid the rapids of the river St Laurence, from Montreal to Segotchy, and the lower end of the Thousand Islands, the navigation to and from that city may become easy and unexpensive; the settlements would increase with such amazing rapidity, as in a few years to cope with the one half of America, and make it even difficult for the whole to gain any advantage over it. The situation of Canada is such, stretched along the back parts of almost every province in America, as makes it easy to give afsistance from Detroit, Niagara, Kingston, and Montreal, to whatever corner of the States they choose; and one or two hundred thousand pounds, I have been well afsured, would mould that venal court of legislators to any fhape fhe pleased. Nor is it easy to foresee the lofs on the part of America, to be thus divided; the contrary seems evident, as it would make the diversity of interests, and the present unweildy mafs, more compact and reconcileable; unlefs they may think it would make them weaker and more dependent on their old friends of Great Britain; who it may be presumed, would feel her interest in giving them every advantage in trade they pofsibly could expect, more than fhe gives even to Portugal, the most favoured nation, which, it is well known, would have been converted into a province of Spain, but for the protection of Great Britain, which might form an interest and friendfhip, that nothing fhort of a miracle could difsolve, and by a treaty of offensive and defensive alliance, procure independence for, and a free trade to South America; and thus both countries together, might be enabled to give commercial laws to all Europe, " and confident against the world in arms." There is not an intelligent man in America, nor do I suppose in Britain, but knows this to be the interest of both nations; and nothing but inattention in the ministry of the latter power, and the blindnefs which the late succefs and independency of the former, keeps them from bringing it about.

Though several Members of the States, have large personal properties, in negroes, stock, and crops, few have any considerable independent fortunes, and few, very few indeed, if any, can boast of having a 1000l. sterling *per annum*, of landed property, payable in cafh. The rents are paid mostly in stock and produce; so that one and all of them must sell, truck, or barter, and become partly brokers or merchants. The laws of the country make it improbable that ever there fhould be men of considerable landed property among them, as the whole estate, both real and personal, of every individual, is at his death divided among the children, fhare and fhare alike: when thus parcelled out into small portions, none can be of great extent, excepting when a family are few in number, which rarely happens.

The virtues and enthusiasm they exhibited in acquiring their independence, have totally subsided, and given way to interest; perfonalities, and a taste for grandeur and fhow now prevail; and Esquire, and Honourable, have taken place of the humble citizen and virtuous farmer; so that they must have cash to support their dignities and new acquired honours in some shape or other.

If the British ministry had paid half the attention to this quarter of the world, and expended the one-third of what they have done in their mocked pretensions to maintain the balance of power, by supporting the Turks in Europe against Russia, they would in all probability have succeeded better, and the public would have been no losers by it; and if such a sum as 10,329l: 15s. Sterling, voted by Parliament for the purchase of merchandise to be given in presents to the inhabitants of Nootka Sound, were to be laid out, and continued annually for a few years, in cutting a canal in Upper Canada, to facilitate the navigation of that charming country, the public would soon by its commerce feel the good effects of it in a tenfold degree, compared to that for which the above sum was intended.

The forces in Canada are at present as follows, *viz.*

Six battalions of regulars.
Ten ditto, Canadian Militia.
Twelve ditto, British and American loyalists.
A Corps of Artillery.

Five hundred workmen and artificers, regularly officered, under military laws and regulations, to work at roads, bridges, &c. brought lately there by Colonel Simcoe, the Governor of the new province of Upper Canada; so that the two provinces will turn out above twenty thousand men in arms on short warning, and double that number in cases of emergency.

If any disturbances arose in the United States in which Britain should take a part, and that she would as liberally reward such as would join her, as she had done on the last occasion, thousands would flock to her standard who were against her before.

The British dominions in America exceed in extent, the fifteen United States collectively, and enjoy almost every climate, but that of the torrid zone.

The superior fisheries, furs, mast and spar trades of British America, if hands enough were in the country to make the proper use of them, might be put in balance with the rice, indigo, and every luxurious article of the States. They have wheat and grain of all kinds, staves, lumber, pot and pearl ashes, hemp, flax, maple sugar, and soap in common with the colonies. The great superiority the colonies have, and will to the end of time, is their temperate sea coast, and population, which the northern parts and frozen sea coast of the British States, though much more extensive, never can admit of. But strange as it may appear, yet true it is, that Nova Scotia and New Brunswick have built more square rigged vessels within these seven years, and have now nearly as many as all the United States together, and will soon be the carriers of all America, especially to Britain and the British West Indies, in the event that the old navigation act is continued in force. There is as much oak in Upper Canada, were there an easy communication by canals to convey it to sea, and as much black birch in Nova Scotia and New Brunswick, not inferior to the oak in quality, as would supply all the dock yards in Europe with ship timber, for 100 years, if not for ever.

There is just now finishing, within a few yards of where I write, a pine log canoe, three feet broad within the gunnel, and from twenty-six to twenty-seven feet long; and this log is by no means to be compared in bulk with those of solid oak trees I have seen in Canada. The gentleman that owns this canoe has another of about eighteen feet long, made out of the same tree; the former will carry at least a ton and an half weight, and the latter in proportion. The common ferry-boat from Point Levi to Quebec, is a log, which carries twenty people at once; I and my servant sat with ease side by side on the seat within her.

The bird's eye maple, the curled maple, and black clouded birch of New Brunswick, and black walnut of Upper Canada, will admit of as fine a polifh and glofs, and is equal for household finifhing and furniture, to any perhaps in the world; and were they generally known in Europe, there is little doubt of their soon becoming articles of commercial intercourse. In the Governor's house, the Chief Judge's house, in Colonel Allan's house, and other gentlemen's houses in New Brunswick, I have seen most beautiful specimens of each kind peculiar to that country. I have seen gun stocks in Upper Canada of the clouded maple, whose light and deep fhades were so variegated, as to exceed the roots of any heather I ever saw in Scotland; and yet so prevalent is custom, and the desire of emulation, the bane of all society, that many of the gentlemen here, who cannot well afford it, have mahogany furniture in abundance, and despise what can be got at their doors, and at no expence but the workmanfhip. The Chief Justice of New Brunswick is an exception to this, as I have not seen a bit of mahogany in his elegant and commodious new house; but he is a man of a very enlightened understanding and the best informed I met with in my travels in that country; and Mrs Ludlow, his lady, seems to be among the mildest and most amiable of her sex. The Chief Judge, an American bred and born, was high in the law department at New York, and a staunch friend to the Britiſh government, is now justly rewarded for his loyalty by his present office, worth 700l. Sterling *per annum*, besides a fine farm, to which he has considerably added by purchases; and though the farm is not above six years standing from the first trees being cut down on it, he can raise from seventy to eighty tons of hay annually, and live on it; and his present salary equal to as many half thousands in other parts of the world.

WITH Colonel Allan I went to see a fine island of 230 acres, which he rents from the Marichet Indians for 100 dollars *per annum*, on a lease of 999 years, on which he has carried on some improvements. On one plot of seventeen acres he had nine in rye, and eight in winter wheat, the rankest and finest crop I ever saw in any country I ever was in. The former was the seventh succeſsive crop, and the latter the third, without his ever laying on a single ſhovelful of manure; and yet the rye was at that time, 20th June, near six feet high, and the wheat above half that height. Captain Lee was along with us, and understands farming inferior to none I have met with in this province. He was partly bred in that line in England, and much so in America, before and after the late rebellion. He said he had not seen any thing like it, and does not doubt but it would return at the rate of thirty fold at least, in the event the wheat was to stand till ripe, but that it ran a great rifk of lodging from the weight of the crop. This island in the river St John's, is 100 miles from sea. We saw another plot, of about twelve acres, of spring wheat, on the main land, raised also without manure, which Captain Lee supposed would nearly equal that of the island. This may stagger the belief of farmers in Great Britain, but it is far from being very uncommon in this country. I was at a French farmer's house, in a settlement called *Madawafkas*, near 200 miles still higher up this river, who told me that he was convinced that he had then in his barn forty-five bufhels of wheat from one bufhel sown, but as it was not then threfhed out he would not say with certainty. These people never make use of any manure, not even to their gardens, though they produce cabbages, onions, beets, pompions, and quafhes, to great perfection; and yet I am convinced this settlement is two miles perpendicular above the level of the sea, as has been already observed on my going up that river the preceding year.

THE time being now drawing near, that the vefsel I meant to take my pafsage in for Scotland, was to sail from St Andrews, I prepared for returning to that place by the way of St John; and after bidding adieu, and thanking the engineer and family, whose house was my home while I resided in this part of the country, the Chief Judge and lady, Captain Lee, and his amiable family, Mefsrs M'Gibbon and Garden, on the river St John, Dr Drummond, Captains M'Lean, Lymon, and French, and Lieutenant Dugald Campbell on the river Nafhwack, all of whom have a claim to my respects, and best thanks for their hospitality, attention, and politenefs to myself, while I had the pleasure of being in their respective parts of the province.

From FREDERICK TOWN *to* ST JOHN *and the* KENNEBECKASIUS.

I SET out from Frederick Town on foot; and walking through Maugerville along the river side, I fell in with a gentleman travelling the same way. As we were conversing along, I heard a great noise in a house at some distance, on which I stopped to listen, and told the gentleman that there were some people fighting in that house; at which he smiled and answered, " That he knew the place well; that it was a house of worſhip, where a number of religious fanatics aſsembled at all hours of the night and day; that no body preached, every one prayed for himself, and the louder they roared, the more sincere and devout they were supposed to be; so that the one vied with the other who ſhould bawl out loudest." When we had come nearer, I was struck with amazement at the hideous noise they made, and which could be heard at a considerable distance; I aſked him if he supposed they would permit me to go in to see them; he said I might, provided I behaved properly, and did not laugh, or offer to ridicule them in any fhape; that they would not prevent me, or give me the least trouble; thus encouraged, I went in, and found they consisted of about three score persons, of both sexes, all on their knees, and in tears, every one praying for himself, as already said, and bawling out, O Lord! O Lord! which were the only exprefsions I understood of what they said. After standing for a few minutes in the house, my hair almost standing on end at the horror of the scene these miserable people exhibited, I returned, and just as I was pafsing the window of their apartment, some one called out, that the devil was among them; upon which they all gave a yell, louder and more horrible than any Indian war hoop I had ever heard; and if the devil himself was to fhow his physiognomy in all the frightful grimaces ascribed to him in the middle of them, every door bolted, so that none pofsibly could escape his clutches, their screaming could not have been louder or more horrible. I returned to the the road with deep imprefsions of the deplorable effects of fanaticism on the human mind, where it gets a hold, and found the gentleman there waiting for me, and proceeded on my journey, and arrived in a few days at the city St Johns.

It however revived in my mind a story I was told that happened in the Jersies, much about the time I was there, and seemed well authenticated, of a set of religious enthusiasts, who were in use of afsembling in a certain house of worſhip, in the neighbourhood of Elizabeth Town, and whose tenets run much on the notion of the devil being fond of money. This article in their creed was admited by all, as also that he made much more use of money to bribe Christians, than Indians, which was clear from the former being greater worſhippers of the Golden Calf, than the latter, wholly owing to his machinations. A wiser head than the rest suggested the idea of bribing the devil himself with money, to prevent his working on the pafsions of any of their sect. The scheme was highly applauded, and approved of as the best that could be devised, and the projector of it, himself, requested to set about collecting sums of money, adequate to the businefs, which he had the humanity to do without losing much time, lest the devil ſhould be at work on them in the interim; and to inforce his arguments, he told them, that each man's ſhare would be placed to his own account; and as they all knew the devil was not to be put off with a trifle, he hoped they would contribute accordingly.

CONTRIBUTIONS went on liberally, and no inconsiderable sum was collected, with which he went off, with the consent and approbation of all concerned, to bribe the devil, as already said; but whether he found him worse to please than he expected, and did not get his business effected, was not known when I was there, but so it was, that he had not returned, though he had then been two or three months away upon that business.

It was affirmed that some respectable people were concerned in this plan, though they are now ashamed to acknowledge it, and deny their having contributed any money towards it.

The diversity of principles, and religious opinions in this country, is great. But when they give no disturbance to the state, the legislature takes no notice of them; and in the course of time the most fantastical of them generally falls into disuse, and goes to pieces of itself.

Being informed by several respectable people in this place, who launched out in great encomiums on a tract of land called the *Kenebecasius*, that it was among the best parts in the province, and fittest for new settlers, the easiest land to clear, and for raising stock with least trouble, I thereupon

R R

resolved to go and see it, and accordingly set out, in company with a Mr Thomson, merchant here. The first sixteen miles of the way to the French village, is timbered with pine and spruce, the land uneven, knolly, barren, and interspersed with many small lakes, in which however are abundance of Trout; yet there are several new settlers stretched along the sides of the road, who have a year or two ago begun to clear this poor and forbidding soil, which had nothing to recommend it but its vicinity to the city of St John, and to a large meadow, consisting of some thousand acres, formerly overflowed by the sea, but now barricadoed out, the joint property of Mefsrs Heason, White, and Symons, who got grants of it before there were any thoughts of settling the country with loyalists. This immense tract of meadow produces such a quantity of hay, that the city and all the neighbourhood consume only a small portion of its produce, and it is sufficient to supply ten times the demand. The remainder of it is pastured, or the grafs allowed to decay upon the sward.

The French village is so called from some of that nation being settled there previous to the close of last war, and who removed from it to Madawaſkar, when a part of the diſbanded Britiſh army and of the American loyaliſts entered and took poſseſsion of this country. It is situated on the banks of the little river Hammond, a beautiful broad, ſhallow, and smooth stream, gliding through a narrow valley in the form of a glen, in which a good many Salmon are speared. The flats on each side of this river are but small, the hills well timbered with hard wood, mostly beech, birch, and maple. The soil thin, dry, and in many parts stony, and not so inviting for cultivation as many other parts of the country.

AFTER dining at this village we proceeded on for about eight miles further, to the house of one Thene, a Scotchman. From this place we croſsed a broad sound to the island of Darling, on which Mr Thomson has a good farm, and where he was then building a ſhip of between two and three hundred tons burden. Paſsing this sound I observed the water muddy, and intermixed with some uncommon substance, that floated along with it. I inquired the cause, and was told it was the spawn of fiſh, and that here a great deal of Herrings or Gasparoes, Baſs, Shed, and some Salmon, were annually caught in seines and trammels. This island, of six or seven miles long, abounds with timber for ſhip building, and as I am informed, could be bought, excepting this farm of Mr Thomson's, for 50l. The soil good, sharp, and fit for cultivation; the wood of the hard kind, thin, but strong and lofty, and from its vicinity to the city of St John, and the easy conveyance by water, could be transported thither, and sold to good advantage for fuel and ship timber. It is customary in this province, at least in such parts as I have seen of it, to permit a ship builder to enter the woods, cut down and carry off whatever parts suit him, on his paying the land owner at the rate of a shilling, or quarter dollar, *per* ton, and these lakes, and the different arms and creeks of this fine river, are quite adapted for navigation. Many ships and vessels are annually built on its borders, at the above rate for the timber. A Captain Smith of this town, lately launched a brig of 200 tons, the cabin of which is finished with black birch; equal to any mahogany in appearance: he has two ships on the stocks, one of which is of 400 tons burden, all built of black birch; indeed there is no other timber used in this province in shipping of any kind. The durability of this timber is such, that in clearing lands, logs have been found of it in the woods, over which trees of considerable size had grown, and though the outside was rotten, and crumbled away into dust at the first touch, yet in the heart it was found to be sound, and hard as ever, which leads some people to suppose, that its decay is almost proof against time itself. At the head of this lake, there are large intervals of land, and spacious meadows, that produce more natural grafs for hay than the inhabitants can make use of; but such as they do cut, and win in the season, they only carry off when frozen, and on the ice. In time of frefhets, it is flooded over, and appears as one large fheet of water; at this time, and in the fall of the year, large flocks of Wild Geese, Brants, and Ducks, resort to it, and afford to such as live in the neighbourhood, a great deal of sport. After Mr Thomson had settled his businefs with the fhip carpenters, and I had taken a cursory view of his farm, we returned with Mr Thene acrofs the lake, (at least a mile over,) in the same log canoe in which we had gone to his house, and we were treated with every attention and great hospitality.

NEXT day, Mr Thene was good enough to mount his Horse, (though very unwell at the time,) and go along with me until he delivered me over to another Scotchman, who lived about ten miles farther up the river Kenebecasius. Here I was treated with equal attention and hospitality, as in that which I had left. On our way to this gentleman's house, whose name is Guthrie, Mr Thene showed me some grist and saw mills of his, and a farm he had lately bought. That on which he lives, seems to be a very good and extensive one; it lies on the side of a hill, descending with an easy slope to the side of the lake. The situation, soil, meadows, fish, and fowls, hills, and dales, navigation, and timber for ship building, make the neighbourhood of this lake pretty eligible for a settlement, and there is little doubt in a few years but they will make out pretty well, and be in a flourishing way.

We crossed the river Kenebecasius in a canoe, swam our Horses, as the scow was out of order, and could not ferry them. Mr Guthrie brought me through his farm, of which I did not think much, being too dry, and partly on the side of a mountain of too steep an ascent, and rather over stony; but Mr Guthrie told me the stones were all on the surface, and that none were to be met with below it. He having a very mechanical turn, showed me a grist mill he mostly built with his own hands. He lived near twenty years in the West Indies, made money, retired here, married, and settled on this farm. After dinner, he was good enough to go along with me to the house of a Mr Symon Baxter, a few miles farther up the river, and preſsed me much to paſs a night with him on my return.

As the story of Mr Baxter is not very common, I cannot help being somewhat particular. He is a Yanky, bred and born in the heart of New England, and as he says himself, of Scotch extraction, his grandfather having emigrated from that country, after the rebellion in 1715, in which he had been engaged. It would seem attachment to the old sovereign, and loyal blood of the family, ran in the grandson's veins, and made him embark early in the late troubles on the king's side. He was taken in arms with Burgoyne's army, and permitted by a paſs of the Commiſſary of prisoners to go to see his family; he had not been two hours at home when his house was surrounded by several scores of the enemy, on which he immediately flew to arms, bolted his doors, and being strong in body and mind, enterprising and bold, dared any soul of them on their peril to set fire to the house, which they threatened, and would not surrender but on promise of good usage, and being delivered to those from whom he came; this being promised him, he gave himself up, but he no sooner was in their power, than some of them flew at him with drawn swords and bayonets, pricked him in the breast in several places, of which he still retains the scars, with threats to run him through the body, put a rope about his neck to hang him, and if any of them could be got to undertake the office of hangman, would be instantly tucked up, but as one of this stamp could not then be procured, he was carried along, and permitted to ride one of his own horses. He had gone but a fhort way when he was dismounted, and another put in his place, and the rope, which was still about his neck, tied to the Horse's tail, and in this way dragged along. From the Horse's tail he was fhifted and fastened to that of a cart, into which he was not allowed to enter. In this way he continued for three day's march, and when they came to the end of their journey, and that none could be got to hang him, they fell foul of him with sticks, clubs, and butt end of mufkets, until he was almost killed. He was then thrown into prison, where he was confined for eighteen months, and, when relieved, made off for this country, and the place he now lives in. His two eldest sons, who staid at home, and did not tread in the footsteps of the father, now enjoy his old property, and live comfortably on it in New England. Mr Baxter is the most succefsful farmer in raising stock and clearing land in this province; this I have heard from others, before ever I saw him. He told me that when he landed in St John he had but two dollars of cash in the world; got a large grant of land from government, on which he now sits in ease and affluence, has about 150 acres of cleared land, twenty milk Cows, with their followers, Oxen, Horses, breeding Mares, and a stock of 100 Sheep. In one clear field of interval, in the front of his house, he cuts about 100 tons of rank grafs, called here *Tymothy*, or *English hay*, at the rate of two tons *per* acre; he has 200 acres more of the same kind of interval, besides a deal of up-land that is not as yet cleared. Of his sheep he gave the following account; that in spring 1786, which is now six years ago, he bought four Ewes in Lamb, and states the produce as under, *viz.*

	Sheep.
Sold,	27
Killed,	72
Given to his daughter,	3
Killed by accident,	3
Remaining on the farm,	102
In all,	207

He says his Sheep have annually twins, and can rear them well; of this I had ocular demonstration, as I could hardly point out one Ewe in his flock that had not two good Lambs by her side; that such as he sold, his bargain was always twenty shillings for each Ewe, in the event she was to have two Lambs at once; but if only one, to give back five shillings of that price; but that he never yet was required to return any of it. After we had returned to the house from viewing his meadow grounds, and some improvements he was carrying on in his farm, he asked me if I would drink tea, and said that he was very fond of a kind of tea he found on his possession. He then brought a small basketful to show me, and Mrs Baxter being present, he added, that his wife could not drink of it because it was found at home; but if it had cost two dollars the pound, she would be very fond of it; that his reason for preferring it to any other, was her's for hating it. Though this was apparently in joke, it had in some measure some reality in it. I requested the home-got tea to be made for him and me, but she and her daughters drank souchong. Ladies here, as well as in other parts of the world, are taxed with being governed by a passion for trifles of this kind, more than by reason; and to be in the fashion, and supposed to be possessed of a good taste, is with them an object of the first magnitude, to which the good of their families, and all other considerations whatever, must give way. Unfortunate the man who is chained to a wife of this description, and bound to such thraldom, as to be obliged to put up with it; he may truly say with the poet:

"The world is a cheat, all things fhow it,
"I thought so once, but now I know it."

NEXT to Mr Baxter's is a Captain Smith, a sea-faring gentleman, on whose farm a very genteel new house was then finifhing. A few miles farther on than Captain Smith's, I entered on the burnt land, which extended as far as I could see on each side of the river. It would appear the wood in this part of the country had caught fire a few years ago, and burnt to the ground, as many of the burnt stumps are still standing, and logs, in a decayed state, lying on the ground; the young fhoots in some parts still thin, and so weak and slender that any ordinary workman could clear an acre of it in two days. The soil fharp, but thin and light, and I have no doubt productive enough. For the space of seven miles I could see no inhabitant. The cattle ranged at large through this young wood, in wild grafs, up to their horns, which would afford summer pasturage for many hundreds, free of all charges but the herding. Next to this uninhabited tract is Major Studholm's, who holds a large tract of land. I called at this gentleman's house, but he being unwell at the time, could not fhow me any thing but such as was about his house, which is situated on the side of a barren hill, with a large mill stream hard by it; he has, however, a deal of interval land on the banks of the river, which seems to be of middling good quality; his whole farm is of the burnt land, and easily cleared.

From Major Studholm's I proceeded to Pleasant Valley, up the same river, from thirty to forty miles up from the lake Kenebicasius. This valley justly deserves its name, and consists of 24,000 acres, surrounded by high hills, or rather low mountains, with two beautiful small streams, abounding with Trout and some Salmon, gliding through it, which meet at a point of land formed by the junction of these two small rivers at the west end of this spacious flat. Having a letter of introduction to Mr Lenard, who purchased a large tract of land in this valley, I directed my course towards his new and genteel house, and was received with much politeſs and hospitality.

Here I staid that night, went over a considerable part of his farm, which is situated on an interval point of land, where these two small rivers meet, and is navigable for flat bottomed boats to his door, excepting when the waters are very low in the heat of summer. In the front of the house is one clear field of sown graſs, consisting of about sixty acres, free of stumps, which most of the fields I have seen in this Pleasant Valley are. Mr Lenard told me that he had a natural meadow of wild hay of vast extent, about two miles, of which he permitted the neighbouring inhabitants to carry off as much as they pleased; that he had pasture enough in his woods for several hundred head of cattle, of which he made no use whatever; that he had 200 Sheep, twenty Milk Cows with their followers, some Mares, Oxen, and Horses, and that he thought these enough on one farm. This fine farm, and large stock of cattle, he would give on fhares to any good man that would take it. What is meant by a farm given out on fhares, which is customary all over America, is, The proprietor gives over a farm, stocked with all sorts of cattle, seed corn, and farming utensils, for a certain term of years agreed upon, generally three years; every thing given out in this way, is numbered and valued much in the form of stilbows in Scotland. At the end of the three years, or lease, of whatever endurance it may be, the tenant returns to the proprietor the same number and kinds of cattle, farming utensils, and quantum of sown land, with the buildings and fences in proper order. The produce of the farm, during that period, is equally divided between them; that is, the one half of the butter, cheese, wool, grain, poultry, Pigs, Sheep, Horses, and black cattle, belongs to the tenant, the other half to the proprietor, which is all he has in lieu of rent and interest of money; yet it generally turns out to good account to him. If the pasture is tolerably good, he gets at the rate of about forty pounds of butter, (sixteen ounces to the pound,) for each Cow, as his proportion, during the season, and one Lamb from every Sheep; the produce of the Sheep, grain, and small articles, are divided annually, and that of the breeding Cows and Mares once in the three years. They have many other ways of letting land here, but rarely for a money rent. Sometimes a proprietor has a farm with a little cabin, barn, and some small portion of cleared land on it, which he lets to a tenant for a term of years, on condition of his clearing and sowing two or three acres annually on it, and frequently gives a yoke of Oxen to enable him to carry on the work; this is continued from time to time, until the farm becomes large enough to be stocked with cattle, and given out on shares; but more frequently given over to one of his sons. If he has only daughters, the property is to be divided among them at his death, but never before it. There is no such thing as tocher, or any compensation whatever given with a wife here, during her father's lifetime, excepting in very rare instances. A good farmer makes up a farm for every son he has in this way, or by purchase, and often sees them all settled around him on their own properties in his lifetime. Children deem themselves bound to work to their fathers like indented servants, until they attain the age, the sons of twenty-one years, and the daughters eighteen, at which periods they are free, and may act for themselves. This practice prevails; but whether by law or custom, I know not.

As every farmer who emigrates to America goes there with a view of bettering his own condition, or that of his posterity, I would recommend to all such as have but small property, to engage in a farm on shares, before he undertakes to sit down and clear land of his own; he will thereby be furnished with as much clear land as will support his family, will become acquainted with the management of Oxen, handling the axe and implements of farming used in that country; and if he has industry, and tolerable management, he can raise stock enough from his proportion of the produce of the farm, to enable him to occupy lands of his own, on which he and his posterity may sit in ease and affluence to the end of time; and if he fixes in either New Brunswick or Upper Canada, he may depend on meeting with thousands who will be glad to employ him on these, or such like terms; but if he should prefer any part of the States' territories, which I am sorry to find many of my countrymen do for want of information, he will find the matter not so easy. The United States are so crowded with inhabitants for several hundred miles from the coast, that a great many of them emigrate to the British colonies, the same as those of Britain and Ireland do to theirs; so that a new comer may wander about a long time, and spend a great deal of money, before he gets a place to sit down on, without paying too dear for it; and his ignorance of their mode of working or farming, is such as will deter them from employing him; whereas it is quite the reverse in the two provinces already mentioned. Any person that asks for land, will be supplied *gratis* by government; and thousands, were they to arrive at once, might depend on finding employment in the manner above set forth, from the inhabitants, who are greatly at a loss for hands to work their farms and give near double wages to that which is given in the States. This is not all; by an act lately canvassed, and much contested in Congress, winter 1791--1792, regarding whether the whole militia of the United States should be made subject to military laws, and put under the immediate command of the **President**. It passed in the affirmative, 28 against 27, carried only by the casting vote of the **President** himself; so that he may order the whole or any part of them to any corner of the United States, on whatever service he pleases. Every new comer is immediately enrolled in the militia, and if called on service must turn out; the Committee will no doubt take care, that in the event there should be but a few wanted, that the lot shall fall on the strangers, rather than on any of their own connections; if he refuses, he is instantly laid up in prison, or tarred, feathered, and driven out of the country. A gentleman assured me, that he knew a man whose son was a militia man, called out last April, to go against the Indians, who offered 100l. and a good Horse to any one that would go in his place, yet could not get one, so disagreeable was that service to the people; if thus to them that are well acquainted with Indian wars and manners, it must be much more so to the natives of Britain and Ireland; and no less so to be compelled to turn out against their own countrymen, friends, and relations, which they will, in the event any dispute shall ever arise between the States, and the British subjects in America; and of the two, I should suppose any man of spirit, and not lost to all sense of honour, gratitude to the country that gave him birth, besides his finding it to his account to be the friend of his friend, rather than his enemy, would of course choose to be a British subject, where he will get lands for nothing, be among his countrymen, and run no risk of being ever molested by the Indians, tarred, or feathered.

The American land of Canaan, to which they emigrate in great numbers yearly from the coast, is supposed to be in the South Kentucky, in the middle provinces, the Genesee country, and in the north, the river St John in New Brunswick; and from all these, excepting Kentucky, which is at too great a distance, they fly to Upper Canada, which is now deemed the paradise of the new world. The soil is clay and loam intermixed, seemingly in equal proportions, and generally from ten to thirty feet deep. The way to observe this is by paying attention to the banks washed by the lakes and rivers, and to those of the creeks and brooks in the more remote and inland parts.

After all, though these be no doubt very great advantages, and what are not to be had in any other part of the world I ever heard of, yet the farmer who can live comfortably in his own country, and can rear his family as becomes his rank in life, would do wrong to leave it for any other country in the world. But such farmers as are so distreſsed by their landlords with over racked rents, and other oppreſsions, as likely to be brought to beggary and ruin, these, and these only, ought to try such justified experiments as may better their conditions.

Mr Lenard is an American loyalist, who had served last war in the Commiſsary Departmant, and is now well rewarded for his loyalty, by a yearly salary, besides his being paid, in common with other loyalists, for the loſs of his former property.

Mr Lenard told me of a curious mound of the plaister of Paris that was in the neighbourhood, and as I signified a great desire to see it, he was good enough to conduct me to a gentleman's house who lived near the place, whose son went along with me to ſhew it. This mound, which appeared to me very singular, is in several pyramidal or spiral forms of various dimensions, some high and some low, such indeed as excite curiosity, and almost defy conjecture; I ſhall however hazard one, that it was occasioned by a volcanic eruption, from a neighbouring bank, thrown up in small particles; little larger than the culm of pit coal, or the droſs of charcoal, and lighted close to the place from whence it came, among large trees, which had been afterwards burnt at the conflagration that happened to the other woods in that corner of the country, as large burnt logs and stumps are in great numbers to be seen rotting about it. In these pyramids are deep cavities or chasms, perpendicular from the top to the bottom, formed as if trees had been standing in the place when that eruption happened.

I am informed the plaister of Paris is to be found in several other places of this pleasant valley, and if ever any manure is to be used, which no doubt will through time, it must turn out to great account to the inhabitants for that purpose, exclusive of the use they make of it at present in finishing and whitening their dwelling houses; but as the Bay of Fundi abounds with the plaister of Paris, it can never become an article of commerce in this place, so remote from sea.

The Agricultural Society of Philadelphia, who have got several ship loads of the plaister of Paris from Nova Scotia, have published in their Transactions, that it is equal to that imported from France; and as this is of the same quality with that, it must be of the like utility to such as use it.

This pleasant valley has advantages not common to be met with in other places, from the salt springs, and the above mentioned plaister of Paris, which is deemed to be among the first stimulants to vegetation. It is a centrical situation between the city St John and the fine grazing country of Cumberland; yet the salt springs can be of little advantage, as, from St John, salt imported there from the West Indies can be bought at an easier rate than I suppose it can be made here; yet some of the inhabitants, I am told, when it happens to be scarce, boil a little for their own immediate use, rather than be at the trouble of going for it to St John: so that this appears to me to be as eligible a situation for a settlement as I have met with in this province, and perhaps as much so as any in North America.

In the counties of Cumberland, Northumberland, Westmoreland, Windsor, and Cornwallis, round the head of the Bay of Fundi, are large dairies, kept on the plan of those of the counties of the same names in Old England, from whence the inhabitants came at the close of the war before last. I have been told that several farmers there have three or four score of Milk Cows, and some many more, and sell annually as many firkins of butter.

The salt marshes, level as the sea, on which the cattle pasture, and which supply the hay for winter, are of considerable extent, in some parts two miles broad and thirty miles long. From these fine grazing counties, the towns of Halifax, Port Campbell or Rosway, Annapolis, Royal, and Digby, in Nova Scotia, and city St John, New Brunswick, are chiefly supplied with beef, butter, cheese, and pork, in great abundance, the former sometimes so low as three coppers a pound; and from thence cargoes are now sent to the Newfoundland Bank fisheries, at as easy a rate as it can be brought from the New England States, the cheapest and most plentiful in America. The up-lands from these spacious flats and salt marshes, are timbered with spruce and pine, and so poor, thin, and barren, as to produce very little grain. From the produce of their dairies alone, the inhabitants live in great affluence; but as I never was there I speak only from information: however, one thing I know is, that a friend of mine, merchant in St John, had been through these countries last summer, buying the above articles for the Newfoundland market, in preference to procuring them from Boston, or any part of the New England States; and as merchants rarely mifs to find out the cheapest and fittest commodities for the markets to which they are bound, is a proof of their being both plentiful and reasonable in that quarter.

AFTER satisfying myself with every thing worth seeing in this place, I took a stroll with this young gentleman through several fields, some of which had been succefsively cropped for six years, without any manure ever being used, and free of stumps, and level almost as a bowling green; the former is an advantage rarely to be met with in new lands, and the latter but on intervals. These plaguy stumps are a great nuisance, and occasion much inconveniency; and yet many good farmers told me they were more an eyesore than any thing else; but one thing I know, is that once they are rotten, and turned off the land, no part of the ground produces better crop than where they stood.

LARGE stumps of oak, pitch pine, hemlock, and black birch, will stand twenty years before they are quite rotten; whereas white pine, spruce, beech, white birch, poplar, and several other kinds, decay in from six to ten years; and young wood, such as is to be met with in this delightful valley, and over all the burnt land, may be turned out in a year, or in two or three at most, which is the cause of the fields being so clear of them. I returned to Mr Lenard's house, and dined in the usual genteel and hospitable stile of that amiable family.

After dinner, the conversation turned on sea-faring matters, which introduced the high compliment paid by Admiral Don Langara to the British nation, on his getting ready to leave Admiral Rodney's ship: it happened to be the duke of Clarance's duty, who was then on board as a midshipman, to get a boat and hands ready for his departure; when Prince William Henry came up, dressed in his midshipman's uniform, and told Don Langara that his boat was ready, he exclaimed, " No wonder Great Britain should have dominion of the sea, they deserve it, when so high a character would serve in so low a station." Mrs Lenard asked what station the prince was then in; I answered, in that which her two sons now were, which must have been very gratifying to any lady whatever, but to none more so than to an American loyalist.

Being now prepared to return to St John, and as I wished to go by a different route from that by which I had come, Mr Lenard directed me by a shorter road, lately lined out through the wilderness, unfrequented, and uninhabited but by one man, who lived about ten or twelve miles from hence, and the next settlement from that man's house, was above twenty miles farther on, and by the direction he gave me, I made no doubt of making it out, trusting at the same time a good deal to my pocket compass. I therefore mounted my little Horse, ascended the first mountain that bounds this pleasant valley, crossed it, descended to a solitary glen, that falls down on the opposite side, about five miles from that which I had left. The unfrequented path was difficult to make out, and so boggy that I had to alight and lead my Horse through. The place was truly romantic, and still as night, rarely the chirping of a bird to be heard, and finding myself in a very defenceless state, I began to be apprehensive lest some savage man or beast should find me in this forlorn situation, and take advantage of it; and wished I had brought my servant, gun, dog, or pistol along with me, which I left at St John. I now began to reflect how unguarded men in general are when no danger is in view, and how little they think of it until it is past recovery. I cut a stout stick with my knife, and being thus fortified, I proceeded on with great confidence. I walked the greatest part of the way up one hill and down another, and came through several of the most romantic glens I had ever seen. The evening was still and soft, and the Mosquetoes so troublesome, that I was under the necessity of holding a bush in my hand to beat them off from my own and Horse's eyes; yet these plaguy insects did not prevent me from admiring the scenes which were beautiful and delightful. From the summit of a mountain I could see a long way round. The fire had not consumed the wood on the top of the mountains, which now appeared like stately old planting, while that which was burnt in the valleys, was wholly a young growth, and had a pretty effect on the sight.

THE sun being now nearly set, and descending a mountain, I saw on the face of an opposite hill something like as if it had been inhabited; here the path became more difficult to make out than formerly, owing to very rank ferns and underwood, through which it led. It was with a good deal of difficulty I made out the place, and when I came up to it, I found only a small Cow and Hog pen, but no appearance of a house; from this I judged that it was the place I had been directed to, but that the man had left it and gone to some other place, I could not tell where. Here I hallowed out, but nobody answered; I proceeded, and had gone but a fhort way when I found the path divide; one led straight forward, while the other descended to a valley which I could see for about a mile below; this last happening to be the most frequented, I kept by it until I came to the links of a small stream that glided slowly through, and on the banks of which some natural hay had been cut and carried off to some other place. Here the path failed, and did not appear to go any farther; I therefore alighted, and left my Horse feeding along with a Mare and Foal I found there,—crofsed the river on logs, traversed the opposite side, found where some ground had been cleared, and a little buck wheat, Indian corn, and potatoes had been sown and planted; but no house or habitation was to be seen. Here I hallowed out again, but to as little purpose,—nobody answered. I returned acrofs the same logs,—got to my Horse,—mounted him, and meant to make the best way I could, while the least light remained, along the road I had lately struck off from. I now saw that I was to be out that night, and not a little dreaded being attacked by a Bear, Lucervi, or Carcaseu, in the event I was to fall asleep; and if the road I was to follow fhould fail, as that in which I now was did, that I would be obliged to leave my Horse in the woods, and make for the next inhabited place, by the help of my pocket compafs. While I was wholly occupied with these thoughts, I heard the jingling of a Cow bell, in a bufh hard by; I alighted, and went to see if any of them had the appearance of having milk; two of them had. I now judged that it was probable somebody would come to look for them, however late it might be. It was now turned dark; I went to the highest knoll in the neighbourhood, and hallowed out again as loud as I could, and, to my no lefs surprise than joy, I was answered by a human voice at some distance; we soon drew nigh each other, and when we met, I found that it was the landlord of the house I had been directed to coming to look after the Milk Cows, as I had conjectured. With him I staid that night, and was very civilly treated. His house was a miserable little hovel, covered with bark, and so low that I could not stand upright in it. I slept on the floor, and was much troubled with Mosquetoes. He told me he had come to live here at the desire of Mr Lenard, for the accommodation of any pafsenger that might be going that way; that he was promised a large tract of land, and expected 1000 acres; and though he had been there very little more than a year, he would not sell his land for lefs than fifty pounds; but in a little time afterwards he came down to 100 dollars, which is no more than twenty-five pounds Halifax currency; and though it was at a considerable distance from any other habitation at the time, it was a great bargain at that price, as it was well adapted by its situation for a considerable settlement. The land is good, lies well for cultivation, and is easily cleared. He said he could easily clear an acre of it in two days, and in some parts in one; the wood was very young, mostly of the burnt kind. I afked him about game; he said Bears were not troublesome; that the great game, such as Moose and Kerraboo Deer, had been totally banifhed; that he had fhot but one of the former all last winter, but that he might kill in the fall of the year as many Pheasants and Hares in snow as he chose.

THE number and diversity of objects which presented themselves to the eye in the preceding day's excursion, as well as in many others, must have naturally created a very rapid succefsion of ideas, more indeed than my memory can retain or pen describe; I fhall therefore only say on the whole, that notwithstanding the trouble, rifk, and charges, unavoidably attendant on such a ramble as mine, through rapid streams, lakes, and wildernefses, the pleasure of having seen them, and so much of nature in its rude state, repays them all. A certain portion of hardfhips and difficulties are necefsary for giving zest to enjoyments. Without them life is apt to become insipid; and we see those, who, independent of any effort of their own, have every enjoyment at their command, are perhaps of all mankind those who have the least. The Indian prayer often recurred to my mind in these excursions, *i. e.* To pray to the Great Spirit to protect me in my travels,--to give me a bright sun, a blue sky, clear untroubled waters, lakes, and rivers; and I doubt not it was as well heard from the deepest recesses of the wilderness here, as if I was kneeling before the altar in St Peter's church in Rome, or that of our Lady at Loretto.

I set out from this man's house, whose name was Smith, early after breakfast, that I might have plenty of day before me to make out the next settlement, which I suppose was at least twenty miles off; and took his directions for finding the road. The path was much better and more easily made out than the preceding day. I crossed several high mountains and deep valleys, some of which were so remarkably gloomy and solitary, that I again became apprehensive I should be attacked by some wild creature; I alighted and cut a stout stick, with which I thought myself so secure, that I went on chearfully, without the least concern, and towards evening came down on the banks of the beautiful small river that runs through the French village. Here I dined and fed my little Horse, who was a good deal fatigued with the up and down hills, and the badnefs of the road; I set out from this place, and arrived at the city St John about nightfall. Here I staid for about three weeks, in the coffee house kept by one Charles Macpherson, originally from Athol, in the fhire of Perth, in Scotland, where I was very well used, and had an opportunity of conversing and afsociating with the strangers and gentlemen that frequented it every night.

BEFORE I leave St John I must acknowledge my very particular obligations to Mefsrs Alderman, Campbell, and Stewart, merchants, from whom I had the highest marks of friendfhip and hospitality, Mr William Pagan, also merchant, and Captʼn Charles M'Lean, mariner. These gentlemen are of the first character and respectability in the place.

IN this province and wintry cold climate, but fertile soil of New Brunswick, I found the country flourifh, and the inhabitants do very well, excepting the Britifh half pay officers; who, it would seem, had neither foresight, industry, nor prudence. The first object of their care when they entered on the lands granted them by government, was to build a genteel house, in which they could entertain their friends in a becoming stile; before that conveniency was finifhed, and a small garden cleared, their money was expended, and now, as the only expedient, recourse must be had to the merchant for credit, to whose fhop they then became thralled, until the next term's half pay fell due. The debt always increasing, and no pofsibility of paying it, a moon-light flitting is thought of, put in execution, and away they set to Great Britain or Ireland, damning the country, and in vindication of themselves, giving out that the devil could not live in it. Others of them judged the best thing they could do, was to take to themselves a wife; never considering how they and their children were to be maintained; therefore the most delicate American ladies were singled out as the only mates, and fit companions for their beds, to pafs the long winter nights with. For that purpose, a gentleman drefsed himself out in his regimentals, powdered from the eyes to the rump. With such a figure, genteel addrefs, and profefsions of eternal love, no lady of the least tender feelings could withstand his solicitations, or refuse his hand; a cottage with such a *dear creature* was preferable to a palace with one not pofsefsed of such accomplifhments. A match was thus made up; the lady brought home, did the honours of the table with a becoming grace, and fhowed away while the credit lasted; when that failed, the miserable property, or rather wilderness, as there was nothing done on it of value, but a house built, is mortgaged to the merchant: Away they set to the States, saying, like those single men who went for Britain or Ireland, that the devil could not live in it. It is said if you take a wife from hell, she will bring you back if she can; the case is here in point with the ladies in question, as it must be a hell on earth to any man of spirit to hear his party, and the side he espoused, king and country, almost daily abused; and there is little doubt if there were any disturbances to arise between Great Britain and the States, but she would prevail on him to engage in the service of *her* country, in preference of *his own*. This had been too much the case last war, and may be so again.

SOME of the gentlemen of the last description, who still continue on their farms, and have had industry enough to make out two or three Milk Cows, have now to milk them with their own hands, lay by the milk, make the churn, muck the byre, sweep the kitchen, and do every menial but requisite office that the family require. My lady was not brought up to such drudgery, and her nerves are too weak to milk the two or three Cows, which ever of them it may happen to be, but rarely more; it is enough for her to take up cream for the tea, rock the cradle, and look after the children; and as he cannot get himself out of debt, so as to afford to keep a single servant, male or female, old or young, he must do all the drudgery himself, or let it alone. To this humiliating state, these dear creatures have brought themselves; whereas the poor soldiers, that had not a shilling in the world when they entered on their lands, have now in general from four to eight Milk Cows, with their followers, and supply the markets with the produce of their farms, live more comfortably than their officers, and as happy as they can wish.

THE *gentlemen* of the American loyalists are of a very different description. They are all men brought up either to the law, or to some mercantile or mechanic business, or farming, to which they severally applied on their entering into this country, and make out in general very well; yet there are even some exceptions among them; some of them made money, cleared a deal of land, sold it after being pretty well improved, went off for the States, and spent their all there; a few have returned back again, and declare this to be the most productive soil, and best place for a settlement they have seen in America. It is clear to myself from what I have seen of it, that it is not owing to the land, soil, or climate, that any resident in it does not do well, but totally to their own mismanagement.

From ST JOHN *to* ST ANDREWS.

BEING desirous of seeing St Andrews, Pasmaquady, and Charlotte County on the west borders of this province, which bounds it and the New England States, I set out in the packet sloop, Captain Magiston; and though the distance from thence to St Andrews be but seventy miles, the calms were so frequent, and the little wind there was so much a-head, that we were four nights on the way. This coast is intersected with deep and small bays, and excellent harbours. In the Bay of Pasmaquady and offing, are said to be as many islands as there are days in the year; Grand Monnan is from eight to ten miles long, and from two to three miles broad; Deer Island about four miles every way; and others of every degree and proportion lefs. On the Deer Island 500 Deer had been killed in one winter, but now there are none. Moose Island, which is also pretty large, and supposed to be within the British lines, has been taken pofsefsion of by the Americans. Though this has been represented to the British ministry they deem it as nothing,* and

* But if this had been done by the French to the Dutch, our ministry would have roused heaven and earth with their

will give themselves no trouble about it. It is inhabited by a band of Yanky smugglers, that carry on a contraband traffic with the colonies on each side.

The Bay of Pasmaquady, betwixt these islands and St Andrews, is from seven to eight miles one way, and from ten to twelve the other. In the islands are many inhabitants, that live mostly on fishing; they bait their hooks with small Herrings, and their method of catching them is somewhat curious; the darkest nights are best for their purpose: The fishers place a torch of lighted birch bark, fixed in a cloven stick, in the bow of the canoe or small boat, and row backwards and forwards through wherever they suppose the fish to be, who, upon seeing the light, spring up to the surface, break and play about the light; a man is then ready with a bag or scoop net, and scoops them up until he fills his canoe, or has as many to bait his hooks as he chooses.

I once asked a parcel of these islanders that came into St Andrews to sell fish, if they were then getting any: they said not; that the moon was so bright they could get no bait, so that they are only got in dark nights, as already said.

From St Andrews I went in a boat with some ladies and gentlemen of that town, to complaints, and would go to war directly to revenge such an insult to our allies;

an Indian sacrament held within the New England States; the service was given out by a French priest, lately arrived in Boston from South America, where he officiated among the natives of that part of this great continent, which it was supposed qualified him for the office he now undertook. He was a decent looking middle aged man, and spoke Englifh pretty well, but not the Indian tongue of this part of the continent. The Indians built a large hall for the occasion, from fifty to sixty feet long, neatly enough made up and covered with bark. In one end of it he had an altar and an Host, and used an uncommon deal of forms and ceremonies, no doubt intended to strike these savages with the more awe in the exhibition of the scene. The Indians were bred by the French in the faith of the church of Rome, when they were in pofsefsion of the greatest part of Nova Scotia, and still continue in the exercise of that religion, and much attached to that nation. To this place the Marafhet Indians of the river St John, and those that inhabit the northern and back parts of the New England States resorted, drefsed in their most fhowy apparel, but made a miserable appearance in comparison to the warlike tribes in Upper Canada. The hoods and caps of the squaws were however among the finest I have seen, made much in the form of a grenadier's cap, ornamented with silver, and beads of various colours. The priest himself had on the most fhowy garment I ever saw, embroidered and inwrought with gold and silver, from the crown of the head to his heels, in a vast variety of forms and figures; but whether he is a man whose propensity for travelling and for seeing the world had made his profefsion the instrument of indulging it, or whether he was one who had committed some crime in his own country, which banifhed or made him forsake it, is not known here; but so it is, that the French Consul at Boston would not see him, probably on account of his not being satisfied in these points.

THIS priest and Indians put me in mind of a story I have been told which seemed to be well authenticated of the Micmac Indians, who inhabit the Bay of Chaleur, and the river Merimafhee in the Gulf of St Laurence.

THESE Indians were, like their neighbours the Marafhets, instructed by the French in the Romifh religion, and much attached to that nation. On hearing that the French had taken part with the Americans in the late war against the Englifh, and judging thereby that they would invade and endeavour to recover their lost pofsefsion in Canada, and this part of the country, they formed a plan of surprising and killing all the English subjects in these parts, to facilitate the conquest of the French; this having come to the ears of their priest, who was an Irishman, he convened many of them, and exclaimed against such a horrible attempt; and told them in plain terms, that he would send every man of them to hell who should be guilty of murder, or embrue his hands in Christian blood, that when they would be roasting in the incessant fires of hell they would feel the just reward of their atrocity, deceit, and murder. These threats of their priest frightened them a good deal, and deterred them for a time; but as they were still sanguine for the plot, the expedient they now fell upon to counteract his threats, was first to kill himself, and thereby put it out of his power to send them to hell, that they might then with impunity go on with the intended massacre. This being resolved upon, and every thing ready to put it in execution, a squaw had compassion on the poor priest, and informed him of it just time enough to betake himself to a boat and set off for Halifax; had he gone by land they would have soon overtaken him, and done his business in the woods; but his going by sea put him out of their reach. On his arrival at Halifax he told what the Indians were about. The country was alarmed and precautions taken to prevent it. The priest was handsomely rewarded with a salary of two or three hundred pounds a-year, and enjoys his former office among the same Indians.

HAVING heard many contradictory and various accounts of the boundary line between the British Colonies and American States, as settled by the treaty of peace, some informed it ran due east, some due north, some due west, and others again said it ran in all the intermediate points of the compass, so that not the least reliance could be made from hearsay of what course it took from the sea, I was therefore resolved to satisfy myself in that particular, and set out in a boat up the Scudiac river, which is that which divides them. This river is in many parts a mile broad, and navigable fifteen miles for vessels of considerable burden. The land on each side is like that on all the other parts of the American coast, poor, thin, barren, and unproductive, timbered mostly with spruce and small pine; but, like that also, the farther you go back in the country, the better and deeper the soil, always covered with hard and lofty wood. I put up at the house of the Reverend Mr Dun M'Coll, a Methodist preacher, a very pious and good man, which I made my head quarters while I staid in this part of the country, and received much attention and hospitality from my countryman and his wife.

Next day after my arrival, I went to see what is called the Falls of the Scudiac, but they are no more than rapids, the water being hemmed in between rocks into a narrow space, which turns it into froth. In these whirlpools a considerable deal of Salmon, Herring, or Gasparoes, are caught in the season with scoop nets, which the fisher dips into the body of the eddies and caves of the rocks, where the water is in such a froth as to prevent the fish from seeing it; here he ranges it about until he feels a fish touch either the hoop, bag, or pole, and scoops it up. I saw one Salmon caught in this way; the water was too low for the fish to get up to the place fittest for the purpose. I returned to Mr M'Coll's that night, and next morning engaged an Indian with a birch canoe to proceed along with me up the river through the wilderness. There are no settlers above the Falls on the New England side, but two families, and these are twelve or fifteen miles up; nor on the British side, but four or five, and these near at hand. We had gone but a short way past the British settlements, when paddling up by the side of long reeds and bushes, I heard an Indian hoop some space a-head of us. I answered, by making a like hoop, which is customary when one party hears another, or wishes to be heard in the wilderness; that instant some wild animal made a plunge in the water among the reeds quite close to us; the Indian immediately stopped, and made a sign for my gun, which I had in my hand; and though I wished to have taken a shot myself, the canoe was so small, and my back being towards the place the animal was in, I could not turn about on my breech or knees, without endangering our oversetting, so that I handed my gun behind me to him: he no sooner got it than he made the *Otter Call*, and had not repeated it but two or three times when an Otter answered by a like call. In this way they continued for a few minutes, calling and answering, but the Otter found out his companion, and had the precaution not to come out from among the reeds; while the Indian stood ready with the gun cocked to his eye, and though he never had a double barrelled gun in his hand before, he understood at first sight how to handle it. The Indian was so attentive that they could not stir a reed which he would not observe. At length he got sight of one of them, and fired, but the powder having got damp it hung fire;

he however hit the Otter, but after searching for it a long time with my Dog among the bushes, we could not find it. I asked him whether it was an Otter or Beaver; he said there were two of them, an Otter and his squaw.

We proceeded up the river, and came to a small lake. After pasing this lake, the river became shoal, full of large stones and rocks. The Indian was obliged to pole up by the sides, and the current was so rapid that the water sometimes came in over the bow and gunwel of the canoe. We pased an Indian encampment, and several islands, two or three of which seemed to be pretty good land and fit for cultivation. The water now became so shoal and rapid that in several places we were obliged to land, and carry the canoe over rocks. Having proceeded in this way, for I suppose fifteen miles, through ugly streams and gloomy wildernesses, and rain having come on, I got myself wet; and sitting in a small canoe, in which I could not stir, or even look about me without the risk of oversetting, I turned tired; and finding by my compass that the course I steered was *westward*, and having thus attained the principal object of my voyage, I resolved to go no farther than the first Falls, which were but a few miles a-head. We came to a landing place where there was a birch canoe and some lumber on the river side; here I landed, got under a large tree to fhun a fhower of rain, and having found a path, and been told by the Indian that there was a house in the wood a fhort way above, I followed the path, and about a mile farther on I came up to a house, around which there was a considerable quantity of new cleared ground. On my entering this house, I found it inhabited by one Baillie and his family, a man of great activity and industry. After partaking of this man's dinner, which was a small piece of pork, and a large parcel of kidney beans, of which I eat pretty heartily, and going through his extensive farm, I returned to our canoe, and continued our course back again. Baillie told me that a surveyor, by order of Congrefs, had been lately there, exploring and ascertaining the course of that river, which they deemed to be the boundary line; that a few miles above his house the river divides into two branches, the one comes from the north west, and the other from the south west; that the former is the largest stream, but that as far as I went, he gave the same account of its course as I did; that is, that it comes in general from the southward of west; so that by this surveyor's report, and by my own observation, I find the account I in general had in St John, totally erroneous, as well as a map I have of the United States, lately publifhed in Boston; and though this map is deemed the best made out of the States' territories, nothing can be more false than its representation of the Britifh lines. If the south west branch of the Scudiac is to be the boundary, the Britifh lines run far down on the back of the northern parts of the New England States, towards the head of the Penobscote river. But it appears to me to be no object to either Britain or America, which of Scudiac branches are to be held as the boundary line, the intermediate space, and the neighbourhood of that river, being so barren that no use will be made of it, at least for some centuries to come, if ever.

BEING not prepared to stay out a night in the woods, and now so late as to have scarcely time to be back with day-light, I returned through the islands, in some places by a different channel from that in which I went up. Proceeding along, the Indian observed a Mufk Rat fifhing among some reeds, which he pointed out to me, and desired I fhould be ready to fire at him, but the Mufk Rat having seen us, dived and disappeared; and notwithstanding the Indian having often repeated his call, we never saw him more.

Having now come to the place from whence we set out, and paid a dollar to the Indian for his trouble, agreeably to promise, I travelled for two miles farther on, on foot, to Mr M'Coll's house.

In this neighbourhood I found a great many settlers, who had sold their lands in the United States and come here to live, where they were in a very thriving condition.

Next morning I set off, and arrived in the evening at St Andrews, where I stopped but a few days, when I set out with Lieutenants M'Dougall and M'Kay, to see their settlements on the Macadevi river, from thence to Captain James Campbell, at Harbour le Tongue. With these gentlemen I paſsed eight days, principally with Lieutenant M'Dougall, who was so obliging as to go from thence along with me to see the settlements on the Digidequaſh river, where we resided some days with Captain James M'Donald, originally from Uist, but now an American loyalist. Here, as well as in every place we had been in, we were treated with marked attention and hospitality.

The plantations on this creek are the neatest I have seen in this country; the inhabitants, mostly diſbanded soldiers from Highland regiments, have cleared a good deal of land, and have stock and crops in proportion, and in a fair way of being in flourishing circumstances. In this place, as well as in every other part of America I have either seen or heard of, every year old Quey takes the Bull, and brings forth young when two years old; so that their stock increases with a rapidity unknown in many other parts of the world, particularly in that corner I had come from.

AFTER bidding adieu to our kind host and respectable family, my good friend Lieutenant M'Dougall, to whose civility and friendship I was much indebted, parted from me, went home, and I proceeded to the house of a Captain Alexander M'Crae, who resides about a mile from St Andrews. Captain M'Crae was originally from Kintail in Rossshire, but now, like Captain M'Donald, an American loyalist. They both emigrated with their families from Scotland some years prior to the breaking out of the late American war in North Carolina, but at the commencement of the war they both embarked in it, and raised each a company of their namesakes and followers for the British government. Captain M'Crae was so active in procuring men, and useful in other lines, that he was offered a Majority all at once; but as he was totally unacquainted with military matters, and supposed the duty of a Major to be so intricate that none but such as were bred early and long in the army were fit to discharge, he for the present declined it, and said he would in the mean time be contented with a Captain's commifsion, and when his services merited promotion, he made no doubt of obtaining it; the company was instantly given him, but in respect to promotion he was mistaken, and without regard to merit or sufferings, people of superior interest were on all occasions preferred to him.

Captain M'Crae now entered on his new profefsion in the Light Horse, and was engaged in all the broils, succefses, and disasters, that happened during the war in the southern provinces; and he being a bold, daring, intrepid man, at the head of a small band of chosen friends and faithful followers, rufhed into the heat of every action or fkirmifh; but had the misfortune of never escaping out of any one of them unhurt, and now bears the marks of sabres, swords, balls, and bayonets. His left arm having been broken in two or three places, he has totally lost the use of it, and it now hangs powerlefs by his side. He told me that once he was taken prisoner in Georgia, and his life despaired of through the severity of his wounds; that Sir Archibald Campbell, then commanding the King's forces in that province, wrote such strong letters in his favour to the commanding officer of the American army in that quarter, that they supposed him to be a man of higher rank and consequence than he ever was; and Sir Archibald requested he might be supplied with all the money he fhould call for, and obtain every chirurgical afsistance that could be given, until he fhould have an opportunity of sending money, and his own surgeon to attend him: that in consequence of that letter, every attention that could be wifhed was given him: that the first people in the place often waited upon him, offered him money, and every service in their power: that they spoke of Sir Archibald with such applause and admiration, that they were on the eve, and publicly spoke of giving up the province, and joining the Britifh cause. When the news came of his being superseded in the command by General Provost, they said that Provost was an old wife, with whom they would have nothing to do.

CAPTAIN M'CRAE is confident from his knowledge of the people, and what he heard them declare, that had Colonel Campbell continued in the command, that province would not have held out ten days longer, and that North and South Carolina would soon have followed. The infatuation that attended the Britiſh cause, on that and many other occasions, cannot well be accounted for but by a planetary influence, that brought disgrace upon every one in high command that was engaged in the war, excepting Sir Archibald Campbell, General John Campbell in Pensicola in the South, and General M'Lean in the North. Is it not a little singular that these three were from the poorest and most remote corner of the Britiſh empire? and does it not verify what the great Lord Chatham said, " That he sought for merit every " where, and found it in the heathy moun- " tains of the North?" to which might be applied, what Ulyſses said of Ithaca, " 'Tis a " barren clime, but breeds a generous race."

The coast from the foot of the river St John to the river Scudiac, is so full of inlets, creeks, bays, and harbours, of various forms and dimensions, that I suppose, if a line was drawn along the water's edge, it would be found to consist of a stretch of several hundred miles in length. The whole of this extensive ſhore is covered with kelp ware, and yet never an ounce of kelp was made here, or in any part of this country.

It often occurred in going along these bays, that it would be a good speculation to bring a parcel of kelp-makers from Scotland to this country. The undertaker would require to indent every one of them for six months at least; otherwise they would all forsake him on coming to this country. He might cut the sea ware wherever he pleased; no one would challenge him. The perpetual sun would make his labour so productive, that he could afford to pay the pafsage of his men, and at the same time allow them higher wages than they get in their own country; as here they could work six months in the year, without being stopped in all that time, ten days by bad weather; whereas in the Hebrides, and west coasts of Scotland, where most kelp is made, it is rare to see six days work go on without being interrupted with rain.

It frequently happens that servants are not to be had here for love or money; and when any happen to be got, they rarely engage but from month to month. The extravagance of their board and wages is such, as to equal, if not exceed, all the benefit that can accrue from their labour; which deters most people from carrying on works that would otherwise be found very advantageous. Every day-labourer must have beef, or what he likes better, pork, twice a-day, tea or chocolate, half a mutchkin of rum for grog, and half a dollar of money *per* day. The undertaker would run no rifk of being troubled with solicitations from his people for returning to their own country, as they could fhift for themselves; his only difficulty would be to keep them from running away, and engaging with others before their time fhould have expired. Ships he could have at St John to carry his kelp to Britain, at 2l. sterling *per* ton; and if kelp were to sell any thing near to what we have seen it in Britain, I am perfectly satisfied that whoever fhould try this experiment would find it answer probably beyond his expectations. I suggested this plan to a Scotch gentleman in St Andrews, who seemed clearly to see the utility of it, and told me some time thereafter that he was determined to try it; but since I returned to Britain, I find kelp has fallen so low in price that it will not answer; but whenever it rises to its former standard, it surely may.

This new town of St Andrews is prettily situated, on a spacious point of land, with an easy slope towards the water, and environed on three sides by the river Scudiac and the Bay of Pasmaquady. It has a good anchorage and bar harbour, with two outlets, the one to the north west, and the other to the south or south east with a low woody island in front, of about a mile long, which makes it very safe mooring. This small town is in its infancy; yet has a smart trade in fhip building, lumber, and fifh, of which Mr Robert Pagan, a Scotchman, is the life and soul. To his activity and enterprising spirit his country is indebted for this colony. He built this year, besides other vefsels, one of four hundred tons, copper bottomed, that has ten state rooms, intended for the West India trade to London. This fhip, as well as all others built here, is of black birch. This settlement is at present in a prosperous state; but it is feared it will not continue long so, on account of the American States being at liberty to export their lumber to Britain on as low a duty as those of our own Colonies; and as their country is full of people, and labour cheap, they can undersell us in our own markets. Of this the merchants of New Brunswick, Nova Scotia, and those of Greenock, that trade in these articles in that country, complain much; and speak of addrefsing the Britifh government on the subject. Unlefs their grievances are redrefsed, it is probable the people will leave this country, which, as formerly, will become a desert, and settle somewhere else; as without a trade in lumber, this town or county cannot subsist. If the Britifh ministry were to pay due attention to the prosperity of our own Colonies, they would prohibit any lumber from the States to enter their ports, until such time as the Colonies were well peopled, and the trade established on a stable footing; whenever that happened, their ports might then be opened to the Americans, as well as to our own people, which would create emulation and a rivalship between them. Temporary inconveniencies ought to be put up with for the sake of future and permanent advantages.

From St Andrews to Greenock in Scotland.

Every thing being now ready for our departure for Scotland, and after bidding adieu, and thanking my worthy friend Captain M'Crae, and his kind family, with whom I lived most of the time I had been in this corner of the country, Messrs Robert Pagan, John M'Kenzie, and Daniel M'Master, merchants, and several other gentlemen in the place, on the 4th of November 1792 I stepped on board the Friendship brig, of St Andrews, of 230 tons burden, loaded with lumber; a new vessel, built by Mr Colin Campbell of this place, for the use of, and by desire of his creditors.

In passing through the islands, in the mouth of the Bay of Pasmaquady, we saw vast flocks of Sea Gulls and Marrats, which indicated the great quantities of fish with which these sounds abound. Cod were so abundant here last summer, that it was said Newfoundland Banks could not exceed it for fishing. We passed Grand Mannan at night, and found ourselves next morning near the entry of the Bay of Fundi; but had we met with contrary winds that detained us for some days beating about. After we had been a little way out from the Bay in a thick fog, we saw a Humming Bird which kept flying about the ſhip for some time, also some land Hawks, one of which followed us for several days, and perched on the mast, yards, and ſhrouds, when tired to rest itself. It once caught a Mother Carries Chicken nearly as big as itself, and brought it on board, and rather than part with it, allowed itself to be taken alive. We kept it for about a week, when it was killed by some accident. Nothing particular happened until we came to the Newfoundland Banks, when the equinoxial gale overtook us, and blew a violent storm; such indeed as none on board had ever experienced the like, excepting one sailor who had been on board the fleet that accompanied the Ville de Paris when ſhe was lost; and as we had been in the very place on the same days of the year that disaster happened, we dreaded not a little to meet with the like fate. The ſhip was put in the best trim poſsible; top gallant masts, and all the yards were struck, to enable us to weather this storm, which continued with very little intermiſsion for about a week: great part of the time we could put up no fire or cook any victuals. Our situation was very disagreeable, scudding before the wind with bare poles. For two weeks after we had rode out the storm we could not say where we were, and kept a sharp look out in hopes of falling in with some homeward bound West India man, who could tell us something about it; but we saw no vessel until we came within two days sail of the south west end of Ireland, when we fell in with an American ship three days out from Liverpool, on her way home to New England. It being then fair weather we immediately launched out a boat, sent her a-board the ship to learn from her where we were. Two days thereafter we fell in with an Irish smuggler hovering on the coast, waiting for night and a fair wind to land and discharge her cargo; we spoke her, when she told us that from the mast head we could see land, which was very pleasant tidings to us. Nothing particular happened farther for four days, when we landed safe in Greenock, after a tedious passage of forty-one days.

During the tiresome days I spent at sea on my passage home, I had time to examine the jottings and memorandums I had picked up in my travels, containing anecdotes of singular persons, which I wrote upon separate pieces of paper, and did not insert them in my journal. Among these the following, selected from a great number, appeared to me so interesting or entertaining, that I thought them not undeserving a place here; especially as they tend to illustrate the manners of the people, and the circumstances of the country which is the subject of these memoirs.

The manner in which the famous Indian chief Pontinac took the Fort of Detroit, is as follows. He being a great adherent to the French interest for a long time after the British had wrested Canada from the crown of France, had formed a plan to retake Detroit: to effect this purpose, he, with his whole nation came, under pretence of hunting in that neighbourhood, and encamped near the fort, and continued there for a considerable time. It was at length agreed among his tribe to have a shinty match in a plain near the fort; of this he sent notice to the governor, and said that a large bet was depending. On the day appointed the whole Indians came, divided themselves into two parties, and began a furious contest. The garrison were at first on their guard; but seeing the game continued for a long time, made them suppose there was no ill intended, and the officers came out to see the sport. One of the Indians struck the ball over the rampart into the fort, and another of them was permitted to go in for it and take it out, and to continue the deception this was done three or four times, till the people were quite off their guard. When the Indians discovered this, the ball was struck in again, on which the whole rufhed in, in a body so thick that it was impofsible to fhut the gates, and made all within prisoners.

AFTER keeping pofsefsion for some considerble time, the troops were ransomed, and a handsome gratification given Pontinac for giving up the fort.

HERE now again the Britifh were in pofsefsion of Fort Detroit, but still Pontinac was difsatisfied, and being yearly in expectation of an army from France to retake Canada, he formed another plan to take the fort. For this purpose he came again with his whole tribe and encamped in the vicinity. Sent notice to the Governor, that as the French had been amusing them yearly with promises of befriending them and retaking Canada, all of which they failed in, and gave him every reason never to believe them more; he therefore wifhed of all things in the world to be in friendfhip and alliance with their great father the king of England, for whom he had the highest respect and veneration, and requested that the Governor would be good enough to draw up a treaty of amity and friendfhip, and even of offensive and defensive alliance if he chose it, most to his own liking, on any terms he thought proper, and that he and all his chiefs would confirm it, and come into the fort on any day he would appoint, to sign and sanction such a treaty. He told his story so speciously that the Governor had not the least doubt of its sincerity, drew up a treaty, and appointed a day for him and his chiefs to come into the fort to sign it. Some days previous to this meeting the Governor gave a Deer ſkin to a squaw to make him a pair of mogazines; when ſhe returned with them he was so well pleased with their make, that he handsomely rewarded her, and desired her to make another pair in the same way. She answered that one pair was enough. This surprised the Governor a good deal, who aſked her reason for saying so; ſhe refused to give any but that ſhe supposed one was enough, carried away the ſkin, and went off with a downcast look, seemingly in a thoughtful musing manner. The Governor upon ruminating on what the squaw had said, and as these people rarely waste words uselefsly or say more than enough, thought ſhe must have had some reason for it, he therefore ſent for her to come and speak to him. When ſhe came he recalled to her memory what ſhe had formerly exprefsed, and begged to know her reason for having done it. She refused to give any for a considerable time, but that ſhe thought so. At last he prevailed by fair-words, promises, and bribes; she told him that if she was to discover it she would be burnt, but that her gratitude for his kindness was such that she could not be easy and see him sacrificed, and that he and all his people were to be killed on the day appointed for their meeting; that for this purpose all the chiefs had cut their guns short, so that they could be hid under their blankets, and were to have them charged and primed, their knives on, and every thing ready for falling, first on him and his officers, and then on the men, on a certain signal to be made by Pontinac, when they were to meet in the Council Chamber, and still added that she would be burnt alive, in the event it was known that it was she that discovered it; for that reason the most inviolable secrecy was necessary in respect to her, which the Governor solemnly promised to observe. To guard against this dreadful attempt he ordered all the garrison out to excercise on the parade without the fort, twice a day for about a week previous to the meeting; this, with a view to deceive the Indians and his own people; but the night preceding the meeting he told his officers of the whole plot, and put them on their guard, and ordered them to have every thing ready for defence, and none to be out of the garrison or look over the ramparts. The next day when the whole Indian chiefs entered the gate, they saw the garrison standing ready under arms. Pontinac afked the Governor why he had his young men armed and all on the parade. The other answered, that it was on account of their health, that it was much better for them than to be loitering in their barracks; and as Pontinac knew it was customary for them to be so, he pafsed on without any further alarm. When they entered the Council Chamber and seated themselves, Pontinac began a speach in the most friendly terms and highest afsurance of affection and friendfhip for the Englifh. At that instant a large party of soldiers with fixed bayonets entered the room, and the officers drew their swords, the whole party without came to the door also and made a great noise with their arms. On seeing this Pontinac turned as pale as linen, but continued his speech, and when he had finifhed it afked the meaning of all this. The Governor then drew his sword and taxed him with his treachery, and told him if any one of them was to stir hand or foot that that moment he and all his party would be sacrificed, and not a single man of them would escape the slaughter. Pontinac still protested innocence until he and his chiefs were desired to throw aside their blankets, which they were obliged to comply with, and discover what they had concealed below them. When this was done it was in vain to deny the plot. Pontinac and all his chiefs sued for mercy, and promised the most inviolable attachment to the Englifh if their lives fhould be spared. The Governor through too much humanity and lenity forgave them, and dismifsed them without any punifhment. The use they made of it was instantly to invest the fort, and continued to blockade it the whole winter until the place was relieved by the arrival of a fhip with stores, and a reinforcement from Niagara next May. I saw several people who know the squaw, and said fhe is still alive at Detroit, that the Governor gave her a pension for some years, but whether it is still continued or not they could not say.

Account of the ACTION *between the* STATES OF A-
MERICA *and the* CONFEDERATE INDIANS, *on the*
4*tb November* 1791.

THE account of the action which took place between the troops of the States of America, commanded by General St Clair, and the confederate Indians, in the Miami territories, on the 4th November 1791, which has been slightly mentioned (page 202,) is, by the best information I could procure from Indians and white people that were in the action on each side of the question as follows, *viz.*

GENERAL ST CLAIR's whole army consisted but of 2500 men. In this number were included two or three hundred Kentucky militia, who, after having gone a considerable way with the army into the Indian country, became restive, and would go no farther. At the time of their departure from the army on their return home, there happened to be a considerable store of provisions, with a small convoy, coming forward for the troops, and for fear the Kentucky militia should seize on it, the General detached the first regiment of continental troops, to guard and escort it to his camp. This reduced St Clair's army to 2000 men.

The Indians had in the field 1300 men, about 300 of which were out a-hunting to procure provisions for the rest, so that they had but 1040 in the action. In the night between the third and fourth of November, the old chiefs and experienced warriors had the utmost difficulty to restrain the ardent young warriors from afsaulting the camp, at night; nor were they able to keep them from sallying, and carrying off several scores of oxen and horses. But no sooner day light appeared in the morning of the 4th, than they attacked and afsaulted their enemies in all quarters at once, many of the Indians penetrating into the middle of the camp, slafhing away on all sides with their tomahawks, as they went along: but as the Indians never make a regular stand, they were beat back, but instantly turned about and kept up a perpetual fire from behind trees and logs, which galled their enemies severely from quarters they could not see where. Sallies were made by the white people frequently, with succefs in beating back the Indians; but no sooner the party returned to the main body than the Indians were at their heels. In this way the action continued from day-light to nine o'clock in the morning, when St Clair's army was reduced to one third of the number he brought to the field. He then ordered a sally to be made to gain the main road; when this was obtained they gave way on it, and it now became a perfect rout. Had the Indians understood his intention was to retreat, they would have prevented it, and neither he himself, nor perhaps any one of his army would have escaped. Another circumstance favourable to him was, that the Indians after their retreat, attended more to plundering the camp than to the pursuit; yet a few of them are said to have followed the chase for ten miles. General St Clair's army had six pieces of cannon and two howitzers, yet not a shot was fired out of either; but they were intended for a different purpose, which the court of St James's was apprised of not many months thereafter *.

* In the baggage taken by the Indians after that action, papers were found, which they immediately sent to the commanding officer at Detroit. Some of these bore General St Clair's private instructions from Congress, that how soon he beat the Indians, he should attack Fort Detroit, for which purpose alone the cannon and howitzers were sent. Though this did not puplicly transpire while I was in that neighbourhood, yet it privately did, and there is little reason to doubt its authenticity, as the cannon were not so much as once charged, and useless if they should, against Indians sculking in a wood behind trees and logs.

The Americans had thirty miles to go from the field of action to their next post at Fort Jefferson, and no doubt had run the greatest part of the way, in which they threw away all their firelocks and accoutrements. Next morning when they mustered up the remains of their army at this fort, by some accounts there were but 300, by others 200; and one officer who was present told me there were but 175. There were about sixty officers killed and wounded, and as there were but three officers to a company, it must have been nearly the whole. I have heard of Bunkers hill, Brooker mill, Brimston hill, and Jew's Burying ground, but such slaughter as this unfortunate army underwent, the annals of history, I believe, will rarely instance. The preceding year the Indians were victorious in two actions, wherein it was said they had killed six or seven hundred of the Americans, which no doubt helped to give a spur to their exertions on this last occasion. Lieutenant Turner told me that at one time they were so galled from a certain quarter, and could not see those that did it, that he himself and between thirty and forty others pushed on to beat them off, but only saw one Indian, who, it would seem, had not perceived their approach until they were near him. He sprung off with such agility and speed, from tree to tree, in a traverse way, that though they all fired at him, he got off and did not seem to have been touched with their shot.

I ASKED what was the matter with him that he did not run as well as the rest. His answer was, that there was not an officer in the army, but he could run with; which I readily believed, as he is a very handsome genteel looking young man of twenty-two years of age, and six feet two inches high, very athletic and active; but that he had carried a wounded companion two or three miles on his back: that on his way he fell in with a pack Horse, on which he mounted the wounded officer: that he ran along with them, but that the Horse outstripped him; and gave the following account of the manner in which he was taken, viz.

THAT after the Horse had left him he was pushing along the best way he could, and almost blind with sweet, and out of breath, about five miles from the seat of action, seven or eight Indians in the pursuit came up with him. On seeing the stoutest of them stop to dispatch him, the rest scoured past. But when the Indian took up his tomahawk to blow out Mr T's brains, he seized upon, wrested it out of his hands, and threw it aside; on which the Indian drew his knife, which

Mr T. also wrested from him, grappled with and dashed him to the ground. All this happened before the other Indians were out of sight, who on seeing their companion down turned back. By this time Mr T. allowed the Indian to rise. On the Indians coming back they took up their tomahawks to kill Turner, but the Indian he had overcome interposing, desired them to desist, and said that he was a brave fellow and deserved his life. Mr T. said that he was perfectly collected all the time, and that he knew his only safety was to spare the Indian's life; which in the end proved to be so. They brought him back through the field of action, made him carry a very heavy burden of the trophies of the field, and ordered him to strip some of the dead and carry more, which he refused. They brought him from thence to the village where he was afterwards as well used as he could wish, and once had gone out on a hunting party with them, and was permitted to visit a French village that was in the neighbourhood *. After being three

---

* There are several French settlements and villages whose inhabitants formerly had spread out from the district of Detroit in the heart of the Indian territories. They trade with and seem to live on the most amicable terms with them. These French make as much red wine as serves themselves, and abundance of rice grows spontanious in their swamps; perhaps no country in the world exceeds it in productions of various

weeks in this way with the Indians, he was permitted to go on his parole to Detroit, under a promise of returning from thence, two eight gallon cags of rum, some powder and fhot, for his ransome; that done he might go to his own country or wherever he pleased, but a Frenchman guarantied his implementing these terms. Mr T. amply performed them, and returned more presents to the Indians than he was engaged for. He gave a high account of his reception from the Britifh officers at Detroit. From thence he had come to Niagara, where he and I lived for three weeks together. Mr T. in the Philadelphia gazettes, which I fhowed him, was returned in the list of the killed in that action, which no doubt greatly distrefsed his friends and relations; but when they afterwards learned of his being still in life, and that he had been permitted to return to the Britifh settlement, they sent an exprefs with a letter to Colonel Gordon at Niagara, requesting that he would be good enough to find him out, and supply him with money, cloaths, and every necefsary, to draw upon them for the

kinds; but its distance from sea and market exceeds 1000 miles, yet there is water communication by small rivers, and the Mifsisippi to the sea on the south, and by other small rivers, the Lakes of Canada, and the river St Laurence in the east.

amount, and that it would be most gratefully honoured. On the receipt of this letter, Colonel Gordon sent for Mr Turner to acquaint him of it, and upon Mr T's return from Colonel Gordon to me, he expressed such joy at his friends hearing of his being in life, and felt such felicity as unfortunately deranged his understanding, and was never more himself, while he continued in that place, and I am extremely unhappy to hear that he was no wise better on his return home, or after his arrival at Philadelphia. The Indians lost in that action as follows, *viz.*

	Men.		Men.
Savanese,	3	Ottowas,	
Delawares,	4	Chipawas,	4
Hurons,	3	Pottawamas,	
		Miamis,	2

Mingoes or five nations some, but not known how many.

So that they did not lose above twenty men in that action.

REFLECTIONS *on the* BRITISH PROVINCES *in* AMERICA, *with regard to their throwing off their allegiance to the* MOTHER COUNTRY, *and their falling into the hands of the* FOEDERAL STATES.

IT is supposed by many people in Britain, and they do not hesitate to say, that how soon our American Colonies find themselves strong enough, they will throw off their allegiance to the Mother country, and become independent, or prior to that event, fall into the hands of the American States. But these assertions and ideas proceed totally from want of information. The example of the Fœderal States, who now pant for a connection with Great Britain, and to have a free trade with our West Indian islands, from which they are totally excluded, is enough to deter them for ever. The British Colonies are so sensible of the advantage they derive from a free trade with Britain, the British laws and Government, the protection of its navy to their shipping and trade, no duty paid, no land tax, no cefs, nor any public burden imposed, no grievances whatever, have many felicities in that line no country in the world enjoys, and

c c c

many others unnecefsary to enumerate here, that were they millions strong, their first and last wifh would be a continuation of their connection with Great Britain. The examples of the Fœderal States as already observed would operate so powerfully as to preclude all idea of the remaining Britifh colonies ever wifhing for a change.

In regard to their falling into the hands of the States of America, I will venture to say, that while the Britifh keep pofsefsion of the out forts, that were the whole power of Congrefs, which is not so very great as some perhaps suppose, over such a free and independent people (that think for themselves,) as the inhabitants of the United States are, were levelled against Canada (even in its present state,) and an attempt made to conquer it, it would be attended with no lefs disgrace and disaster, than that which had lately befallen the Britifh arms in endeavouring to subdue themselves. The Canadians would take fire to a man at such an attempt, to which the recent sufferings of the loyal Americans, some of whose fathers, brothers, and nearest relations were killed (or hanged,) in cold blood, would give such an additional spur to their resentment, as would make it nearly if not as bloody to them as that in which they are now engaged with the Indians, and end in the like disaster to themselves.

THE rifk and difficulty of carrying provisions and stores through a wildernefs of some hundred miles, and that distant from resources and supplies of all kinds would be subject to embarrafsments easily foreseen, but ill to surmount, and liable to the fate of Burgoin and his army, in every corner the attempt could be made on that province. " Whoever seeketh to attain unto this end by crooked cunning, will find that by this left handed wisdom he will at least lose his way," nor is it likely that such an attempt will be made, while it is well known that half a dozen of Britifh frigates, and as many bomb ketches, could lay every town of note in America in afhes in one day.

To explain this article it may be necefsary to mention that all the old fortifications were erased to the ground, and not a gun now mounted in that whole continent but such as are in the pofsefsison of the Britifh.

FINIS.

ERRATA.

Page 1 line 11 for *monday* read *day*.

P. 15 l. 24 for *Grandaman* r *Granmanan*.

P. 41 l. 5 for *Nashwack* r *St John*.

P. 43, 45 and 47 for *Symon* r *Lymon*.

P. 72 l. 18 for *length* r *weight*.

P. 97 l. 13 for *the* r *a*.

P. 99 l. 8 and 9 for *port* r *fort*.

P. 111 l. 15 for *come* r *been*.

P. 153 l. 24 for *young* r *little*.

P. ib. l. 27 for *glad* r *he*.

P. ib. l. ib. for *and* r *he*.

P. 160 l. 18 for *bushels* r *bolls*.

P. 232 l. 14 for *him* r *me*.

P. ib. note l. 2 insert after the word house, " *they must have starved.*"

P. 268 l. 4 for *Glencoe* r *Gleno*.

P. 269 l. 20 for *leafy* r *lofty*.

P. 272 l. 21 and afterwards, for *M'Jons* r *M'Ians*.

P. 276 last line for *still* r *now*.

DIRECTIONS TO THE BINDER.

	PAGE.
Place the portrait of the author to front	1
The large plate	86
The small plate	102
The table of distances at the end.	

TABLE of the DISTANCES in the British Provinces in North America, to which Letters may be conveyed through the Post Office. The Distances, by later Measurements, are found to be greater than in this Table, but all Letters are paid according to it.

Michilimakinac	Detroit	Fort Erie	Niagara	Kingston	Augusta	Matilda	Cornwall	Cote du Lac	Montreal	Berthier*	Three Rivers	Quebec	Fredericktown	St Johns	Digby	Annapolis	Horton	Windsor	Halifax
317	Detroit																		
547	230	Fort Erie																	
582	265	35	Niagara																
722	405	175	140	Kingston															
772	455	235	190	50	Augusta														
806	489	259	224	84	34	Matilda													
841	524	294	259	119	69	35	Cornwall												
882	565	335	300	160	110	76	41	Cote du Lac											
927	610	380	345	205	155	121	86	45	Montreal										
972	655	425	390	250	200	166	131	90	45	Berthier*									
1017	700	470	435	295	245	211	176	135	90	45	Three Rivers								
1107	790	560	525	385	335	301	266	225	180	135	90	Quebec							
1536	1219	989	954	814	764	730	695	654	609	564	519	429	Fredericktown						
1626	1309	1079	1044	904	854	820	785	744	699	654	609	519	90	St Johns					
1662	1345	1115	1080	940	890	856	821	780	735	690	645	555	126	36	Digby				
1680	1363	1133	1098	958	908	874	839	798	753	708	663	573	144	54	18	Annapolis			
1755	1438	1208	1173	1033	983	949	914	873	828	783	738	648	219	129	93	75	Horton		
1767	1450	1220	1185	1045	995	961	926	885	840	795	750	660	231	141	105	87	12	Windsor	
1813	1496	1266	1231	1091	1041	1007	972	931	886	841	796	706	277	187	151	133	58	46	Halifax

N. B. Where the Angle between any Town meets, is the exact distance in English miles; viz. from Detroit, in the Horizontal Line, to St Johns, 1309 Miles; or from Matilda to Annapolis 874.

* Letters may be sent across the River St Laurence from Berthier to William Henry, formerly Lorel.

www.ingramcontent.com/pod-product-compliance
Lightning Source LLC
Chambersburg PA
CBHW051743300426
44115CB00007B/679